# Technology, Information and Market Dynamics

# Technology, Information and Market Dynamics

Topics in Advanced Industrial Organization

*Edited by*

## Patrizio Bianchi

*Professor of Industrial Economics and Public Policy and Dean, Faculty of Economics, University of Ferrara, Italy*

## Luca Lambertini

*Professor of Economics, University of Bologna, Italy*

**Edward Elgar**
Cheltenham, UK • Northampton, MA, USA

Published by
Edward Elgar Publishing Limited
Glensanda House
Montpellier Parade
Cheltenham
Glos GL50 1UA
UK

Edward Elgar Publishing, Inc.
136 West Street
Suite 202
Northampton
Massachusetts 01060
USA

A catalogue record for this book
is available from the British Library

**Library of Congress Cataloguing in Publication Data**

Technology, information, and market dynamics : topics in advanced industrial organization / edited by Patrizio Bianchi, Luca Lambertini.
  p. cm
  Includes bibliographical references and index.
  1. Industrial organization (Economic theory) I. Bianchi, Patrizio, 1952- II. Lambertini, Luca.

  HD2326 .T43 2003
  338.6—dc21

                                                        2002037941
  ISBN 1 84376 049 5

Printed and bound in Great Britain by MPG Books Ltd, Bodmin, Cornwall

# Contents

# List of Figures

# Contributors

**Silvia Baranzoni** BA (Economics), 00:am Sas, via Mazzini 150/2, 40138 Bologna, Italy, zerozero.am@tin.it

**Patrizio Bianchi** Professor of Industrial Economics and Public Policy, Faculty of Economics, University of Ferrara, via del Gregorio 13, 44100 Ferrara, Italy, bianchi@economia.unife.it

**Roberto Cellini** Professor of Economics, Dipartimento di Economia e Metodi Quantitativi, University of Catania, Corso Italia 55, 95129 Catania, Italy, cellini@mbox.unict.it

**Luca Lambertini** Professor of Economics, Department of Economics, University of Bologna, Strada Maggiore 45, 40125 Bologna, Italy, lamberti@spbo.unibo.it

**Michele Moretto** Professor of Economics, Department of Economics, University of Padua, via del Santo 33, 37100 Padova, Italy, moretto@decon.unipd.it

**Sougata Poddar** Assistant Professor of Economics, Department of Economics, National University of Singapore, 10 Kent Ridge Street, Singapore 119260, ecssp@nus.edu.sg

**Gianpaolo Rossini** Professor of Economics, Department of Economics, University of Bologna, Strada Maggiore 45, 40125 Bologna, Italy, rossini@spbo.unibo.it

**Dan Sasaki** Associate Professor of Law and Economics, Institute of Social Science, University of Tokyo, 7-3-1 Hongo, Bunkyo-ku, Tokyo 113 0033, Japan, dsasaki@iss.u-tokyo.ac.jp; and Reader in Economics, Department of Economics, University of Exeter, Exeter, Devon EX4 4PU, United Kingdom, d.sasaki@exeter.ac.uk

**Marco Trombetta** Assistant Professor of Finance and Accounting, Departamento de Economia de la Empresa, Universidad Carlos III, Calle Madrid, 126, 28903, Getafe, Madrid, Spain, mtrombet@emp.uc3m.es

# Preface

Over the last three decades, the economics of industry has gone through a radical process of change and evolution, driven by the massive use of the toolbox of game theory. Starting from the seventies, the growing amount of attention devoted to strategic interaction generated a wide stream of theoretical literature recasting the formerly established views on firms and markets within a completely new paradigm compared to that of Bain, Sylos-Labini and Modigliani.

Even a quick overview of Tirole (1988), Schmalensee and Willig (1989), Martin (1993) and Shy (1995) suffices to grasp the essence of the revolution brought about by game theory taking the centre stage in industrial economics. The so-called New Industrial Economics, subsequently re-labelled as the Theory of Industrial Organization or IO for short, grew up alongside the existing applied discipline based upon industry and case studies[1] with a theoretical setup aimed at building formal structures on the basis of a set of noncooperative equilibrium concepts, such as the Nash equilibrium and subgame perfection. Although theoretically solid and rigorous, the new approach generated a plethora of models and equilibria over a relatively short time span. After a while, economists became acquainted with the idea that, in the IO models, almost anything can be an equilibrium. This, in turn, generated a countervailing need, that for a selection of results compatible with the data. Fascinating accounts of this view can be found in Sutton (1991, 1998).

The same references cited above also reveal that summing up the achievements of IO theory along all its lines of research is a tremendous task. Indeed, many relevant streams of research are just outlined or are left out of the picture, and the speed of evolution of the discipline makes it even more difficult for professionals to keep pace.

Moreover, an obvious requirement for any mature branch of scientific research is to keep in line with the evolution of its object in the

---

[1]Applied industrial economics is still a vital discipline, with several promising intersections with the theory of industrial organization. See, *inter alia*, Stiglitz and Mathewson (1986); Geroski, Gilbert and Jacquemin (1990); Geroski (1994); Dowrick (1995); and Davies and Lyons (1996).

real world. Industrial organization is becoming increasingly complex as time goes by. This is due both to the evolution of the internal organization of firms, and to the multiplicity of market strategies implemented by firms in a global economy.

The collection of essays proposed in the present volume aims to offer a comprehensive perspective on firms' behaviour, adopting an angle that enables the reader to grasp some essential lines along which our understanding of firms and markets is currently evolving, and to assess the role of firms in the new economy where the relevance of information creation and transmission is often more relevant than physical features, such as installed capital or product ranges, in determining the long run performance of enterprises. Although the toolbox employed by the professional economist in modelling firms' behaviour in the new economy is basically borrowed from the formal approach to the theory of markets which, by now, we are well accustomed to (Shapiro and Varian, 1999), the object of analysis is substantially different, in that (i) the market value of a firm is often much higher than the value of its installed capital assets; and therefore (ii) a firm's global strategies can be explained in terms of information management at least as much as in terms of R&D efforts or capital commitments. In addition to that, the relevance attached to information also requires a properly dynamic approach to the description of firms' choices. This involves accounting for the role of calendar time in a way that often remains beyond reach for the usual tools of multistage games.

The volume sets out with a classic topic in the IO literature, that is, entry deterrence, which is investigated here – in the chapter by Sougata Poddar – in connection with demand uncertainty. This is an essential feature of real-world markets, though not sufficiently highlighted so far in the theoretical literature. This is followed by the analysis of strategic investments by Sougata Poddar and Dan Sasaki. Building on the long debated idea of using excess capacity as an entry deterring device, in chapter 2 Poddar and Sasaki give an exhaustive theoretical account of the topic, from strategic investment in inventories to investment in process or product innovation.

Then, multiproduct firms enter the picture in the chapter by Silvia Baranzoni, Patrizio Bianchi and Luca Lambertini. The analysis of multiproduct firms involves the interplay of economies of scale and scope, with competition taking place in several dimensions, including product variety and product quality.

So much for the strategic uses of the capital input, be that installed capacity, R&D in process innovation or product innovation. However, capital inputs are used in combination with labour inputs, and this opens a perspective on the internal organization of the firm. In the fourth chapter, Michele Moretto and Gianpaolo Rossini review the literature on labour participation in the management of firms, and the related issue of profit sharing.

An additional factor is the role of information, that can be treated along two lines: (i) financial reporting for the evaluation of a firm's tangible as well as intangible assets, and (ii) information sharing among firms involved in research activities. In chapter 5, Marco Trombetta presents a detailed analysis of the economics of financial reporting, while in chapter 6 Dan Sasaki offers a viewpoint on information sharing.

Surprisingly enough, the most part of the theory of industrial organization has been worked out along static approaches. This is clearly at odds with real-world behaviour, which is inherently dynamic. In the last chapter, Roberto Cellini and Luca Lambertini illustrate differential game models of oligopoly, that is, the application of dynamic optimization tools to strategic settings. The chapter sets out by outlining the foundations of differential game theory, and then offers a brief survey of relevant results in the field of industrial organization.

### Entry under uncertainty

Poddar sets out by briefly summarizing the literature of the late seventies and early eighties on the strategic investment in productive capacity. These contributions, however, assume that demand is certain, which appears, in retrospect, rather restrictive. Since demand changes over time both in quantitative and in qualitative terms, any excess capacity used at some point as an entry deterring tool may then trap a firm that hasn't duly accounted for a fluctuating demand. Building on this observation, the author checks the feasibility conditions for entry deterrence (or accomodation) under demand uncertainty, with and without excess capacity. The most recent contributions in this field confirm that demand uncertainty drives incumbents to install a larger capacity compared to what would be optimal under perfect certainty. The issue of endogenous timing of investment is also assessed. This problem is related to the theme of the second chapter.

### Strategic investment

Poddar and Sasaki explore the time dimension in models of strategic investment. On the one hand, their chapter connects the issue of building up capacity with the optimal management of inventories. On the other hand, it reviews the literature on R&D investment either for process or for product innovation.

Under either perfect competition or monopoly, the assumption of perfect certainty leaves no scope for accumulating inventories. As casual observation suggests, if there are non-negligible scale economies and products are sufficiently homogeneous, then inventories may play an entry deterring role under uncertainty, since the optimal response to demand fluctuations may well consist in accumulating inventories in periods of low demand, and conversely. In other words, the business cycle can be smoothed by using inventories.

Experience shows that, under persistent conditions of uncertainty, accumulating large inventories may represent a trap to the dominant firm(s) in the case where competitors introduce new product varieties. This entails a twofold cost for the incumbent(s). One is the sunk cost associated with large unsold volumes of a good which is now obsolete to the consumers' eyes. The other is the cost associated with the entry of outside competitors, that cannot be foreclosed using excess capacity or inventories. Over the last twenty years, these considerations have triggered large investments in process and product innovation by dominant firms, so as to make their production more flexible. Potential competition has thus proved to be effective in inducing incumbents to accelerate technical progress and decumulate inventories.

## Multiproduct firms

Baranzoni, Bianchi and Lambertini deal with the delicate relationship between firms' marketing strategies and the organization of production, which is the object of the theory of multiproduct firms. A few decades ago, the usual approach to this topic consisted in the supply-side analysis of the interplay between economies of scale and entry deterrence. Between the late fifties and the early sixties, Bain (1956), Modigliani (1958) and Sylos-Labini (1962) confined to the description of a single-product firm facing the perspective of entry by a rival with the same characteristics. This was in line with the mass production characterizing the second industrial revolution and the period from the thirties to the oil crises in the seventies. Not surprisingly, the first contributions to a theory of multiproduct firms were produced in the early eighties, with the theory of contestable markets. This framework relates scale and scope economies with the supply of product ranges to a market which is regulated by the potential threat associated with outside competitors. Thereafter, the theory of multiproduct firms, which is now so relevant for our understanding of firms' behaviour in the global economy, has evolved along four main lines.

The first, building upon some of the reflections born out of the contestability theory, focuses upon the supply side, where the product range is the result of the interplay between scale and scope considerations. The second view considers product differentiation and proliferation as a tool for discriminating across consumers with different tastes and incomes. The third one explains multiproduct firms as the result of competition in R&D for product innovation between incumbents and outsiders. The fourth stream of literature takes a demand-side perspective by considering brand loyalty and switching costs which make it difficult for consumers to patronize new goods and profitable for the existing firms to expand their product range so as to exploit such phenomena.

Hence, the theory of product differentiation allows us to understand how firms can acquire and possibly increase their market power by crowding the product space with new varieties. Such a strategy must trade off the advantages of scale economies associated with the production of a single variety against the scope economies associated with wide product ranges. In turn, this hinders competition and yields excess variety (or excess differentiation) which is socially harmful.

**Labour participation**
The relationship between the organization of production (i.e., technology) and market strategy goes along with the participation of workers in the management of the firm, and eventually with the issue of profit sharing. This is what Moretto and Rossini deal with in the fourth chapter.

The analysis of labour participation in the firm has produced a large literature where the profit-maximizing firm is evaluated against the labour-managed firm. While the first is affected by static inefficiency, in that it does not provide workers with the correct incentives, the second cannot sustain an optimal growth path. The PM firm yields a superior performance, as compared to the LM firm, when capital assets are specific and the labour input is not, while the opposite holds when labour is specific. That is, the role of a productive factor in managing the firm becomes more relevant as its specificity becomes higher. However, these are polar settings, while in real-world cases a range of intermediate situations usually arises, with some degree of specificity characterizing all factors of production. That is where profit sharing comes into the picture, as pointed out by Aoki (1984). However, the firm described by Aoki is rather rigid with respect to external shocks. Therefore, under uncertainty, the problem of collective decision-making faced by the firm becomes almost overwhelming.

These themes are extremely relevant to our understanding of industries where the value of a firm is measured by intangible assets, and the specific knowledge associated with specific labour inputs is in itself a crucial asset.

### Financial reporting
Marco Trombetta deals with the strategic use of information through financial reporting. In a world of perfect certainty, financial reporting would be immaterial to firms as well as any other agent. Under uncertainty, manipulating and transmitting this kind of information becomes extraordinarily relevant. Thousands of analysts devote a lot of time and energy every day to analyse financial reports so as to produce forecasts on the future behaviour of stock market prices.

Balance data disclose valuable information to investors as well as competitors, who can work out optimal strategies in response to their evaluation of a firm's behaviour and performance as emerging from those data. This entails that a firm, on the one hand, should disclose as little information as possible to rivals, while giving as much information as possible to shareholders, on the other.

These considerations are of vital importance in the new economy, where the market value of a firm is largely linked to intangible assets and accounting methods become crucial communication tools. The disclosure and signalling value of accounting can reveal relevant aspects of a firm's strategy, which are not conveyed by the dividend or investment policy, as the connection between tangible assets and profits is scarcely, if at all, revealing.

### R&D and information sharing
Another perspective on information is given by Dan Sasaki: information becomes a production factor in innovative industries where firms activate R&D investment either for process or product innovation, and may find it convenient to share information about the status of their respective research projects and the efficiency of their respective technologies.

This creates an interesting paradox. A standard view on information maintains that a piece of information is valuable to any given agent as long as it is exclusively held by that agent. However, activities of information transmission may accelerate the process that transforms such information into new technological knowledge. Accordingly, R&D in oligopoly markets is the most relevant framework, although of course not the only one, where the analysis of incentives towards information sharing plays a role.

Information transmission, and the evolution of the stock of technical knowledge of an industry through R&D investments, lead us to consider the role of time in shaping firms' strategies and the evolution of the market where they operate. This is the theme of the last chapter.

**Differential oligopoly games**
Using the toolbox of differential game theory, Cellini and Lambertini offer an overview of some key factors for the understanding of dynamic competition, focusing upon three specific problems: (i) the determination of optimal intertemporal production in a market with sticky prices; (ii) optimal accumulation of capital (or productive capacity); (iii) R&D investment for product or process innovation. This yields a dynamic description of firm behaviour which is richer and more realistic than the picture we are accustomed to from the existing literature on static (multistage) models. Such a framework can be fruitfully adopted to investigate the optimal design of regulation and competition policy.

This set of survey articles, worked out by a group of young theoretical researchers, offers useful tips for applied research. In particular, this is done by building a theoretical setup which stresses the dynamic behaviour of firms with respect to several features of crucial relevance from the applied point of view as well as for the optimal design of policy measures.

We would like to thank Enrico Cesari for cajoling Scientific Workplace to properly execute our commands. And, last but absolutely not least, during the preparation of the final manuscript we were very fortunate in working with Caroline McLin, Alexandra Minton, Francine O'Sullivan and Alison Stone of Edward Elgar, whose constant and extremely efficient assistance allowed us to manage the project most easily.

# References

1] Aoki, M. (1984), *The Co-Operative Game Theory of the Firm*, Oxford, Oxford University Press.

2] Bain, J.S. (1956), *Barriers to New Competition: Their Character and Consequences in Manufacturing Industries*, Cambridge, MA, Harvard University Press.

3] Davies, S. and B. Lyons (1996, eds), *Industrial Organization in the European Union: Structure, Strategy, and the Competitive Mechanism*, Oxford, Clarendon Press.

4] Dowrick, S. (1995, ed.), *Economic Approaches to Innovation*, Aldershot, Elgar.

5] Geroski, P. (1994), *Market Structure, Corporate Performance and Innovative Activity*, Oxford, Clarendon Press.

6] Geroski, P., R. Gilbert and A. Jacquemin (1990), *Barriers to Entry and Strategic Competition*, Fundamentals of Pure and Applied Economics Series, vol. 41, London, Harwood Academic.

7] Martin, S. (1993), *Advanced Industrial Economics*, Oxford, Blackwell.

8] Modigliani, F. (1958), "New Developments on the Oligopoly Front", *Journal of Political Economy*, **66**, 215-32.

9] Schmalensee, R. and R. Willig (1989, eds), *Handbook of Industrial Organization*, Amsterdam, North-Holland.

10] Shapiro, C. and H. Varian (1999), *Information Rules. A Strategic Guide to the Network Economy*, Boston, MA, Harvard Business School Press.

11] Shy, O. (1995), *Industrial Organization. Theory and Applications*, Cambridge, MA, MIT Press.

12] Stiglitz, J.E. and G.F. Mathewson (1986, eds), *New Developments in the Analysis of Market Structure*, Cambridge, MA, MIT Press.

13] Sutton, J. (1991), *Sunk Costs and Market Structure: Price Competition, Advertising, and the Evolution of Concentration*, Cambridge, MA, MIT Press.

14] Sutton, J. (1998), *Technology and Market structure: Theory and History*, Cambridge, MA, MIT Press.

15] Sylos-Labini, P. (1962), *Oligopoly and Technical Progress*, Cambridge, MA, Harvard University Press.

16] Tirole, J. (1988), *The Theory of Industrial Organization*, Cambridge, MA, MIT Press.

# Chapter 1

# Entry under uncertainty

Sougata Poddar[1]

## 1.1 Introduction

In this chapter, we focus on the theme of entry deterrence under demand uncertainty in an oligopolistic industry. Generally speaking, in any industry, entry would take place whenever a potential entrant finds it profitable to enter the market. A great deal of literature has been devoted to study the economic incentives of firms towards entry in an industry. Researchers tried to model the behaviour of the incumbent firm(s) and/or the potential entrant(s) involved in many such situations. Most often, a game theoretic model is adopted where firms are the players and the resulting strategic interactions among the players are studied in great detail. Various issues regarding entry or deterrence have been studied in various contexts. In this particular chapter, we will mainly focus on the issue of strategic capacity investment by the competing firms when there is demand uncertainty. The issue of capacity investment under deterministic (certain) demand has been carefully studied by Spence (1977), Dixit (1979, 1980), Spulber (1981), Schmalensee (1981), Bulow *et al.* (1985), Saloner (1985), Basu and Singh (1990) among many

---

[1]I am most indebted to Luca Lambertini, whose continuous encouragement and suggestions made this chapter possible. I would like to thank Dan Sasaki for numerous stimulating discussions and comments on this subject matter. I would also like to thank Jean Gabszewicz, who introduced me to this topic. Parts of this research have been presented in CORE, Louvain-la-Neuve; Institute of Economics and Centre for Industrial Economics, University of Copenhagen; Indian Statistical Institute, New Delhi and Calcutta. The author has prepared this chapter while being with the Department of Economics, National University of Singapore. Financial assistance from National University of Singapore is gratefully acknowledged.

others.

One debate that comes out from the above studies is about the level of pre-entry capacity that an incumbent firm would like to install when it faces a threat of entry in the market. In a two firm setting, Spence (1977) argued that in order to maintain its monopoly position, the incumbent firm may install a level of capacity that may remain unutilized if the entry of the new firm is successfully deterred. In other words, the incumbent firm would like to hold idle capacity as a threat to the potential entrant in order to deter entry. The idea is that, in the event of entry, the incumbent will use all its capacity to produce output, which eventually drives down the price to such a level that makes entry unprofitable. The straightforward implication is that, in the event of no entry, idle (or excess) capacity will be observed. However, later Dixit (1980) argued that such behaviour, namely, holding idle capacity is not an optimal action for the incumbent firm, and also emphasized the fact that entry prevention should not be a prior constraint, because in some situations, the established firm can be better off by accommodating the entrant. More importantly, he showed that under all circumstances, irrespective of entry accommodation or deterrence excess (idle) capacity will never be observed and proved that Spence's argument was based on a non-credible threat from the incumbent towards the entrant.

So far, the debate whether an incumbent firm will hold excess capacity or not (in the literature, this feature is also known as the *excess capacity hypothesis*) when there is a potential entrant in the market has been carried out in various directions. Most of the latter models used different assumptions of demand, costs, strategies and timing of the moves by the players. This strand of literature comes out with a wide variety of conclusions, sometimes supporting the excess capacity hypothesis and sometimes invalidating it. For example, Bulow *et al.* (1985) showed that instead of a linear downward sloping demand function (as in Dixit) if the firms face a constant elasticity demand function, then actually, it is optimal for the incumbent to hold idle capacity in order to deter entry. A unified theory on the issue of strategic investment by an incumbent firm under the threat of entry can be found in Fudenberg and Tirole (1984). Studies have been done in a static framework as well as in a dynamic framework. The most involving study in a dynamic framework was done by Spulber (1981), where he showed that whether excess capacity will be observed or not depends on the nature of the post-entry game. He showed that if the post-entry game is Cournot-Nash, the incumbent firm will never hold excess capacity whereas if the post-entry game is of Cournot-Stackelberg type, with the incumbent acting as a leader, then excess capacity will be observed.

The brief survey proposed above refers to models where the demand is certain. Now, in reality this assumption may sound somewhat restrictive, since, after all demand changes with time and the firms must take into account this fact while choosing their strategies. As a result, this chapter mainly focuses on the issues of entry when there is demand uncertainty. The very presence of demand uncertainty changes many results, which were obtained in a framework of no demand uncertainty. For example, it can be shown through a simple model that the excess capacity hypothesis in the Spence-Dixit model can also be revived when demand uncertainty is introduced. In a typical situation with demand uncertainty, a firm usually chooses the capacity for production before the actual demand is realized. Now, in a strategic framework, this implies that firms must adjust their capacity not only in view of meeting output demand levels varying across the states of nature, but also for providing best output replies against the capacity and output strategies chosen by the rival firms. In this random environment, each firm plays a game *simultaneously* against nature and against their rivals. This certainly makes the firms' behaviour more complicated as opposed to the situation where there is no demand uncertainty. In the forthcoming analysis, we will study and analyse various models around this particular theme.

The plan of the chapter is as follows. In section 1.2, we look into the analysis of holding excess (idle) capacity by the incumbent firm when it faces a threat of a potential entrant under demand uncertainty. In section 1.3, we focus on the issues of strategic investment when the timing of entry of the competing firms is *exogenous* as well as *endogenous* in the market. The issues of entry deterrence and entry accommodation are analysed in detail. In section 1.4, we discuss the aspects of informational advantage of knowing the true demand before entering the market versus commitment power of being the first-mover (without knowing the demand) in a leader-follower type framework. Here, we see under what condition the informational advantage of a follower is comparable with the commitment power of the leader. We also outline some further progress of ongoing research on strategic investment under demand uncertainty. Finally, in section 1.5, we conclude with some remarks on the chapter.

## 1.2 Excess capacity with demand uncertainty

In this context, I define the notion of *excess capacity* in the following way. Suppose

a] there are two states of demand (namely, high and low) where each state might realize with some probability, and b] an incumbent firm installs capacity before the actual demand is realized. It also anticipates a potential entrant in the market after the demand realizes.

Now consider a situation where the incumbent installs a level of capacity such that part of the installed capacity remains unutilized after production of output in the actual state, then naturally, the incumbent firm ends up with idle capacity, i.e. excess capacity is observed. For example, the capacity needed to produce output corresponding to an equilibrium at some low state of demand is obviously less than the capacity needed to produce output corresponding to some high state of demand. So if any capacity is installed in anticipation to meet a demand in the high state, a realization of low state of demand will inevitably lead to excess capacity. On the other hand, we also assume that the incumbent may add on its capacity after demand is realized, if needed. Hence, the natural question arises, why in the first place the incumbent firm should be interested in installing a capacity that may remain idle when the incumbent has the option to add on its capacity in future if high demand is indeed realized. The answer is that, in doing so, the incumbent firm can position itself so as to maintain a strategic cost advantage over the potential entrant at the time of producing output in the later stage of the game. So, *a priori*, it is not clear whether an incumbent firm should hold a capacity that may remain unutilized in some state when there is a potential entrant in the market under demand uncertainty. In fact, in this analysis, it has been shown that the result of holding *no excess (idle) capacity* may not necessarily hold when there is some uncertainty in the demand. To this end, it should be emphasized that in a similar situation, a monopoly firm facing no threat of entry would never hold a capacity that may remain idle, because the incentive to have a strategic advantage is completely absent and it always has the option to increase its capacity if a high demand state is realized. So the phenomenon of holding a high level of capacity under demand uncertainty by the incumbent is precisely to get a strategic advantage over the potential entrant when there is a threat of entry. We describe such a situation formally using the following model (Poddar, 1999).

## 1.2.1   The setup

Consider a model with an incumbent firm and a potential entrant. Both firms produce a single homogeneous good. The demand for the good is given by the usual linear demand function: $P(Q) = a - Q$, where $Q$ is the aggregate supply.

There is uncertainty over the realization of market demand. For the sake of simplicity, suppose there are two states of demand that may realize. The demand can be high ($a = a_H$) with probability $\theta$ or low ($a = a_L$) with probability $1 - \theta$. The game is as follows. There are two time periods, $t = 1, 2$. The demand realizes at $t = 2$. Firm 1 (the incumbent) is there at $t = 1$ and firm 2 (the entrant) arrives at $t = 2$, after demand realizes and it becomes common knowledge to firms.[2] The incumbent firm chooses a pre-entry capacity level $k_1$ in the first period ($t = 1$). This capacity may subsequently be increased, but cannot be reduced. We assume that both firms compete in quantities in the second stage à *la* Cournot-Nash irrespective of the level of capacity installed by the incumbent firm in the first stage.

## 1.2.2 Cost

Suppose that firm 1 has installed capacity $k_1$ in period 1. If it is producing output $q_1$ within its capacity limit, i.e., if $q_1 \leq k_1$, then its total cost is:

$$C_1 = rk_1 + wq_1 \tag{1.1}$$

where $r$ is the unit cost of capacity and $w$ is the unit cost of output.

However, if it wishes to produce output greater than its pre-planned capacity in the second period, it must acquire additional capacity in period 2, i.e., if $q_1 > k_1$, its total cost becomes:

$$C_1 = (r + w)q_1 \tag{1.2}$$

Since firm 2 (the entrant) arrives at time period 2 and has no prior commitment in capacity for all positive levels of output $q_2$, it acquires capacity $k_2$ to match its output, yielding

$$C_2 = (r + w)q_2 \text{ for all } q_2 \geq 0 \tag{1.3}$$

## 1.2.3 Entry

Here we will analyse the case of entry deterrence and entry accommodation separately and address the following question. Will the incumbent firm ever choose a level of capacity at period 1 that might remain unused if the low state of demand is realized in period 2, and hence, excess capacity is observed?[3]

---

[2]Thus, the incumbent firm faces demand uncertainty only while choosing pre-entry capacity.

[3]Notice that, if a high state of demand realizes, then excess capacity will never be observed because no firm installs a capacity that will remain unutilized after producing the optimal output corresponding to an equilibrium in the high demand state.

The incentive for holding excess capacity is the following. In the first period, if the incumbent firm installs a capacity beyond or at least equal to the level needed to produce output in the second period, then it actually enjoys a cost advantage over the entrant while producing the output. For example, if the incumbent firm installs a capacity, beyond or at least equal to the level needed to produce output corresponding to an equilibrium in low demand, then naturally, if low demand is realized the incumbent produces output within its pre-planned capacity level and incurs a marginal cost of $w$ only, while the entrant has to bear a marginal cost of $(r + w)$ for production. At the same time, if the incumbent installs *exactly* the level of capacity needed to produce output corresponding to an equilibrium in low demand, then it does get a cost advantage if low demand realizes, but unfortunately, *does not* get any cost advantage in case the high state of demand arises. It is for this latter eventuality that it is worth building a capacity larger than what is needed in a low demand state; and this opens up the possibility of excess (idle) capacity. Now, this cost advantage, in turn, gives the incumbent firm a strategic advantage over the entrant by shifting its reaction function outwards in period 2, while output is produced.

Note that if the incumbent firm does not face the threat of entry, i.e. in a monopoly situation, it would never choose a capacity that may remain idle since it has got the flexibility of adding to its capacity in the second period according to the actual demand need. So holding excess capacity (relative to low demand output) is *only* for getting strategic advantage when there is a potential entrant in the market.

We solve this entry game in the usual way by moving backwards (i.e., first by considering period 2, then period 1) in order to find a subgame perfect equilibrium. First, we will consider the case of entry deterrence.

### 1.2.4   Entry deterrence

Assume that the potential entrant faces a fixed entry cost $F > 0$.

#### Holding excess capacity

Suppose the incumbent installed a level of capacity $k_1$ at time period 1 which enables it to get a strategic advantage in cost in the second period in *both* states of demand. This means, under the realization of demand in the second period the incumbent incurs a unit cost of production $w$ whereas the entrant's per unit production cost remains $(w + r)$. This leads to an incumbent's entry deterring output equal to $(a_L - w - r - 2\sqrt{F})$ in the low state and $(a_H - w - r - 2\sqrt{F})$ in the high state of demand. Now if the incumbent installs a capacity $k_1^e = a_H - w - r - 2\sqrt{F}$ (superscript $e$ stands for *excess capacity*) in time period 1 to get a strategic advantage in costs over the entrant in both states of demand, then the expected profits of the incumbent become:

$$E\pi_1^e = \theta\left(r + 2\sqrt{F}\right)\left(a_H - w - r - 2\sqrt{F}\right) \qquad (1.4)$$
$$+ (1-\theta)\left(r + 2\sqrt{F}\right)\left(a_L - w - r - 2\sqrt{F}\right)$$

The corresponding subgame perfect equilibrium of the two stage game has the incumbent playing the strategy $(k_1^e, (q_L^e, q_H^e))$, where $k_1^e = q_H^e = a_H - w - r - 2\sqrt{F}$ and $q_L^e = a_L - w - r - 2\sqrt{F}$, and the entrant stays out, i.e., $q_2 = 0$ in both the high and the low states of demand. Now this level of capacity installation by the incumbent firm naturally leads to an excess capacity equal to $k_1^e - q_L^e$ if the low state of demand realizes.

**Holding no excess capacity**

Now consider the case where the incumbent installs a capacity level $k_1$ in period 1 which is just large enough to give a strategic advantage in costs only if the low state of demand is realized. If a high state of demand is realized then the incumbent must increase its capacity level in order to deter entry. This implies, in the second period, if a high state of demand is realized the incumbent does not enjoy any strategic cost advantage while producing output. This leads to an expected profit of

$$E\pi_1^{ne} = 2\theta\sqrt{F}\left(a_H - w - r - 2\sqrt{F}\right) \qquad (1.5)$$
$$+ (1-\theta)\left(r + 2\sqrt{F}\right)\left(a_L - w - r - 2\sqrt{F}\right)$$

The corresponding subgame perfect equilibrium has the incumbent playing the strategy $(k_1^{ne}, (q_L^{ne}, q_H^{ne}))$, where $k_1^{ne} = q_L^{ne} = a_L - w - r - 2\sqrt{F}$ and $q_H^{ne} = a_H - w - r - 2\sqrt{F}$, and the entrant stays out, i.e., $q_2 = 0$ in both the high and low states of demand. The superscript $ne$ in all the above expressions denotes the phenomenon of *no excess capacity*.

Now, we would like to see whether the expected gain in order to have a strategic advantage from installing more capacity dominates (or not) the expected loss from ending up with idle capacity if the low state of demand is realized. In case the former dominates the latter, we come to a situation where excess capacity may be observed and thus Dixit's conclusion gets reversed. To see this, we proceed as follows.

Comparing (1.4) and (1.5), we get the expected gain ($EG$) from strategic advantage as:

$$EG = \theta r\left(a_H - w - r - 2\sqrt{F}\right) \qquad (1.6)$$

while the expected loss $(EL)$ of holding excess capacity is:

$$EL = r\left(1 - \theta\right)\left(k_1^e - q_L^e\right) = r\left(1 - \theta\right)\left(a_H - a_L\right) \qquad (1.7)$$

so that

$$EG > EL \text{ iff } \theta\left(a_H - w - r - 2\sqrt{F}\right) > \left(1 - \theta\right)\left(a_H - a_L\right) \qquad (1.8)$$

Below I construct a numerical example, which shows that in some situations it is indeed profitable for the incumbent firm to hold excess capacity.

**Example** Let $a_H = 7$, $a_L = 3$, $\theta = 0.6$, $r = 1$, $w = 1$ and $F = 1$.

Plugging these values in (1.6-1.7), we get $EG = 1.8 > 1.6 = EL$.

Hence, under these parameter values, it is optimal for the incumbent to choose a level of capacity that may remain idle if a low demand state is realized. As a result, excess capacity may occur in the equilibrium.

## 1.2.5 Entry accommodation

Now assume the entry cost $F = 0$, and the entry takes place with certainty. After entry, we assume both firms compete with each other à la Cournot-Nash.

**Holding excess capacity**

As before, suppose the incumbent installed a level of capacity $k_1$ in period 1 which enables it to get a strategic advantage in cost (by shifting its reaction function outwards) in the second period in both states of demand. This leads to an incumbent's output equal to $(a_L - w + r)/3$ in the low state and $(a_H - w + r)/3$ in the high state of demand.

In order to attain these output levels the incumbent must install a capacity at least equal to $(a_H - w + r)/3$ in period 1. So, the subgame perfect equilibrium of this two stage game has the incumbent playing the strategy $(k_1^e, (q_L^e, q_H^e))$, with $k_1^e = q_H^e = (a_H - w + r)/3$ and $q_L^e = (a_L - w + r)/3$, and the entrant playing the strategy of selecting the state contingent reaction function $R_s(q_s) = (a_s - w - r - q_s)/2$; $s = L, H$. As a result, in the event of realization of low demand the incumbent is left with an idle capacity equal to $(k_1^e - q_L^e)$.

The expected profit of the incumbent at the equilibrium is given by:

$$E\pi_1^e = \theta\frac{(a_H - w + r)^2}{9} + (1 - \theta)\frac{(a_L - w + r)^2}{9} \qquad (1.9)$$

## Holding no excess capacity

Now consider the case where the incumbent installs in period 1 a capacity level $k_1$, which is just large enough to give a strategic advantage in costs *only* if the low state of demand is realized. If a high state of demand is realized then the incumbent must increase its capacity level in order to meet the increased demand for output in the second period. As before, this implies that in the second period the incumbent does not enjoy any strategic cost advantage in that state while producing output. In this case, the subgame perfect equilibrium is given by the incumbent playing the strategy $(k_1^{ne}, (q_L^{ne}, q_H^{ne}))$, where $k_1^{ne} = q_L^{ne} = (a_L - w + r)/3$ and $q_H^{ne} = (a_H - w - r)/3$, and the entrant playing the strategy of selecting the state contingent reaction function $R_s(q_s) = (a_s - w - r - q_s)/2; \ s = L, H$.

Under these conditions, the expected profit of the incumbent at the equilibrium is given by:

$$E\pi_1^{ne} = \theta \frac{(a_H - w - r)^2}{9} + (1 - \theta) \frac{(a_L - w + r)^2}{9} \tag{1.10}$$

Notice that, if the incumbent firm does not install enough capacity (i.e., for any $k_1 < k_1^{ne}$) in period 1, in order to gain the strategic cost advantage even in the low state of demand, then its expected profit remains:

$$E\pi_1 = \theta \frac{(a_H - w - r)^2}{9} + (1 - \theta) \frac{(a_L - w - r)^2}{9} < E\pi_1^{ne} < E\pi_1^e \tag{1.11}$$

Thus, installing capacity at least to the level $k_1^{ne}$ in period 1, indeed improves the strategic position of the incumbent firm in the product market competition.

Now, since $E\pi_1^e > E\pi_1^{ne}$, installing even higher capacity, $k_1 = k_1^e > k_1^{ne}$ indeed gives rise to a higher expected profit. But, by doing so, the incumbent faces the risk of ending up with idle capacity (viz., $k_1^e - q_L^e$) if the low state of demand is realized.

Once again, we would like to check whether the expected gain in order to have a strategic advantage from installing more capacity dominates (or not) the expected loss from ending up with idle capacity if the low state of demand is realized. In case the former dominates the latter, we again come to a situation where excess capacity is observed and thus Dixit's conclusion does not remain valid. To see this we compare the following.

By comparing (1.9) and (1.10), we get that the expected gain from strategic advantage is:

$$EG = \theta \frac{(a_H - w + r)^2 - (a_H - w - r)^2}{9} = 4\theta r \frac{(a_H - w)}{9} \tag{1.12}$$

On the other hand, the expected loss associated with holding idle capacity is given by:

$$EL = (1 - \theta)(k_1^e - q_L^e)r = r(1 - \theta)\frac{(a_H - a_L)}{3} \tag{1.13}$$

Now, $EG > EL$ iff $4(a_H - w) > 3(1 - \theta)(a_H - a_L)$, i.e.:

$$\theta(a_H - w) > \frac{3}{4}(1 - \theta)(a_H - a_L) \tag{1.14}$$

For a given $\theta$, it is clear from the right-hand side of the above inequality that, as the probability of realizing a low state increases (i.e., as $\theta$ becomes small), naturally, the expected cost of holding excess capacity increases. So the incumbent firm tends to hold idle capacity only when the strategic advantage (which is showing in the left-hand side) is big enough to outweigh the cost of excess capacity. Of course, when $\theta$ increases (i.e., the probability of the occurrence of the high state increases) then obviously the incumbent is more likely to hold idle capacity.

To capture such a situation where $EG > EL$, a numerical example follows.

**Example** Let $a_H = 7$, $a_L = 3$, $\theta = 0.6$, $r = 1$ and $w = 1$.

Plugging these values into (1.12) and (1.13), we get $EG = 3.6 > 1.2 = EL$.

Hence, under these parameter values, again we find that it is optimal for the incumbent to choose a level of capacity that may remain idle if a low demand state is realized. As a result, excess capacity may arise in the equilibrium.

We can therefore conclude that the result of holding excess capacity in equilibrium may generally arise if some uncertainty prevails over the states of demand; and this is true irrespective of the fact that the incumbent deters or accommodates entry. Thus, Dixit's (1980) conclusion under deterministic demand does not necessarily hold true when we allow for demand uncertainty. The foregoing discussion produces the following results.

**Result 1** *Under demand uncertainty, the presence of the strategic advantage in costs may force the incumbent firm to choose a capacity level that may remain idle in the low states of demand. More specifically, in a Spence-Dixit type model of entry deterrence, the result of holding no idle capacity by the incumbent firm under deterministic demand does not necessarily hold under demand uncertainty.*

Comparing (1.8) and (1.14), we also get the following.

**Result 2** *Under demand uncertainty, excess capacity is more likely to be observed under the case of entry accommodation as opposed to the case of entry deterrence.*

The intuition is as follows. From the analysis, it turns out that the magnitude of the possible excess capacity, i.e., $k_1^e - q_L^e$, is much higher in the case of deterrence as opposed to accommodation. Hence the cost associated with idle capacity becomes significantly higher in the case of deterrence as compared to accommodation. Thus, excess capacity is less likely to obtain in the case of deterrence.

## 1.3 Entry deterrence and demand uncertainty

The issue of entry deterrence under demand uncertainty has also been studied by Perrakis and Warskett (1983), Kim (1996), Sadanand and Sadanand (1996) in a dynamic framework, and more recently by Maskin (1999) in a static framework. All these models assume *exogenous timing* of entry of the competing firms in the market, namely, the incumbent moves first (say, by installing capacity) and then the entrant moves after observing the incumbent's installed capacity. In the next section, we will first review the main findings in the literature under this assumption of *exogenous* timing of entry. After that, we will continue our discussion when the timing of entry decision is *endogenous* to the model.

### 1.3.1 Strategic investment decision under exogenous timing of entry

Maskin (1999) shows that the uncertainty about the demand would force the incumbent to choose a higher capacity level to deter entry than it would do under certainty. Hence, the act of deterring entry by the incumbent becomes more costly and unattractive to the incumbent firm when there exists some demand uncertainty compared to the situation where there is no such uncertainty. The main intuition behind this result is the following. To deter entry, the incumbent must install enough capacity so that, if entry occurred, the entrant's profit would be zero (or negative). Now suppose the uncertainty about the demand is of the following type, namely, the mean inverse demand remains the same as under certainty. When demand is high, an incumbent that has installed the certainty level of capacity still continues to produce at capacity; price simply rises to reflect the higher demand. But when demand is low, the incumbent will wish to produce at less than full capacity. This means that the fall in price when demand is low is not so large as the rise in price when demand is high, and so if the entrant's profit is zero under certainty, it is positive with uncertainty. To deter entry, therefore, the incumbent must increase capacity above the certainty level to ensure that when demand is high it produces enough to drive an entrant's expected profit back down to zero. This finding can be illustrated using the following simple framework (Maskin, 1999).

### The setup

Suppose that to produce at all a firm must install $k_0$ units of capacity. The unit cost of capacity is $r$, and $w$ is the unit cost of output. A firm that installs $k$ units of capacity $(k \geq k_0)$, can produce up to $k$ units of output. Inverse demand is given by the stochastic function $p(x, \widetilde{\varepsilon})$, where $x$ is the output and $\widetilde{\varepsilon}$ is a random variable. There are two firms, an incumbent and a potential entrant. The incumbent moves first and selects its capacity level $k_1$. The entrant then moves and either chooses to stay out of the market or else selects capacity $k_2$. After capacity is installed, firms observe the realization of $\widetilde{\varepsilon}$. Then, they choose output levels simultaneously. Of course, if the entrant has stayed out, its output is zero.

The following example will suffice for the result.

### Example

First, we proceed with the analysis of the situation where there is no demand uncertainty. Assume $p(x) = 3 - x$, and $r = w = 1$. Then, the *deterrence capacity* $k_d$ must satisfy $3 - k_0 - k_d - 2 = 0$.

That is, $k_d = 1 - k_0$, provided that $1 - k_0$ exceeds the monopoly capacity $k_M = 1/2$, i.e., $k_0 < 1/2$.[4]

Hence, the incumbent's profit when it deters entry is:

$$\pi_d = [1 - (1 - k_0)](1 - k_0) = k_0(1 - k_0) \tag{1.15}$$

If instead the incumbent accommodates entry and sets capacity $k_1$, the entrant responds by setting $k_2$ to maximize profits $\pi_2 = (3 - k_1 - k_2) - 2k_2$,

---

[4]Note that, since

$$\frac{\partial [(3 - k_0 - k_d)k - k]}{\partial k} = k_0 \geq 0$$

at $k = 1 - k_0$, the incumbent would produce at full capacity should entry occur.

i.e., $k_2 = (1 - k_1)/2$. Hence, the incumbent maximizes

$$\pi_{ea} = \left[3 - k_1 - \left(\frac{1 - k_1}{2}\right)\right] - 2k_1 \tag{1.16}$$

with respect to $k_1$. Subscript $ea$ stands for *entry accomodation*. Solving firm 1's maximum problem we get $k_1 = 1/2$, and its profit with accommodation is thus

$$\pi_{ea} = \frac{1}{8} \tag{1.17}$$

Hence, comparing (1.15) and (1.17), we conclude that deterrence occurs if and only if $k_0(1 - k_0) > 1/8$. That is, the incumbent accommodates entry for all

$$k_0 \in \left[0, \frac{2 - \sqrt{2}}{4}\right] \tag{1.18}$$

and deters entry for all

$$k_0 \in \left(\frac{2 - \sqrt{2}}{4}, \frac{1}{2}\right] \tag{1.19}$$

Let us now introduce uncertainty about demand. We would like to show that the cut-off point to deter entry in this case is higher than $\left(2 - \sqrt{2}\right)/4$. Suppose that, with equal probabilities, the intercept is $a = 3 + t$ (high demand) and $a = 3 - t$ (low demand), where $t = 2/3$. If the entrant has installed $k_0$ units of capacity and demand turns out to be low, then the incumbent faces the following problem:

$$\max \ \pi_1 = \left(\frac{7}{3} - k_0 - k\right)k - k \tag{1.20}$$

and so will choose output

$$k = \frac{2}{3} - \frac{k_0}{2} \tag{1.21}$$

However,

$$\frac{2}{3} - \frac{k_0}{2} < 1 - k \ \text{iff} \ k < \frac{2}{3} \tag{1.22}$$

So, unlike in the case of certainty, the incumbent will not produce up to capacity when demand is low. This implies that, to deter entry, the incumbent must install capacity greater than $1 - k_0$, so profit is less than $(1 - k_0)k_0$.

By contrast, if the incumbent accommodates entry, and if it and the entrant have installed capacities $1/2$ and $1/4$ respectively, then the incumbent chooses output to solve the following problem:

$$\max \ \pi_1 = \left(\frac{7}{3} - \frac{1}{4} - k\right)k - k \tag{1.23}$$

where $k \leq 1/2$.

Now, the solution to the above problem is $k = 1/2$. That is, even when demand is low, the incumbent produces up to capacity. Hence, output and therefore expected profit are unchanged w.r.t. the case of certainty. Thus, we conclude that $k_0 = \left(2 - \sqrt{2}\right)/4$ is no longer the cut-off point between accommodation and deterrence; under uncertainty, $k_0$ must be somewhat greater than $\left(2 - \sqrt{2}\right)/4$ for deterrence to be worth the effort.

**Result 3** *Under demand uncertainty (with mean preserving spread) entry deterrence is more costly (lower expected profit to the incumbent), hence less attractive to the incumbent firm as opposed to the situation with no demand uncertainty.*

## 1.3.2  More on exogenous entry timing

Perrakis and Warskett (1983) studied the general conditions for entry deterrence and entry accommodation by the incumbent firm under demand uncertainty. They examined the effects of random demand upon the decision to enter into a sector dominated by a monopoly, as well as the actions that such a monopoly firm may take in order to discourage entry. A two period model is considered where the monopolist enters initially and enjoys an uncontested monopoly for one period, while the entrant may enter and compete during the second period. The main features of the two period model are the intertemporal separation of the capacity investment and the production decisions of the competing firms and the mutual independence of the random demands in the two periods.

However, in both these models (Maskin, Perrakis and Warskett), one restrictive feature was that the incumbent only had the option to install a capacity *before* the true demand is realized. Notice that, in section 2.3 while discussing the issue of excess capacity, we allowed the incumbent to increase its capacity level if needed *after* the demand is realized. After all, if the entrant can install capacity after the demand is realized, there is no reason why the incumbent would not be able to do so. The model by Kim (1996) allows this flexibility for the incumbent to increase its capacity after the demand is realized, if needed. In that study, he essentially revived the excess capacity hypothesis using Spulber's (1981) dynamic framework under demand uncertainty. He showed that the incumbent firm may hold excess capacity in the pre-entry stage even if the post-entry game is Cournot-Nash when market demand in future is greater enough than current demand. Recall that under deterministic demand Spulber (1981) showed no excess capacity under any circumstances will be observed when the post-entry game is Cournot-Nash.

Kim also argued the fact that if the discount rate for the future is sufficiently high under a booming prospect of the market, the incumbent may choose to give up its first-mover advantage (i.e., the cost advantage gained by not needing to pay capacity cost in the second period) by delaying installing of capacity until the post-entry phase and thus competing on an equal footing with the new entrant. The intuition of these results is as follows. When market demand remains constant over time, the established firm's production capacity at its monopoly level is likely to be more than sufficient to meet the output needed for the equilibrium of the post-entry game. The established firm naturally finds itself owning the first-mover advantage of not having to pay capacity cost. When future demand is high enough, however, the current monopoly output is likely to fall short of the output needed to fulfil the post-entry equilibrium. So the incumbent must decide whether to install the additional capacity now or after the new entry occurs. If the discount rate is not high, holding excess capacity now costs the incumbent little but confers upon it a cost advantage over its rival in the post-entry stage. If the discount rate is sufficiently high, however, the incumbent may be better off renouncing its first-mover advantage by delaying capacity instalment until the post-entry phase and competing on even terms with the new entrant. This paper thus modifies the received conclusion that the excess capacity choice is inconsistent with the post-entry game rule of Cournot-Nash, and presents the new result that an established firm's first-mover advantage is a matter of choice, not a predetermined condition.

Now we will turn to the case where the competing firms endogenously choose the timing of entry into the market under demand uncertainty.

### 1.3.3 Strategic investment decision under endogenous timing of entry

The importance of endogenizing the timing of moves by the competing firms under deterministic demand has been closely studied and formalized by Hamilton and Slutsky (1990), where they propose an extended game with observable delay. The firms announce when they will decide their production levels and commit to their announcement. After their production timings become common knowledge, they select their production level. Such a game is called an extended game with observable delay. They show that in this extended game a simultaneous play will be observed in the equilibrium. A sequential play will be observed if and only if the outcome of sequential play Pareto dominates the outcome associated with simultaneous play.

Sadanand and Sadanand (1996) made an analysis along this line under demand uncertainty. They extend the Hamilton and Slutsky (1990) paper in two directions. First, they introduce demand uncertainty into the model, and discuss how the results are affected by the amount of uncertainty. Second, they model the role of relative firm sizes in determining the order of moves. In their setup firms can choose to pre-commit to an output level under uncertainty or choose to remain flexible and make production decisions after the resolution of uncertainty. Since pre-commitment is crucial, there would be no strategic value to this pre-commitment if firms were able to freely adjust production levels *ex post*. Uncertainty and firm sizes provide trade-offs between commitment and flexibility and they show that both relative firm size and amount of uncertainty *jointly* determine the equilibrium moves. The main results of this analysis can be characterized as follows. First, with symmetric sized firms, a symmetric equilibrium is obtained with any amount of uncertainty. At the extremes of uncertainty the outcome is identical to a standard Cournot with no temporal randomization. For moderate amounts of uncertainty there is temporal randomization under the symmetric equilibrium. When firm sizes become disparate the temporal random symmetric equilibrium converges to a deterministic asymmetric equilibrium. With moderate uncertainty, the more disparate the firm sizes the more likely it is that larger firms are Stackelberg leaders and smaller firms are followers.

## 1.4   Ongoing research

In the course of writing this chapter, the author has come across with some of the most recently ongoing research in this area. Much of it is still in the form of unpublished manuscripts or working papers. In this section, we look into a few of these recent studies, and discuss the newest frontier of research on strategic investment under demand uncertainty.

A paper by Hirokawa (1999) borrows the model from Sadanand and Sadanand (1996) with two symmetric firms, but considers a situation when the demand uncertainty is resolved after at least one firm engages in production. In Sadananad and Sadanand (1996), the demand uncertainty resolves in the second period irrespective of a firm's production timing decisions. Here uncertainty resolves *endogenously* by at least one firm's entry into the market, and not exogenously by the passage of time. If neither of the firms enters the market, the uncertainty regarding demand remains unresolved. This could be a more realistic assumption since it is very well observed that only after launching a new product in the market, the industry gets fairly accurate estimates about the level of demand for that particular good. So the point in the Hirokawa (1999) paper is to see the trade-off between leadership advantage under uncertainty versus informational advantage without any strategic advantage. A firm chooses its optimal entry time by taking into account these two effects simultaneously. The main finding of the paper is that two *a priori* identical firms can voluntarily choose Stackelberg behaviour (i.e. the leader-follower behaviour) under demand uncertainty. This finding could be described using the following framework (Hirokawa, 1999).

## 1.4.1 Informational advantage versus leadership advantage

Consider two firms producing one homogeneous good. There is a demand uncertainty, the demand could be large (with probability $\theta$, $0 < \theta < 1$) or small (with probability $1 - \theta$), and is described as follows:

Large market:

$$p = \begin{cases} a - b(q_1 + q_2) & \text{if } q_1 + q_2 < \dfrac{a}{b} \\ 0 & \text{otherwise} \end{cases} \tag{1.24}$$

Small market:

$$p = \begin{cases} \psi a - b(q_1 + q_2) & \text{if } q_1 + q_2 < \dfrac{\psi a}{b} \,, \quad \text{where } \psi \in (0,1) \\ 0 & \text{otherwise} \end{cases} \tag{1.25}$$

Demand uncertainty is resolved only if at least one firm chooses its quantity or, in other words, if at least one firm enters the market. Each firm has the option to choose quantity at the first instant without knowing the true demand but in the process get the advantage for being a leader; or wait to get to know the true demand (if the other firm enters) but in the process lose the advantage of being a leader. If neither of the firms enters in the first instant, then the true demand is not revealed and firms produce simultaneously under uncertainty in period 2. This behaviour can be represented as in matrix 1.1.

|  |  | Firm $j$ | |
|---|---|---|---|
|  |  | Enter now | Wait |
| Firm $i$ | Enter now | Simultaneous Nash | Stackelberg |
|  | Wait | Stackelberg | Simultaneous Nash |

**Matrix 1.1**

The main result of this analysis is that the degree of demand uncertainty determines the importance of the second-mover's informational advantage. If such an advantage is unimportant, no firm wants to wait to be a follower. On the other hand, if the follower's advantage is so large that it entirely dominates the first-mover's advantage, then no firm wants to be the leader. Only under a moderate degree of uncertainty, the informational advantage of the follower is comparable to the commitment power of the leader, and then Stackelberg behaviour can be observed.

**Result 4** *Two firms, a priori symmetric, would behave asymmetrically (i.e. endogenously choose as being leader or follower) when there is a moderate degree of uncertainty. Otherwise, a symmetric behaviour (i.e. both firms enter or wait) will be observed in choosing outputs.*

An extension of the above analysis is found in Hirokawa and Sasaki (2000) when they consider the same framework (as of Hirokawa, 1999) with more than two firms. That opens up the possibility of co-leadership or co-followership. Under a simple linear demand, they establish that the number of co-leaders monotonically decreases in the magnitude of demand uncertainty relative to the expected level of demand. However, at least one firm always becomes a leader under all circumstances.

## 1.4.2   Dynamic market

Similar results are also found in the dynamic version of the model of Hirokawa and Sasaki (2001a), where the first entrant (leader) enjoys one period of uncontested monopoly before it competes with the follower in the later period. In another related paper, Hirokawa and Sasaki (2001b) modelled a two period dynamic market, where instead of assuming only the first-mover (leader) enjoys the uncontested monopoly for the initial period, both the firms produce in the initial period. The difference between the firms could be, in the beginning of the initial period, each firm either chooses a quantity-sticky production mode or a quantity-flexible production mode. The demand is observable only after the price and quantities are realized at the end of the first period. Now, once the state of demand is observed, a firm can make use of this information to optimize its second period supply if and only if the firm has chosen the flexible mode in the beginning. On the other hand, if only one of the firms has selected the sticky mode whilst the other has selected the flexible mode, then the stickiness entitles the firm to Stackelberg leadership in the second marketing period. Therefore, at the beginning of the game, firms face the trade-off between the strategic advantage of commitment and the adjustability to the demand realization. Under certain conditions, authors show that the trade-off between these two effects can give rise to a *posteriori* asymmetric Stackelberg-like behaviour, even if the firms are a *priori* identical. The explicit presence of pre-Stackelberg first period profits plays an important role in generating leader-follower behaviour as a pure strategy equilibrium.

## 1.5 Concluding remarks

In this chapter, we tried to depict a picture of strategic responses of the competing firms (the incumbent and the entrant) under various situations with demand uncertainty. On no account, this chapter should be seen as an attempt to give a comprehensive literature survey of this area. The main purpose of this chapter was to selectively focus on the main understandings as well as the main findings of the fundamental research that has been done or is going on in this topic. The other purpose of this study was also to provide a road map for future research to understand more about entry under demand uncertainty. It should be noted that the very presence of demand uncertainty changes many results significantly that were obtained under certainty. Consequently, it is safe to claim that the presence of demand uncertainty has a very significant impact on each firm's actions in a strategic environment.

# References

1] Bulow, J., J. Geanakoplos and P. Klemperer (1985), "Holding Idle Capacity to Deter Entry", *Economic Journal*, **95**, 178-82.
2] Basu, K. and N. Singh (1990), "Entry Deterrence in Stackelberg Perfect Equilibria", *International Economic Review*, **31**, 61-71.
3] Dixit, A.K. (1979), "A Model of Duopoly Suggesting a Theory of Entry Barriers", *Bell Journal of Economics*, **10**, 20-32.
4] Dixit, A.K. (1980), "The Role of Investment in Entry Deterrence", *Economic Journal*, **90**, 95-106.
5] Fudenberg, D. and J. Tirole (1984), "The Fat Cat Effect, the Puppy Dog Ploy, and the Lean and Hungry Look", *American Economic Review, Papers and Proceedings*, **74**, 361-8.
6] Hamilton, J.H. and S.M. Slutsky (1990), "Endogenous Timing in Duopoly Games: Stackelberg or Cournot Equilibria", *Games and Economic Behavior*, **2**, 29-46.

7] Hirokawa, M. (1999), "Endogenous Stackelberg Equilibrium under Demand Uncertainty", mimeo, University of Melbourne.

8] Hirokawa, M. and D. Sasaki (2000), "Endogenous Co-Leadership When Demand is Uncertain", *Australian Economic Papers*, **39**, 278-90.

9] Hirokawa, M. and D. Sasaki (2001a), "Endogenously Asynchronous Entries into an Uncertain Industry", *Journal of Economics and Management Strategy*, **10**, 435-61.

10] Hirokawa, M. and D. Sasaki (2001b), "Strategic Choice of Quantity Stickiness and Stackelberg Leadership", *Bulletin of Economic Research*, **53**, 19-34.

11] Kim, H.S. (1996), "Strategic Excess Capacity and First Mover Advantage under Variable Demand", *Seoul Journal of Economics*, **9**, 105-22.

12] Maskin, E. (1999), "Uncertainty and Entry Deterrence", *Economic Theory*, **14**, 429-37.

13] Perrakis, S. and G. Warskett (1983), "Capacity and Entry Deterrence under Demand Uncertainty", *Review of Economics Studies*, **50**, 495-511.

14] Poddar, S. (1999), "Excess Capacity Hypothesis Revisited under Demand Uncertainty", mimeo, National University of Singapore.

15] Sadanand, A. and V. Sadanand (1996), "Firm Scale and the Endogenous Timing of Entry: a Choice between Commitment and Flexibility", *Journal of Economic Theory*, **70**, 516-30.

16] Saloner, G. (1985), "Excess Capacity as a Policing Device", *Economics Letters*, **18**, 83-6.

17] Schmalensee, R. (1981), "Economics of Scale and Barriers to Entry", *Journal of Political Economy*, **89**, 1228-38.

18] Spence, A.M. (1977), "Entry, Capacity, Investment and Oligopolistic Pricing", *Bell Journal of Economics*, **8**, 534-44.

19] Spulber, D. (1981), "Capacity, Output and Sequential Entry", *American Economic Review*, **71**, 503-14.

# Chapter 2

# Strategic investment

Sougata Poddar and Dan Sasaki[1]

## 2.1  Introduction

This chapter is devoted to recent developments in research on strategic investment. We start with a brief overview on the past theoretical research in this field, and then move on to the state-of-the-art, including our most recent studies on *strategic inventories* and *product innovation.*

The chapter starts with a very brief overview of bibliographic background in section 2.2. Then we proceed to a slightly more specialised discussion about the existing studies on *capacity investment* which is closely related to, and in some sense gave rise to, relatively recent microtheoretic studies on strategic inventories. A review (and *preview* to some extent) of our current research on strategic inventories is presented in section 2.4, and its potential

[1]We are most indebted to Luca Lambertini, without whose patient encouragement the completion of this chapter would not have been possible. We also thank the Institute of Economics and Centre for Industrial Economics at the University of Copenhagen, where all three of us (Lambertini, Poddar and Sasaki) were affiliated during the year 1996-97, which gave us the invaluable opportunity to commence our collaborative research project. Parts of our research project have been presented at: EARIE Conference at Leuven, Belgium, September 1997; University of Sydney, May 1998; Far Eastern Meeting of the Econometric Society at Singapore, July 1999; research seminars at University of Melbourne, August 1999; and LaTrobe University, September 1999. Generous financial assistance from Faculty of Economics and Commerce, University of Melbourne, and from School of Business and Economics, University of Exeter, should also be acknowledged. Much of the material presented in this chapter is on the state-of-the-art frontier of research which is still actively developing. The authors assume the sole responsibility for any remaining shortcomings found in this chapter, and are open to further comments and discussions which may help us enhance our research in the future.

interrelation to macroeconomic problems is illustrated in section 2.5.

Another kind of investment which is theoretically closely related to capacity investment is *innovation*, or *R&D investment*. Essentially, if we replace the quantity axis in analysing capacity investment with the time axis in analysing R&D investment, there arises a parallel relation between these two kinds of investment to a large extent. This, in conjunction with the theoretical difference between *product innovation* and *process innovation*, is presented in section 2.6. There are differences between capacity and R&D, however, reflecting the intrinsic difference between the quantity space and the time space. Some of the similarities and differences between capacity investment and product innovation are briefly discussed in section 2.7. There also are similarities and differences between *inventory investment* and *process innovation*, as we show in section 2.8.

## 2.2   Overview

Investment, in the context of industrial organisation, is generally conceptualised as a sunk payment made by a firm in an attempt to alter the firm's variable cost structure. This should be expressly distinguished from the "investment" in its macroeconomic sense, which is dual to "saving".

In order for an investment (in the industrial organisation sense) to be *strategic*, it needs [1] to alter the firm's *marginal* costs, and [2] to be embedded in an oligopoly situation. One of the pioneering contributions on strategic investment is Fudenberg and Tirole (1984), where a monotone comparative statics exercise is conducted in a taxonomy classified according to the effects of investment on the production function (or, put differently, on the variable cost structure) on the one hand, and the form of strategic interaction between oligopolistic firms on the other hand.

A game-theoretic analysis of capacity investment, which is closely related to the material we present heretofore, is founded by Kreps and Scheinkman (1983). In general, quantity competition (à la Cournot) and price competition (à la Bertrand) on a homogeneous product yield very different equilibrium outcomes. However, Kreps and Scheinkman first established a nice correspondence between the Cournot equilibrium and the Bertrand equilibrium. They reinstated the Cournot equilibrium through a different and more compelling route than taken by Cournot (1838) himself. Following the Marshallian (1920) idea (as opposed to Walras, 1874) that prices are easier to change than quantities, Kreps and Scheinkman constructed a particular environment in a two-period game. In the first period, firms produce outputs (accumulate inventories). This production then forms the upper limits of what the firms can sell. In period two, the firms simultaneously choose prices. They showed that quantities chosen by firms in the first period and the price chosen in the second period are exactly the Cournot outcome, i.e., in the subgame perfect equilibrium of this two-period game, in period one firms choose the Cournot equilibrium outputs and in period two they choose the Cournot equilibrium price.

On the other hand, strategic effects of capacity investment had indeed been known in more specific contexts, as in Spence (1977), Dixit (1980), Spulber (1981), Bulow *et al.* (1985), *inter alia*.

The general idea in analysing investment, or strategic investment in particular, is as follows. Investment is modelled as a sunk cost incurred in return to the resulting reduction in *variable* production costs. Thereby its first-order effect is a trade-off between the initial sunk cost and subsequent variable costs. This can be viewed either as intertemporal substitution, or as a trade-off in favour of the relative advantage in large-scale production in exchange for the relative disadvantage in small-scale production (or *vice versa*). In the second order, in an oligopolistic environment, such an investment brings a strategic effect. That is, a reduction in one firm's variable production costs serves to *shift the firm's reaction function*, which in turn affects other firms' actions. Furthermore, depending upon the nature of the oligopolistic environment and of the investment *per se*, there can be a third-order effect which can be conceptualised broadly as a commitment effect. This is not only to say that the investment is pre-committed, but also that the incentive for (or against) such an investment may in itself involve interactive forces between the oligopolist firms in question.

To find the role of investment in capacity on entry deterrence in an incumbent-entrant model, Dixit (1980) showed that investing in capacity by the incumbent firm prior to entry gives a (limited) Stackelberg leadership to the incumbent firm. He considered a simple two-stage game, where in the first stage the incumbent chooses the level of capacity (which can be increased in the second stage, if needed), and in the second stage chooses the level of output. He showed that in a subgame perfect equilibrium of this two-stage game the incumbent firm will be left with no idle capacity since holding excess capacity has no entry deterring effect. The purpose of this study by Dixit is to challenge the view of Spence (1977), who suggested that an incumbent should hold excess capacity under the threat of entry, meaning if the entrant enters the market the incumbent will use all its capacity to produce output which will eventually drive down the price to such a level that will make entry unprofitable. This is a kind of limit pricing argument. At the same time, in case of no entry, the incumbent will be left with costly idle capacity. That is, excess capacity will be observed in the event of no entry.

Dixit, using Spence's framework, argued that such a limit pricing behaviour or holding excess capacity is not an optimal behaviour of the incumbent firm. At the same time, he also emphasised the fact that entry prevention should not be a prior constraint, because in some situations, the established firm can be better off by accommodating the entrant. However, later, Bulow *et al.* (1985) re-established Spence's original intuition that firms might in some circumstances rationally hold idle capacity to deter entry. They argued that Dixit's conclusion very much depends on the assumption that each firm's marginal revenue is always decreasing in the rival's output (i.e. the firm's reaction curve is always downward sloping). If this assumption is violated the result does not hold any longer. For example, instead of a linear demand (or in general, a concave demand), if a constant-elasticity demand is considered, the excess capacity hypothesis is indeed revived. More generally, they argued that if firms' reaction functions are strategic complements to each other, then there arises the possibility of holding idle capacity to deter entry. This is not going to be true if firms' reaction functions are strategic substitutes to each other (as in Dixit's model).[2]

So far, we have discussed static models, i.e., no consideration of time preferences is assumed and also in these models the established firm installs capacity without any production in the pre-entry phase. Spulber (1981) presented a dynamic model of entry in which the established firm pursues a Cournot-Nash (alternatively a Stackelberg) strategy towards a potential entrant. Spulber considered a two-period framework in which the established firm is engaged in production in each period. He showed that if the post-entry game is Cournot-Nash, the incumbent never holds excess capacity whether or not it allows entry. On the other hand, holding excess capacity to deter entry is shown to occur when the established firm is a Stackelberg leader.

When discussing strategic investment, one of the interesting directions is to consider whether oligopolistic market power entails overinvestment or underinvestment perceived from a *social* point of view. A *monopolist* would generally underinvest, as it tends to produce less than the socially optimal quantity. In *oligopoly*, there are two counterforces. On the one hand, there remains an element of underinvestment as oligopolists tend to exercise market power and thus produce less than the social total surplus maximal quantity. On the other hand, there are strategic effects which, as Fudenberg and Tirole show, can provide either overinvesting incentives or underinvesting incentives

---

[2]Let there be two firms with strategies $x_1$ and $x_2$ and respective profit functions $\pi_1[x_1, x_2]$ and $\pi_2[x_2, x_1]$. Definition: we call $x_2$ a *strategic substitute* for $x_1$ if $\partial^2 \pi_1 / \partial x_2 \partial x_1 < 0$ and a *strategic complement* if $\partial^2 \pi_1 / \partial x_2 \partial x_1 > 0$ (note the analogy with the definition that products are *substitutes* if $\partial \pi_1 / \partial x_2 < 0$ and complements if $\partial \pi_1 / \partial x_2 > 0$).

depending upon the monotone comparative statics of the oligopoly game. In capacity investment, which has similar (albeit not the same) implications to quantity setting, these strategic effects between competing oligopolists tend to provide overinvesting incentives.

A similar analysis can be made on *innovation*, or *R&D investment*. A monopolist tends to invest less, entailing slower innovation, than socially desirable. This is because the monopolist maximises only its own profit without regard to consumers' surplus which, too, forms part of the social total surplus. This makes the monopolist's private marginal return from investment lower than the social marginal return, resulting in an underinvesting incentive.

Oligopolists have similar underinvesting incentives on the one hand, whilst they also have competitive overinvesting incentives which sometimes serve to correct the underinvestment problem but sometimes overcorrect it, giving rise to hypercompetition in R&D investment.

## 2.3 Production capacity investment

Capacity in its strictest sense, sometimes explicitly referred to as a "hard" capacity constraint, is the absolute maximum feasible production quantity, beyond which the production costs explode up to infinity.

A cost function under this hard capacity constraint is a cost function *truncated* at the maximum admissible production level, referred to as the *capacity*. Hence, capacity investment in its narrowest sense is a sunk investment which is to shift this "capacity" outwards. The higher the investment level is, the higher the capacity is. When the underlying total variable cost function is $VC[q]$ ($q \geq 0$) and the capacity is $\bar{q}$, the capacity constrained total variable cost function is

$$VC[q|\bar{q}] = \begin{cases} VC[q] & \text{if} \quad 0 \leq q \leq \bar{q}, \\ \infty & \text{if} \quad q > \bar{q}. \end{cases} \quad (2.1)$$

Diagrammatically, this is illustrated in figures 2.1 and 2.2. Capacity in its weaker sense, referred to as a "soft" capacity constraint, does not stipulate that the total cost should explode to infinity at a specific level of production. As is straightforwardly observed from the diagrams, capacity investment in its broad sense refers to the choice between a low level of investment which entails relative advantage in small-scale production in exchange for relative disadvantage in large-scale production, and a high level of investment entailing the converse.

**Figure 2.1:** Hard capacity

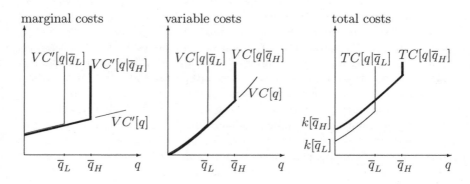

**Figure 2.2:** Soft capacity

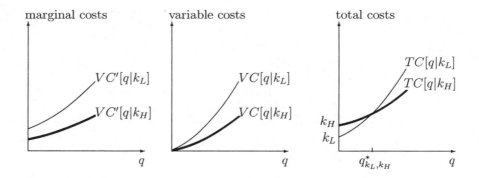

In order for an investment to qualify as a *capacity investment*, this **single crossing property** must be satisfied. That is, for any levels of investment $k_L$, $k_H$ where $k_L < k_H$, there must exist a *unique* $q^*_{k_L,k_H}$ such that the total cost function (inclusive of the cost of investment) $TC[q|k] = VC[q|k] + k$ satisfies

$$TC[q|k_L] < TC[q|k_H] \text{ for all } q < q^*_{k_L,k_H},$$
$$TC[q|k_L] > TC[q|k_H] \text{ for all } q > q^*_{k_L,k_H}. \tag{2.2}$$

This monotone trade-off between relative advantages in small-scale production and in large-scale production is the key feature in distinguishing *capacity investment*, broadly defined, from other forms of investment which can affect the cost structure in a non-monotone way. Obviously, in the case of hard capacity constraints, $q^*_{k_L,k_H} = \min\{k_L, k_H\}$ for any $k_L$, $k_H$.

As is well known in standard microeconomic theory, the *envelope* of the total cost curves in the right diagram of figure 2.1 or figure 2.2 as $k$ varies gives the **long-run total cost curve**. This implies that the most economical level of capacity investment $k$ varies as the contemplated production level $q$ varies, *even in the absence of multi-firm strategic interactions*. This contrasts with *inventory investment* as we discuss in the following.

## 2.4 Inventory investment

### 2.4.1 Preliminaries

Inventory, defined as *advance* production (or purchase) of marketable goods, is considered as a form of investment. This is because the cost of advance production (or acquisition) is *sunk*, so that the *instantaneous* marginal cost of the goods which have been stored as an inventory, evaluated at the time when the goods are marketed, is nil. Hence, there is a trade-off between the advance sunk cost and instantaneous variable costs.

However, inventory is considered as a different kind of investment from capacity. The reason is precisely because it generally does not satisfy the aforementioned single crossing property (see section 2.3). Contrary to capacity investment, advance production typically costs more than instantaneous production for any production level. First, if goods are produced in advance, they must be stored, which typically incurs storage costs. Second, if production costs are intrinsically time-invariant, in the presence of time preferences, those production costs incurred ahead of time are relatively magnified in terms of the time-discounted value. In addition, if the time lag between advance production and instantaneous production is large enough to make the technological progress non-negligible, the earlier production under the less advanced production technology is less economical in and by itself. These factors render advance production *uniformly* more expensive than instantaneous production *for any level of production*.

This immediately implies that neither a monopolist nor a perfectly competitive firm would invest in inventories, at least in an environment where there is no demand uncertainty or serial demand fluctuation. Namely, unlike capacity investment (see section 2.3), inventory investment offers no intertemporal cost trade-off.

Therefore, if there are any incentives for inventory investment, it should be attributed either to demand fluctuation or uncertainty, or to strategic interactions between competing oligopolists. The former has been studied by Dixit (1980), *inter alia*. The latter has been studied by Saloner (1987) and Pal (1991). Saloner disregards the cost differential between advance production and instantaneous production, and focuses exclusively on the strategic advantage of advance production as a quantity commitment device. Pal, on the other hand, takes the cost disadvantage of advance production explicitly into account and nevertheless derives those (subgame perfect) equilibria where at least one firm engages in advance production which, obviously, is a stronger result than Saloner's. What is common in these two pathbreaking contributions on strategic advance production, however, is the key assumption that advance production entitles the firm to Stackelberg leadership in the ensuing marketing stage. In particular, it deserves heightened attention that this is imposed as an assumption in both of these two contributions.

At the same time, it is noteworthy that the literature has not always treated the order of moves between oligopolists as exogenously given, in a closely related yet slightly different context. Seminal results by Henderson and Quandt (1971) and Gal-Or (1985) show that, if firms were to choose their timing of moves, there would inevitably arise a conflict of interests and hence the firms could never "agree" upon a fixed deterministic order. This is known as "Stackelberg disequilibrium". Attempts to model the choice of timing as one of the strategic variables have been pioneered by d'Aspremont and Gérard-Varet (1980) and, more formally and explicitly, by Hamilton and Slutsky (1990) where largely two categories of endogenous timing games are defined: the "extended game with observable delay" is an explicitly two-stage game where firms can choose their marketing actions *after observing* each other's timing decisions and hence, the follower (later mover) can pick its marketing variable (e.g., a price, or a quantity) in response to that of the leader (earlier mover), whilst the "extended game with action commitment" is a game where information is more imperfect in that firms can no longer take timing-contingent marketing actions. In fact, the aforementioned Pal also deals with the issue of endogenising the order of firms' moves in his more recent paper (1996). Effectively all of the existing game-theoretic attempts to endogenise the order of moves between oligopolists are to take into account some auxiliary factors affecting the first- or second-mover advantage,[3] advance production being one of these possible factors.

Now, what if advance production does not automatically entitle the firm

---

[3]These studies include, but are by no means limited to: Albæk (1990) taking into account cost uncertainty; Robson (1990) and Matsumura (1997) introducing higher costs associated with earlier actions; Mailath (1993) and Normann (1997) assuming *a priori* informational heterogeneity between firms; and Sadanand and Sadanand (1996) and Maggi (1996) considering demand uncertainty.

to Stackelberg leadership? As is well known, Stackelberg leadership by itself yields an unambiguous profit improvement compared to simultaneous-move Nash equilibria. Thereby in the preceding literature, the advance production effect is assisted by the Stackelberg leadership effect in contributing to the firm's profit. To separate the former effect from the latter, in Poddar and Sasaki (2002) we construct a model where the order of moves in the marketing stage is independent of the timing of production. Namely, firms engage in simultaneous-move oligopoly irrespective of the levels of their pre-committed investment. The intuition to our results is summarised in the following.

### 2.4.2 Analysis

To keep the model as simple as possible, we consider a two-stage duopoly game. The first stage is the stage for inventory investment. The second stage is where the market opens and Cournot oligopoly takes place. The cost structure is illustrated in figure 2.3.

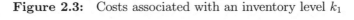

**Figure 2.3:** Costs associated with an inventory level $k_1$

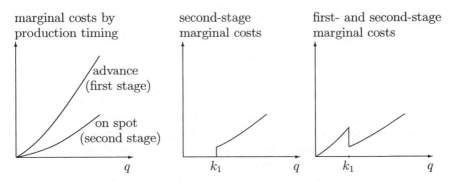

The middle diagram of figure 2.3, second-stage on-spot marginal costs, determines the *reaction function* of each firm in the market stage. Under this cost structure, the reaction function typically has a *flat spot* (vertical segment) at $q = k_1$, as shown by the thick kinked locus in figure 2.4. Namely, by means of advance production, a firm (firm 1 in the diagram) can shift its second-stage instantaneous reaction function outwards over the output range $0 \leq q_1 \leq k_1$.

**Figure 2.4:** Firm 1's reaction function with advance production $k_1^a$

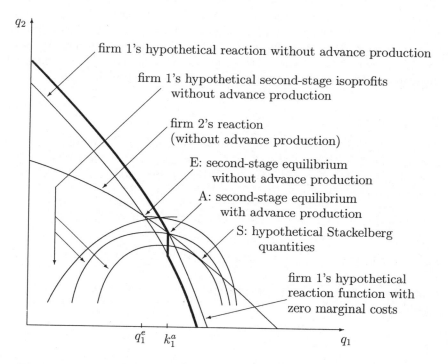

Figure 2.4 shows that, in general, the second-stage equilibrium when firm 1 produces a sufficient quantity ($k_1^a$) in advance (point A) brings a higher instantaneous profit than the second-stage equilibrium without advance production (point E), *insofar as firm 2 does not produce in advance*. Hence, as long as this improvement in second-stage profits overcompensates the cost increment required for advance production, firm 1 has a strict incentive for advance production. A similar argument holds when it is more profitable to produce a quantity which is between $q_1^e$ and $k_1^a$. Depending upon the cost differential between advance production and on-spot production, the relative locations of point A and point S can vary. If marginal costs are relatively low and thus the reaction function over the range $0 \leq q_1 \leq k_1$ can shift out only slightly, then it is likely that point A lies *between points E and S* as shown in the above diagram. Otherwise, if marginal costs are sizeable and therefore the reaction shift is also substantial, then point A is likely to lie

*beyond* (i.e., to the right of) point S. Note that, in the latter case, our result here is identical to Pal (1991), whilst in the former case, the fact that we do not install the artificial assumption of automatic Stackelberg leadership by means of advance production makes a substantive difference. In this sense, our result is stronger in that we derive a similar result, i.e., expensive advance investment may gain a strategic incentive, without having to summon any assistance by Stackelberg leadership.

### 2.4.3 Extensions

Curiously, this result generally does not extend to the case where the competing firm (firm 2 in our example) is already engaged in advance production. This situation is illustrated in figure 2.5. The intuition is as follows. When firm 2 produces $k_2$ in advance, its reaction function has a flat spot (horizontal segment) at $q_2 = k_2$. Hence, first, there is no guarantee that firm 1 can improve its second-stage profits by expanding production (the left diagram). Second, even when it can, the resulting second-stage quantity profile will no longer lie on the flat segment of firm 2's reaction function (the right diagram).

**Figure 2.5:** Firm 1's reaction function given $k_2 > 0$

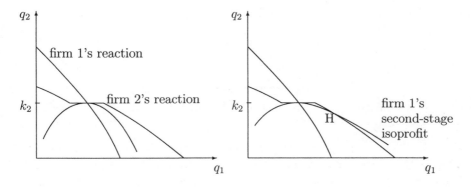

Given that advance production is uneconomical *per se*, if firm 2 were to sell *strictly less than* $k_2$ then advance producing as much as $k_2$ would be suboptimal. Hereby *there is no* (pure strategy subgame perfect) *equilibrium where both* (all, in the case of more than two firms' Cournot oligopoly) *firms advance produce*.

These results can extend to more general $n$-firm oligopoly with similar cost structures. Namely, a firm may have a strategic incentive for costly advance production *when at least one other firm does not engage in advance production*, whilst no such incentive can exist when all other $n - 1$ firms are already advance producing.

Our results can also apply to a situation where "oligopolists" are selling *complement products*. This is diagrammatically illustrated in figure 2.6. In the diagram, the *upper side* of firm 1's isoprofit is now the higher-profit side, reflecting the fact that firms are supplying mutually complementary products. Hence, advance production undertaken by firm 1, shifting its reaction function outwards, can shift the resulting equilibrium in a profitable direction for firm 1.

**Figure 2.6:**  Complementary products

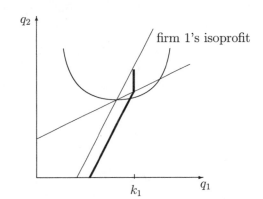

On the other hand, in *Bertrand* oligopoly, there cannot be any incentive for costly advance production, whether the firms' products are substitutes or complements. This is intuitively shown in figure 2.7. The left diagram illustrates duopoly with imperfect substitute products. When inventories are held, *price reaction functions generally shift inwards*, which shifts the resulting market equilibrium to the lower-profit side of the market-stage isoprofit. A similar observation can be made in the case of complement products, as in the right diagram of figure 2.7. Hence, there is no strategic advantage gained by means of advance production.

It is hereby shown that the presence or absence of incentives for strategic inventory hinges *not upon strategic complementarity or strategic substitution*, but upon the strategic *variables per se*.

**Figure 2.7:** Bertrand oligopoly

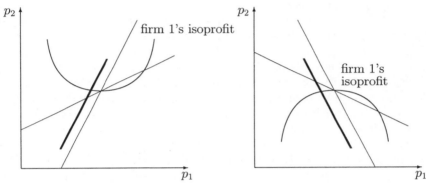

In a more general case where price-setting firms and quantity-setting firms coexist, it can be shown that a firm can gain strategic incentives for advance production only if there is a *quantity-setting competitor who does not engage in advance production*. For instance, in a duopoly with one price-setter and one quantity-setter, it is only the price-setter not the quantity-setter who can possibly have a strategic incentive for costly advance production.

## 2.4.4 Discussion

In real markets and industries, it is difficult to determine whether firms are price-setters or quantity-setters. Most often the truth is somewhere in between, that is, firms are setting *upward sloping supply functions* which are generally neither vertical (Cournot) nor horizontal (Bertrand).

Our foregoing analysis should therefore be interpreted as, in general, firms are more likely to engage in strategic inventory investment by means of advance production [1] in an industry where technological givens induce supply functions to have steep slopes, i.e., the industry being closer to Cournot than to Bertrand, and/or [2] when the firm faces those competitors who, for either strategic or non-strategic reasons, *choose* steep Cournot-like supply functions.

## 2.5   Macroeconomic implications

Inventory behaviour has long been studied by both microeconomists and macroeconomists. In this section we attempt a quick glance at how our foregoing microtheoretic findings can be potentially utilised to disentangle some of the lasting puzzles in macroeconomics.

In almost any economy in the world, the breakdown of the GDP shows the following pattern. Its largest fraction, usually above 80%, is consumption, and the remainder is broadly defined investment (or saving). Within investment, inventory is only a tiny fraction, typically less than 1% of the GDP. In accounting for the *fluctuation* of the GDP, on the other hand, the fluctuation of investment tends to be much more substantial than that of consumption. In particular, it has been universally observed that inventory investment is so much more volatile than the remainder of investment that it alone can weigh as much as 40 to 50 % of the total variation of the GDP (for further details, see Blanchard and Fischer, 1989, chapter 6).

The fact that consumption is proportionately smoother than investment, has been explained by the **consumption smoothing** theory. That is, utility maximisation of each individual consumer entails the tendency of absorbing intertemporal income fluctuations into saving and dissaving, in an attempt to smooth out the consumption level, making investment (which should theoretically equal saving) fluctuant relative to consumption. The difference between inventory and the remainder of investment, however, is less transparent.

An analogue of consumption smoothing theory in an attempt to explain disproportionate volatility of inventory investment is the theory of **production smoothing**. A pioneering research in this direction can be found in Holt *et al.* (1960). In the presence of capacity and other constraints, it tends to be more economical to keep the level of production constant over time, so that the intertemporal fluctuations in demand, or in sales, tend to be absorbed by inventories. If this is the truth, then it should be expected that the fluctuations in inventories are *countercyclical*. An empirical criticism cast against this theory is the fairly general finding that inventories are statistically not countercyclical.

Another theory of inventory investment, which can explain *procyclical* fluctuations, is the **stock out** theory. The importance of procyclical inventories is established empirically by Blanchard (1983) and Blinder (1986), and much of the theoretical establishment of the stock out theory is due to Kahn (1987). This theory is simply based upon the common observation that most commodities *cannot be shortsold*. Hence, whenever the market is booming, suppliers must increase inventories in order to prevent the loss of sales caused by stock out. However, it remains puzzling why inventories need to be disproportionately more fluctuant than the remainder of the economy, given that all suppliers should rationally expect the overall magnitude of fluctuations in the market, taking into account every consumer's consumption smoothing.

What macroeconomics, by definition, does not teach us is the relation between inventory behaviour and each industry's specific structure. Here is the role of inventory studies in industrial economics. In particular, we focus on the strategic aspects of oligopolistic industries. Namely, it is highly conceivable that some industries in the macroeconomy are oligopolistic where firms may have strategic advance production incentives *depending upon demand levels*. In addition, if such advance production incentives arise when and only when demand levels are high, then the resulting inventories become procyclical.

## 2.5.1 Analytical example

To develop a quick intuition, revisit our duopoly model in the previous section, with linear (inverse) demand $p = a - q_1 - q_2$ where $a > 0$ is the indicator of the demand in the market, which varies over time but is assumed, for simplicity, to be commonly known to both firms. Each firm's total costs, discounted to the beginning of the game, are $\gamma k_i$ if $q_i \leq k_i$, or $\gamma k_i + \delta\gamma(q_i - k_i)$ if $q_i > k_i$, where $\gamma > 0$ is the unit cost of production, and $\delta \in (0,1)$ is the discount factor. The overall characterisation of the equilibria of this two-stage linear duopoly game depends upon the discount factor $\delta$, as well as upon the relative magnitude of production costs $\gamma$ to the demand intercept $a$. It can be proven (interested readers are encouraged to refer to our paper, Poddar and Sasaki, 2002) that there is a threshold $\bar{a}$ where:

- if $a < \bar{a}$ neither firm invests in advance production and each firm sells the same quantity $q^{CN}$ produced on-spot only, at the price $p^{CN}$;

- if $a \geq \bar{a}$ one of the firms produces $q^{AP}$ in advance, and sells this quantity (i.e., does not engage in any additional on-spot production) whilst the other firm produces on-spot and sells $q^{OS}$, both at the price $p^{AP}$.

For further concreteness, we choose some benchmark numbers and see how our "strategic explanation" of the extreme volatility of inventory investment appears. Macroeonomically, inventories are kept on average about three to six months, but note also that our $\delta$ includes obsolescence of products, and storage costs. Hence, if we assume an annual interest rate of 4%, an annual obsolescence of 10%, with negligible storage costs, then our $\delta$ should be in the neighbourhood of 93% per half year.

Also, as a rough approximate benchmark, let the *status quo* mass of inventory investment be 0.5% of the economy's gross production (GDP or GNP), and the de-trended fluctuations in the economy be in the order of 0.2% of the GDP. The macroeconomic fluctuations are assumed to be reflected on the demand intercept in every industry (whether oligopolistic or not). Considering the fact that the economic indicators are measured on the basis of the amount of transaction not the quantity of production, the 0.2% de-trended fluctuations in money amount correspond to a demand intercept fluctuation in the order of 0.1%.

When this skimpy 0.1% increment in the demand intercept occurs in our duopolistic industry, it can make the intercept $a$ just cross the threshold $\bar{a}$ if its *status quo* level happens to be near $\bar{a}$. When $\delta \approx 0.93$, this threshold turns out to be $\bar{a} \approx 3.5\gamma$. When the intercept $a$ actually crosses the threshold $\bar{a}$, the industry's total sales amount stays approximately unchanged (i.e., $(q^{AP} + q^{OS})p^{AP} \approx 2q^{CN}p^{CN}$) whilst the amount of advance production suddenly grows from nil to $q^{AP}p^{AP}$, constituting the fraction $q^{AP}/(q^{AP} + q^{OS}) \approx 64\%$ of the industry's total production.

Let $v$ be the weight of the duopolistic industry relative to the economy's GDP. Suppose, for further simplicity, that the inventory fluctuations in all other industries are just proportional to the fluctuation of the total production, that is, 0.2% of the amount of inventories which is 0.5% of the production. In this economy, if aggregate inventory fluctuations represent 40% of the aggregate GDP fluctuation which is 0.2% of the GDP,

$$v \times 64\% + (1 - v) \times 0.5\% \times 0.2\% = 40\% \times 0.2\%, \qquad (2.3)$$

i.e., the weight $v$ needs to be no more than 0.1234%, merely 1/810 of the economy. Note further that, if the inventory fluctuations in other industries are proportionately larger, the required weight of the duopolistic industry $v$ becomes even smaller.

## 2.5.2   Discussion

Our numerical example has demonstrated that the strategic incentives for inventory investment in an oligopolistic industry can explain the widely observed extreme volatility of macroeconomic inventories, even if the weight of such an oligopolistic industry is no more than a tiny — almost negligible — fraction of the economy.

One way to test empirically whether this explanation fits the reality is to focus on the industry's price fluctuation patterns. That is, at our benchmark numbers $\delta \approx 0.93$ and $a \approx 3.5\gamma$, the industry is approximately neither pro-cyclical nor countercyclical in terms of the sales amount, whereas its quantity is procyclical, $q^{AP} + q^{OS} > 2q^{CN}$, which is intuitively similar to Stackelberg quantity outcomes, with *countercyclical prices* $q^{AP} < q^{CN}$. Namely, if there is an oligopolistic industry of which strategic inventories can account for a dis-proportionately large portion of the macroeconomic inventory fluctuations, then such an industry should show a pattern of countercyclical pricing.

## 2.6   Product and process innovation

Thus far, we have focused on those kinds of investment which are to alter the *static* cost structure. Namely, the cost function is conceptualised as a univariate function of which the production quantity is the sole argument.

Now, if we reconceptualise the cost structure by representing it with a bivariate function in both the production quantity and time, then we are able to encompass a broader class of investment, including what is ordinarily referred to as *innovation*.

Innovation is broadly classified into two categories : **product innovation** and **process innovation**. When product innovation (sometimes called "invention") takes place at time $t_0$, the production cost of the product is infinity at any $t < t_0$. This is not the case if the innovation at time $t_0$ is process innovation instead of product innovation.

Innovation, in its strict definition (occasionally referred to as "drastic" innovation), refers to a *discontinuous jump* of the bivariate cost function with respect to time. Namely, if the innovation occurs at time $t_0$, there is a non-negligible range of $q$ such that the instantaneous variable cost function $IVC[q,t]$ has

$$\lim_{t \uparrow t_0} IVC[q,t] > \lim_{t \downarrow t_0} IVC[q,t]. \tag{2.4}$$

Now that the cost function is *multivariate*, the *cost surface* can no longer be drawn on a two-dimensional plane. However, we can draw its $\{IVC, t\}$-slice given any $q > 0$, as well as the slice of the *total* cost function $ITC[q,t|k] = IVC[q,t|k] + k$. Drastic product innovation is illustrated in figure 2.8.

**Figure 2.8:** Drastic product innovation

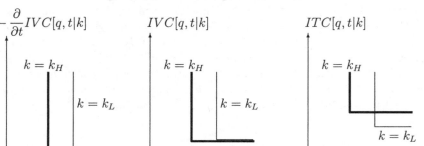

Innovation in a looser definition (sometimes called "incremental" innovation) refers to an investment that alters the time-dependence of the cost structure, as illustrated in figure 2.9. A general conceptual model of product innovation can be presented as follows. For any level of investment in product innovation $k > 0$, the instantaneous variable cost function $IVC[q,t|k]$ satisfies

$$\lim_{t \downarrow 0} IVC[q,t|k] \;=\; \infty\,, \; \frac{\partial}{\partial t} IVC[q,t|k] < 0\,, \tag{2.5}$$
$$\lim_{t \uparrow \infty} IVC[q,t|k] \;\geq\; 0 \; \forall \; q > 0$$

and, for any $t > 0$,

$$\lim_{k \downarrow 0} IVC[q,t|k] = \infty\,, \; \frac{\partial}{\partial k} IVC[q,t|k] < 0\,, \tag{2.6}$$

$$\lim_{k \uparrow \infty} \frac{\partial}{\partial k} IVC[q,t|k] = 0 \; \forall \; q > 0\,.$$

**Figure 2.9:** Incremental product innovation

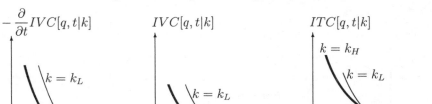

Here arises a straightforward analogy to the monotone trade-off between relative advantages in small-scale production versus large-scale production in our previous case of (static) capacity investment (see section 2.3). Fixing any $q > 0$ and replacing our previous quantity axis with the newly introduced time axis, if we draw the $\{ITC, t\}$-slice of the surface $k = k_L$ and that of the surface $k = k_H$, there exists a *unique* $t^*_{k_L, k_H}[q]$ at which these two loci intersect, that is, there arises the monotone trade-off between relative advantages in *fast production* versus *slow production*

$$ITC[q, t|k_L] > ITC[q, t|k_H] \text{ for all } t < q^*_{k_L, k_H}[q],$$
$$ITC[q, t|k_L] < ITC[q, t|k_H] \text{ for all } t > q^*_{k_L, k_H}[q]. \tag{2.7}$$

Unlike in product innovation, in process innovation the product already exists and has been produced under the *status quo* production technology. Process innovation can also be categorised into drastic innovation and incremental innovation. Drastic process innovation is illustrated in figure 2.10.

**Figure 2.10:**   Drastic process innovation

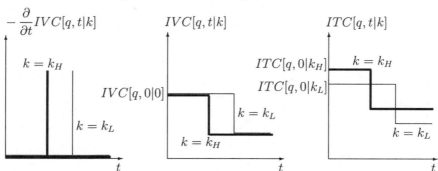

As is unmistakable from the far right diagram, a major difference from product innovation is that, even when the level of investment $k$ in process innovation varies, the total cost function $ITC[q, t|k] = IVC[q, t|k] + k$ does not generally demonstrate the *monotone* trade-off between the cost advantage in fast production and that in slow production. Namely, the $\{ITC, t\}$-slices of the total cost surfaces $k = k_L$ and $k = k_H$ may not be single-crossing. Incremental process innovation is illustrated in figure 2.11.

Likewise, a general abstract model of process innovation, given the *status quo* variable cost function $IVC[q, 0|0]$, is

$$\lim_{t \downarrow 0} IVC[q, t|k] \;=\; IVC[q, 0|0] \,, \; \frac{\partial}{\partial t} IVC[q, t|k] < 0 \,, \qquad (2.8)$$
$$\lim_{t \uparrow \infty} IVC[q, t|k] \;\geq\; 0 \; \forall \; q > 0$$

and, for any $t > 0$,

$$\lim_{k \downarrow 0} IVC[q, t|k] = IVC[q, 0|0] \,, \; \frac{\partial}{\partial k} IVC[q, t|k] < 0 \,, \qquad (2.9)$$

$$\lim_{k \uparrow \infty} \frac{\partial}{\partial k} IVC[q, t|k] = 0 \; \forall \; q > 0 \,.$$

**Figure 2.11:** Incremental process innovation

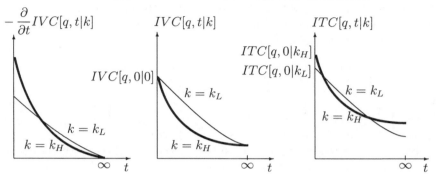

Note that, in the presence of market competition, drastic product innovation has the same effect as a process innovation allowing for very low production costs of the same (already existing) good, so that the innovating firm can fix a monopoly price below the marginal cost of the loser. Observational equivalence between process and product innovation when innovation is drastic is established by Futia (1980).

## 2.7  Product innovation and capacity

There exists a certain degree of similarity, or conceptual interchangeability, between capacity investment and innovation. If we replace the quantity axis with the time axis, drastic product innovation corresponds to hard capacity. As producing any quantity $q > \bar{q}$ was infeasible in the presence of the hard capacity $\bar{q}$, now in the case of product innovation at time $\bar{t}$ it is impossible to produce at any time $t < \bar{t}$.

Dissimilarities between product innovation and capacity investment include their *strategic* implications. As has been known, capacity investment can serve as an enforcement device in support of tacit collusion in repeated Bertrand oligopoly. Can product innovation play a similar role?

The most spontaneous answer to this question would be to contemplate a straight analogue between the *production possibility set* due to the hard capacity constraint and the *production timing set* due to the drastic innovation constraint. This analogy unfortunately does not hold, precisely because of the fact that the innovation constraint is embedded in the time dimension. Any enhancement in innovative investment is to extend the production timing set in the direction of *preponement*. Hence, it cannot serve to deter price wars which are to occur *later*.

On the other hand, a "collusive" outcome in the development stage may be sustained in the following sense, which is unique to the intertemporal nature of innovative investment.

### 2.7.1 Illustrative model

Consider a discrete-time dynamic duopoly for simplicity. Time periods are indexed by $t = 0, 1, 2, ....$ Each of the two firms begin to develop the product mutually independently at time $t = 0$, and start selling it as soon as development is complete. There can be two methods to develop the product: the "fast" method requires the level $I_H$ of investment each period for $T_H$ periods, whilst the "slow" method requires only the amount $I_L$ per period but takes $T_L$ periods to develop the product, where $T_L > T_H \geq 1$, and yet $T_H I_H > T_L I_L > 0$, thus obviously $I_H > I_L > 0$.

Assume further that the market "opens up" as soon as the first of the two firms starts selling the product, and then diminishes exponentially. The economic situation embodied in this assumption is that *potential* demand for the product has existed for a long time, so that the demand is the highest when the product is newly introduced to the market and then quickly declines as these queued-up consumers clear away. To maintain as much generality as possible, we avoid imposing any explicit forms for demand functions and for firms' marketing strategies, abstracting profits by introducing the notation $\pi^M$ for monopoly and $\pi^D$ for duopoly. Namely, a firm's profit from marketing the product as a *monopolist* is $\beta^s \pi^M$, where $\beta \in (0, 1)$ is a parameter for the persistence of demand in the market, and $s$ is the lag between the first introduction of the product to the market and the period in question. Aside from this market depreciation parameter $\beta$, no time discounting is introduced for further simplicity. Hence, each firm's profit stream as a function of the two firms' innovative investment is as follows.

- If both firms invest in the fast method, then each firm pays $I_H$ for the first $T_H$ periods ($t = 0, 1, ..., T_H - 1$) and thenceforth earns $\beta^s \pi^D$ in period $t = T_H + s$, which totals

$$\Pi[H, H] = \frac{1}{1 - \beta} \pi^D - T_H I_H. \tag{2.10}$$

- If one firm invests in the fast method whilst the other the slow method, then the fast firm pays $I_H$ for the first $T_H$ periods ($t = 0, 1, ..., T_H - 1$)

and then becomes a *monopolist* for the next $T_L - T_H$ periods ($t = T_H, ..., T_L - 1$), and then finally a duopolist from period $T_L$ onwards, earning the total of

$$\Pi[H, L] = \frac{\beta^{T_L - T_H}}{1 - \beta} \, \pi^D + \frac{1 - \beta^{T_L - T_H}}{1 - \beta} \, \pi^M - T_H I_H \,, \qquad (2.11)$$

whereas the slow firm pays $I_L$ for the first $T_L$ periods ($t = 0, 1, ..., T_L - 1$) and then becomes a duopolist in period $T_L$ *when the market is already $T_L - T_H$ periods old*, earning

$$\Pi[L, H] = \frac{\beta^{T_L - T_H}}{1 - \beta} \, \pi^D - T_L I_L \,. \qquad (2.12)$$

- If both firms invest in the slow method, then each firm pays $I_L$ for the first $T_L$ periods ($t = 0, 1, ..., T_L - 1$) and then immediately becomes a duopolist from period $t = T_L$, raising the profit stream

$$\Pi[L, L] = \frac{1}{1 - \beta} \, \pi^D - T_L I_L \,. \qquad (2.13)$$

Hence, it is possible to assume further that $\Pi[H, H] > \Pi[L, H] > 0$, $\Pi[H, L] > \Pi[L, L] > 0$ so that the fast method *strategically dominates* the slow method. It is nonetheless clear, from our initial assumption $T_H I_H > T_L I_L > 0$, that $\Pi[L, L] > \Pi[H, H]$. Hence, we have a prisoners' dilemma.

Now, consider whether these firms can possibly sustain the profitable profile {slow, slow} as an equilibrium outcome, by means of the following "trigger strategy". The prescribed equilibrium path is for both firms to adopt the slow method. However, if a firm deviates and switches to the fast method in period $t$, then in period $t + 1$ the other firm also switches to the fast method subject to incentive compatibility. Assuming that switching from the slow method to the fast method nullifies the cumulative investment already made in the slow method and hence makes the firm start the fast method afresh, switching in any period $t \geq T_L - T_H$ is clearly incentive incompatible. In period $t = 0, 1, ..., T_L - T_H - 1$,

- If a firm deviates to starting the fast method, and is immediately "punished" by the other firm's following to the fast method a period later, then starting from period $t$, the deviator pays $I_H$ for $T_H$ periods, subsequently raises the monopoly profit $\pi_M$ for one period only, and then raises the duopoly profit $\pi_D$ for good, earning in total

$$\Pi^{\times\times} = \pi_M + \frac{\beta}{1 - \beta} \, \pi_D - T_H I_H \,. \qquad (2.14)$$

- If a firm deviates to the fast method, but is left unpunished with the other firm staying on the slow method, then the deviator pays $I_H$ for $T_H$ periods starting from period $t$, followed by $T_L - T_H - t$ periods of monopoly, and duopoly for good, totalling

$$\Pi^\times = \frac{\beta^{T_L - T_H - t}}{1 - \beta} \pi_D + \frac{1 - \beta^{T_L - T_H - t}}{1 - \beta} \pi_M - T_H I_H \,. \qquad (2.15)$$

- If neither firm deviates, each firm's profit stream from period $t$ onwards is to continue to pay $I_L$ for $T_L - t$ periods and then to earn the duopoly profit permanently, which totals

$$\Pi^\circ = \frac{1}{1 - \beta} \pi_D - (T_L - t) I_L \,. \qquad (2.16)$$

In the meantime, if a firm deviates to the fast method at time $t = 0, 1, ..., T_L - T_H - 1$, then in period $t + 1$ if the other firm:

- also switches to the fast method paying $I_H$ for $T_H$ periods and then earning the duopoly profit $\pi_D$ *a period behind the deviator*, the profit stream totals

$$\Pi^{\dagger\dagger} = \frac{\beta}{1 - \beta} \pi_D - T_H I_H \,, \qquad (2.17)$$

- does not follow the deviation and continues to pay $I_L$ for $T_L - t - 1$ periods and then earns the duopoly profit $T_L - T_H - t$ *periods behind the deviator*, the profit totals

$$\Pi^\dagger = \frac{\beta^{T_L - T_H - t}}{1 - \beta} \pi_D - (T_L - t - 1) I_L \,. \qquad (2.18)$$

To sustain our contemplated trigger strategy with subgame perfection, it turns out necessary and sufficient that

$$\begin{aligned}
\Pi^\circ &\geq \Pi^{\times\times} \, \forall t \in \{0, 1, ..., T_L - T_H - 1\} \text{ such that } \Pi^{\dagger\dagger} \geq \Pi^\dagger, \\
\Pi^\circ &\geq \Pi^\times \, \forall t \in \{0, 1, ..., T_L - T_H - 1\} \text{ such that } \Pi^{\dagger\dagger} < \Pi^\dagger. \qquad (2.19)
\end{aligned}$$

When $T_L - T_H = 1$, these conditions are clearly incompatible with our initial assumptions $\Pi[H, H] > \Pi[L, H] > 0$ and $\Pi[H, L] > \Pi[L, L] > 0$. The longer $T_L - T_H$ grows, the more likely it is for these conditions to be satisfied.

The economic implication of this finding is that, in a prisoners' dilemma where it is more profitable in terms of oligopolists' *joint profits* to keep the level of R&D investment low and thereby the progress of product innovation slow whilst it is more profitable for *each individual firm* to outinvest its competitors, there is a prospect for a *collusive* subgame perfect equilibrium in which jointly profitable underinvestment is sustained by means of trigger strategies. Such a prospect gains greater feasibility when the faster, high-investment alternative entails *much faster* product innovation than the slow alternative, than when the alternative is only incrementally faster. This collusive incentive can jeopardise the efficiency-enhancing effect of R&D competition and thereby drag the equilibrium result back to socially inefficient "monopolistic" underinvestment.

### 2.7.2 Discussion

Even though our analysis in the above may appear hardly analogous to the well known relation between capacity and tacit collusion, there is a key similarity. That is, the fact that firms' investment levels, be they capacity or product innovation, are influenced by the imperfect competition in the ensuing product market. Relative to the overwhelming mass of existing research in R&D races (for a survey, see Reinganum, 1989 and Martin, 1993), attempts to relate collusive incentives (however defined) in R&D with the ensuing product market are considerably less numerous, leaving ample room for further research.

Note that (tacitly) collusive R&D should be expressly distinguished from *cooperative* R&D. The former is, game-theoretically, a purely non-cooperative outcome. The latter, on the other hand, is carried out through multiple firms' *collective decision making*.

## 2.8 Process innovation and inventories

If there is an analogy between capacity investment and product innovation, inventory investment should be likened to *process innovation*. For both inventories and process innovation are to lower instantaneous marginal costs.

A straightforward application of Fudenberg and Tirole (1984) suggests that the monotone comparative statics of the oligopolistic market determines whether strategic incentives for process innovation favour over- or underinvestment. Namely, in ordinary oligopoly where firms are supplying substitute products, if the market is Cournot (quantity setting), cost-reducing process innovation will shift the firm's market reaction function outwards. *Ceteris paribus*, this induces competitors' quantity contraction, boosting the firm's profit further. Hence an *overinvesting* incentive (see, e.g., Brander and Spencer, 1983). If the market is Bertrand (price setting), cost reduction entailed by process innovation will shift the firm's market reaction function inwards, inducing competitors' price reduction, which interferes with the firm's profit. In this case, there arises an *underinvesting* incentive (e.g., Dixon, 1985).

A curious extension of our findings on strategic inventories, presented in section 2.4, is whether we can meaningfully conceptualise negative inventory holding. Perhaps its most immediate association with a realistic economic institution can be found in *shortsales*, or sometimes called *future contracts*. When a firm shortsells its product, the firm delays the delivery of the product. This implies that the firm can also delay the production, or acquisition, of the shortsold product, which can possibly save some of the production costs. Obviously, shortsales are made possible by adequate provision of the market mechanism including credit facilities and legal contractual enforcement.

Another major institutional difference between future sales, or negative inventories, and ordinary (positive) inventories is that the shortseller usually has to offer a discount, or a rebate, adjusting the sales price for the buyer's time preferences, whilst in the case of ordinary inventories the buyer is generally not responsible for the inventory costs which have already been borne by the supplier firm.

## 2.8.1   Analytical exercise

A mirror image to our previous two-stage inventory model (see section 2.4) can be as follows: it is an advance sales model instead of advance production. Firms can choose whether to sell the product in advance by means of future contracts, or to sell it on spot. There are two stages. In the first stage, firms simultaneously choose whether, and how much, to sell in advance, at a future price. In the second stage, production takes place. If production exceeds advance sales, then the remainder is sold on spot.

Consider the following simple linear duopoly example. Assume negligible production costs, two stages, no discounting. Unlike our advance production model, now production can take place only once, in the second stage. The first stage is exclusively for future contracts, where each firm $i$ $(i = 1, 2)$ can *shortsell* a quantity $f_i \geq 0$. Commonly observing $f_1$ and $f_2$, in the second stage each firm chooses a quantity of *spot sales* $s_i \geq 0$, produces $f_i + s_i$, and the market determines the price $p = 1 - f_1 - f_2 - s_1 - s_2$, except that shortsales must offer a fixed rebate $r$ per unit quantity. Each firm's profit is therefore $\pi_i = (p - r)f_i + ps_i$.

Solving backwards, the subgame perfect equilibria of this two-stage game are:

- $f_1 = f_2 = 0$, $s_1 = s_2 = \dfrac{1}{3}$ when $r \geq \dfrac{1}{2} - \dfrac{\sqrt{2}}{3}$ ;

- $f_i = \dfrac{1 - 2r}{2}$, $f_j = s_i = 0$, $s_j = \dfrac{1 + 2r}{4}$ $(\{i, j\} = \{1, 2\})$ when $r \leq \dfrac{1}{2} - \dfrac{\sqrt{2}}{3}$ .

In words, there is a strategic pre-emption incentive in favour of an advance future sales contract when the required rebate is relatively low.

## 2.8.2 Discussion

Analogously to strategic inventories presented in sections 2.4 and 2.5, the incentives either for or against strategic future sales depend upon the size of the rebate $r$ *relative to* the demand intercept (unity in the exercise above). This implies that, *ceteris paribus*, future sales tend to attract *procyclical incentives*. Namely, a high demand intercept makes the rebate relatively insubstantial, which makes future sales affordable.

Note that the straight analogy between future sales and inventories fails in two ways. First, although future sales can be interpreted as negative inventories on the production side, they play a similar, not an opposite, strategic role to inventories. That is, both positive and negative inventories serve as a *pre-commitment device*. Second, macrostatistically, future sales do not count as negative inventories, hence are hardly relevant in explaining the stylised fact of extremely procyclical inventory investment. However, the strategic aspect can most certainly be helpful in shedding light on the reason why the institution of future sales exists, without resorting to credit imperfection or heterogeneous time preferences among traders.

## 2.9 Conclusion

This chapter has taken a brief game-theoretic (albeit mathematically informal) overview on strategic investment, with relatively strong emphasis on some of the state-of-the-art research topics including *strategic inventories* and *product innovation*.

Generally, investment games are dynamic in nature, where some element of **intertemporal substitution** is always present. This has the potential to relate to those topics including **production smoothing** (see section 2.5) and **risk aversion** (in terms of its parametric relation to the elasticity of intertemporal substitution) which are of broad interest in both microeconomics and macroeconomics.

Alternatively, further research can also be built in the direction of generalising firms' oligopolistic market interactions. In this chapter, following much of the existing tradition in theoretical industrial economics, it has mostly been assumed that firms are either quantity setters or price setters. The reality is apparently that most firms are neither quantity setters nor price setters but somewhere intermediate, setting "nicely" upward sloping supply curves. This may, to a certain extent, relate to the old concept of **conjectural variation** (existing theoretical research in this direction includes Møllgaard, 1994).

Finally, this chapter has deliberately refrained from one specific kind of investment, which is investment in *information*. This is because there is another chapter in this book devoted specifically to that topic.

# References

1] Albæk, S. (1990), "Stackelberg Leadership as a Natural Solution under Cost Uncertainty", *Journal of Industrial Economics*, **38**, 335-47.

2] Blanchard, O.J. (1983), "The Production and Inventory Behavior of the American Automobile Industry", *Journal of Political Economy*, **91**, 365-400.

3] Blanchard, O.J. and S. Fischer (1989), *Lectures on Macroeconomics*, Cambridge, MA, MIT Press.

4] Blinder, A. (1986), "Can the Production Smoothing Model of Inventory Behavior be Saved?", *Quarterly Journal of Economics*, **101**, 431-53.

5] Brander, J. and B. Spencer (1983), "Strategic Commitment with R&D: The Symmetric Case", *Bell Journal of Economics*, **14**, 225-35.

6] Bulow, J., J. Geanakoplos and P. Klemperer (1985), "Holding Idle Capacity to Deter Entry", *Economic Journal*, **95**, 178-82.

7] Cournot, A. (1838), *Recherches sur les principes mathématiques de la théorie des richesses*, Paris, Hachette (*Researches into the Mathematical Principles of the Theory of Wealth* (1897), New York, Macmillan).

8] d'Aspremont, C. and L.-A. Gérard-Varet (1980), "Stackelberg Solvable Games and Pre-Play Communication", *Journal of Economic Theory*, **23**, 201-17.

9] Dixit, A.K. (1980), "The Role of Investment in Entry Deterrence", *Economic Journal*, **90**, 95-106.

10] Dixon, H.D. (1985), "Strategic Investment in an Industry with a Competitive Product Market", *Journal of Industrial Economics*, **33**, 483-99.

11] Fudenberg, D. and J. Tirole (1984), "The Fat Cat Effect, the Puppy Dog Ploy, and the Lean and Hungry Look", *American Economic Review, Papers and Proceedings*, **74**, 361-8.

12] Futia, C. (1980), "Schumpeterian Competition", *Quarterly Journal of Economics*, **94**, 675-95.

13] Gal-Or, E. (1985), "First Mover and Second Mover Advantage", *International Economic Review*, **26**, 649-52.

14] Hamilton, J.H. and S.M. Slutsky (1990), "Endogenous Timing in Duopoly Games: Stackelberg or Cournot Equilibria", *Games and Economic Behavior*, **2**, 29-46.

15] Henderson, J.M. and R.E. Quandt (1971, 2nd edn), *Microeconomic Theory — A Mathematical Approach*, New York, McGraw-Hill.

16] Holt, C., F. Modigliani, J. Muth and H. Simon (1960), *Planning Production, Inventories and Work Forth*, New Jersey, Prentice-Hall.

17] Kahn, J. (1987), "Inventories and the Volatility of Production", *American Economic Review*, **77**, 667-79.

18] Kreps, D.M. and J. Scheinkman (1983), "Quantity Precommitment and Bertrand Competition Yield Cournot Outcomes", *RAND Journal of Economics*, **14**, 326-37.

19] Maggi, G. (1996), "Endogenous Leadership in a New Market", *RAND Journal of Economics*, **27**, 641-59.

20] Mailath, G.J. (1993), "Endogenous Sequencing of Firm Decisions", *Journal of Economic Theory*, **59**, 169-82.

21] Marshall, A. (1920), *Principles of Economics*, London, Macmillan.

22] Martin, S. (1993), *Advanced Industrial Economics*, Oxford, Blackwell.

23] Matsumura, T. (1997), "A Two-Stage Cournot Duopoly with Inventory Costs", *Japanese Economic Review*, **48**, 81-9.

24] Møllgaard, H.P. (1994), "Strategic Inventories in Two Period Oligopoly", Memo 1994-29, Økonomisk Institut, Aarhus University.

25] Normann, H.T. (1997), "Endogenous Stackelberg Equilibria with Incomplete Information", *Journal of Economics* (Zeitschrift für Nationalökonomie), **66**, 177-87.

26] Pal, D. (1991), "Cournot Duopoly with Two Production Periods and Cost Differentials", *Journal of Economic Theory*, **55**, 441-8.

27] Pal, D. (1996), "Endogenous Stackelberg Equilibria with Identical Firms", *Games and Economic Behavior*, **12**, 81-94.

28] Poddar, S. and D. Sasaki (2002), "The Strategic Benefit from Advance Production", *European Journal of Political Economy*, **18**, 579-95.

29] Reinganum, J. (1989), "The Timing of Innovation: Research, Development, and Diffusion", in R. Schmalensee and R. Willig (eds), *Handbook of Industrial Organization*, vol. 1, Amsterdam, North-Holland.

30] Robson, A.J. (1990), "Duopoly with Endogenous Strategic Timing: Stackelberg Regained", *International Economic Review*, **31**, 263-74.

31] Saloner, G. (1987), "Cournot Duopoly with Two Production Periods", *Journal of Economic Theory*, **42**, 183-7.

32] Sadanand, A. and V. Sadanand (1996), "Firm Scale and Endogenous Timing of Entry: a Choice between Commitment and Flexibility", *Journal of Economic Theory*, **70**, 516-30.

33] Spence, A.M. (1977), "Entry, Capacity, Investment and Oligopolistic Pricing", *Bell Journal of Economics*, **8**, 534-44.

34] Spulber, D. (1981), "Capacity, Output and Sequential Entry", *American Economic Review*, **71**, 503-14.

35] Walras, L. (1874), *Eléments d'Économie Politique Pure*, Lausanne, Corbaz (*Elements of Pure Economics* (1954), Homewood, IL, Irwin).

# Chapter 3

# Multiproduct firms

Silvia Baranzoni, Patrizio Bianchi
and Luca Lambertini[1]

## 3.1 Introduction

The choice on the part of firms to supply product lines rather than single goods is commonly observed in several markets. However, industrial economists started investigating this aspect of firms' behaviour relatively late. Neither the theory of monopolistic competition, nor the Sylos Labini-Bain-Modigliani paradigm, offered a satisfactory description of market interaction among multiproduct firms (for a discussion, see Robinson, 1953). The early studies in this direction justified the supply of product lines on the grounds of production costs: within the theory of contestable markets (Baumol *et al.*, 1982; see also Bailey and Friedlander, 1982), the existence of multiproduct firms seemed to be a consequence of economies of scope. A subadditive cost function,[2] combined with the absence of sunk costs, would make it optimal for firms to operate on several markets, supplying several goods.

However, the theory of contestable markets devotes a limited amount of attention to demand-side incentives towards product proliferation. This is the viewpoint adopted by Brander and Eaton (1984), who focus on the interplay between a consumer's demand for differentiated goods on the one side, and the strategic and technological effects affecting firms' behaviour on the other side. Relying on a theoretical model where the analysis confines to

---

[1] We thank Dan Sasaki for useful comments and suggestions. The usual disclaimer applies.

[2] Let $x_i$ define the output level of good $i$. A cost function $C(x_i)$ is subadditive if $C(x_i + x_j) \leq C(x_i) + C(x_j)$, for all $x_i$ and $x_j$.

Cournot competition, Brander and Eaton verify that firms' strategic decisions as to product range and output level may lead to market equilibria where firms supply product ranges characterised by a high degree of substitutability. This result is derived under the assumption that each firm's product range consists of a given number of varieties, and is therefore subject to a fairly natural critique, namely, that firms may endogenously alter the span of their product range for strategic reasons.[3] This is the route taken by several subsequent contributions (Wernerfelt, 1986; De Fraja, 1992).

We intend to supply a summary of the advances achieved by the literature on multiproduct firms, under the alternative assumptions of exogenous and endogenous product differentiation, emphasising in particular the incentives towards product proliferation on the demand side. This implies that we will not proceed to a detailed illustration of (i) supply-side incentives[4] (although they will pop up occasionally in the remainder of the survey); and (ii) the foundations of the theory of multiproduct firms, guaranteeing the existence of equilibrium.[5]

The theory of multiproduct firms has evolved along four main lines of research. The first is marked by a clear heritage from the theory of contestable markets: firms choose the span of the product line on the basis of the trade-off between economies of scope and scale, but they are unable to choose the characteristics of products. The second considers endogenous differentiation, introducing thus a tradeoff between specialisation and the ability to discriminate among consumers with different incomes and preferences. The third focuses on the issue of the persistence of monopoly in settings where the entry of new firms is conditional upon the acquisition of production rights over new varieties. The fourth introduces the idea that consumers may bear switching costs, either real or perceived as such, related to the purchase of product lines. Consequently, consumers' brand loyalty can be so high that they purchase goods from one firm only. The switching costs approach allows us to nest the former three approaches into a unique picture.

The remainder of this chapter is structured as follows. Sections 3.2 and 3.3 contain a review of Brander and Eaton (1984), where product substi-

---

[3] This idea is closely related to the literature on endogenous differentiation (Hay, 1976; Prescott and Visscher, 1977; Eaton and Lipsey, 1978; Lane, 1980; Judd, 1985; Bonanno, 1987), where firms may adopt product proliferation as a foreclosure strategy. This view has found some empirical support (Schmalensee, 1978).

[4] We refer the reader to the seminal contributions due to Panzar and Willig (1981); Baumol et al. (1982); or to the exhaustive surveys by Brock (1983) and Spence (1983).

[5] As to the theorems on concavity of the profit function and the existence of equilibrium in both perfectly and imperfectly competitive markets with multiproduct firms, see Mac-Donald and Slivinsky (1987); Okuguchi and Szidarovsky (1990); Anderson and de Palma (1992); Anderson et al. (1992); De Fraja (1994).

tutability is an exogenous parameter, and no brand loyalty effect is operating. Endogenous differentiation is dealt with in sections 3.4-3.6, considering both models of horizontal differentiation (Bonanno, 1987; Martinez-Giralt and Neven, 1988) and models of vertical differentiation (Mussa and Rosen, 1978; Champsaur and Rochet, 1989, *inter alia*). The strategic use of product proliferation, with or without an explicit description of R&D competition, is analysed in section 3.7 (Gilbert and Newbery, 1982; Shaked and Sutton, 1990). Section 3.8 reviews the literature on switching costs (Klemperer, 1992, 1995). Concluding remarks are in section 3.9.

## 3.2 Demand-side vs scale economies

The contribution by Brander and Eaton (1984) is closely related to the contestability theory, but for the fact that they abandon the assumption of scope economies in production, and introduce an analogous assumption concerning demand, in order to investigate the interaction between this and economies of scale in determining the firms' optimal choices of their respective product lines.

Consider a duopoly where each firm produces two goods. The available goods are indexed 1, 2, 3 and 4. Suppose each good in the pairs $(1, 2)$ and $(3, 4)$ are close substitutes for the other good in the same pair, while pairs $(1, 3)$, $(1, 4)$, $(2, 3)$ and $(2, 4)$ are formed by weakly substitute goods. To determine the extent of substitutability, examine the inverse demand functions. Define $p_i$ the market price of variety $i$, and $x_i$ the demand for the same variety. The demand vector is thus $X = (x_1, x_2, x_3, x_4)$. The inverse demand function for good $i$ writes $p_i = p_i(x_1, x_2, x_3, x_4) = p_i(X)$. Now define:

$$p_{ij} = \frac{\partial p_i}{\partial x_j}; \; p_{ik} = \frac{\partial p_i}{\partial x_k}; \; p_{ii} = \frac{\partial p_i}{\partial x_i} \; . \tag{3.1}$$

If we say, e.g., that goods 1 and 2 are reciprocally closer substitutes than goods 1 and 3, we mean that the reaction of $p_1$ to a variation in $x_2$ is, in absolute value, larger than the reaction of $p_1$ to a change in $x_3$. Hence, in general, we can state that $|p_{ij}| > |p_{ik}|$ if $i$ and $j$ are close substitutes while $i$ and $k$ are weak substitutes.

As to production technology, each firm bears a sunk cost $k$ for each variety. The unit variable cost is assumed to be constant, and the total cost of producing $x_i$ units of variety $i$ is:

$$C_i = cx_i + k. \tag{3.2}$$

From (3.2), it follows that average production cost is decreasing:

$$AC = \frac{C_i}{x_i} = c + \frac{k}{x_i} . \tag{3.3}$$

Notice that this cost function is not subadditive. Hence, product line decisions depend solely upon the interaction between demand incentives and economies of scale. As an illustration, consider first the behaviour of a monopolist.

## 3.2.1   The monopolist's optimal product line

First of all, it can be established that, if the monopolist decides to offer two products, she will find it profitable to supply imperfect substitutes. To grasp the intuition at the basis of this result, suppose the monopolist produces goods 1 and 2, which are close substitutes, and let $x_1 = x_2$. Now, for a given $x_1$, imagine that the monopolist switches from good 2 to good 3, with $x_3 = x_2 = x_1$. Define the two product vectors as $X' = (x_1, x_2, 0, 0)$ and $X'' = (x_1, 0, x_3, 0)$. The effect of the variation in the product vector on the price of good 1 is:

$$\Delta p_1 = p_1(X'') - p_1'(X'). \tag{3.4}$$

The mean value theorem (Rosenlicht, 1968) allows us to rewrite (3.4) for a vector $X^* \in [X', X'']$, as follows:

$$\Delta p_1 = [p_{13}(X^*) - p_{12}(X^*)]\, x_i , \ i = 1, 2, 3. \tag{3.5}$$

Since $|p_{ij}| > |p_{ik}|$, that is, $p_{ij} < p_{ik} < 0$, the price variation observed for good 1 must be positive. By symmetry, this must hold for variety 2 as well. Consequently, for a given pair of output levels, both prices and profits must increase. Hence, the two-product monopolist, in the absence of entry threats, finds it optimal to supply two varieties characterised by low substitutability. Doing otherwise would increase price competition with her own product range.

To verify this result, consider the following demand functions (Singh and Vives, 1984):

$$\begin{aligned}
p_1 &= a - x_1 - dx_2 - g(x_3 + x_4) \\
p_2 &= a - x_2 - dx_1 - g(x_3 + x_4) \\
p_3 &= a - x_3 - dx_4 - g(x_1 + x_2) \\
p_4 &= a - x_4 - dx_3 - g(x_1 + x_2),
\end{aligned} \tag{3.6}$$

where parameters $0 < g < d < 1$ measure the degree of substitutability between products. In particular, parameter $d$ measures the substitutability between goods 1 and 2 or goods 3 and 4, while parameter $g$ measures the substitutability within pairs $(1, 3)$, $(1, 4)$, $(2, 3)$ and $(2, 4)$. Suppose the monopolist supplies a pair of close substitutes, e.g., products 1 and 2. In this case, $x_3 = x_4 = 0$ and the profit function is $\pi^M = (p_1 - c)x_1 + (p_2 - c)x_2 - 2k$. The solution of first order conditions (FOCs)

$$\frac{\partial \pi^M}{\partial x_i} = a - c - 2x_i - 2dx_j = 0, \quad i, j = 1, 2; \; i \neq j \qquad (3.7)$$

is $x_1 = x_2 = (a - c)/[2(1 + d)]$, and the resulting profits are $\pi^M = (a - c)^2/[2(1 + d)] - 2k$. The same obtains if the monopolist supplies goods 3 and 4. Replacing $d$ with $g$ in output levels and profits gives the equilibrium magnitudes when the monopolist produces any pair in $\{(1, 3), (1, 4), (2, 3), (2, 4)\}$. As $g < d$, observing that monopoly profits are inversely related to the degree of substitutability suffices to confirm the above conclusions.

### 3.2.2 The duopolists' optimal product lines

Duopoly competition takes place in three stages. In the first, each firm decides how many products to supply; this choice affects the exploitation of scale economies. In the second, each firm chooses which products to supply, on the basis of their reciprocal substitutability. In the third, market competition takes place, either in quantities or in prices. In principle, one can imagine that these decisions may be taken either sequentially or simultaneously. However, firms' behaviour in the real world suggests that decisions concerning product line should precede those related to the marketing stage.[6] The solution concept of the whole game is the subgame perfect equilibrium by backward induction (Selten, 1975).

For the sake of simplicity, let's bypass the first stage and focus on the more relevant case, where each firm supplies two products. Label firms $A$ and $B$, and suppose they compete in quantities. If firm $A$ produces the pair $(1, 2)$ and firm $B$ produces the pair $(3, 4)$, we have what Brander and Eaton call *market segmentation*. Alternatively, each firm might supply a pair of weaker substitutes, e.g., $(1, 3)$ and $(2, 4)$. If so, product lines are *interlaced*. Consider firm $A$'s profits in the two settings, starting with the segmentation case:

$$\pi_A^S = p_1 x_1 + p_2 x_2 - c(x_1 + x_2) - 2k. \qquad (3.8)$$

---

[6]We strictly follow the authors' procedure (Brander and Eaton, p. 325). Moreover, a sequential solution by backward induction ensures the existence of an equilibrium in pure strategies.

Superscript $S$ stands for *segmentation*. The FOC for profit maximisation
with respect to product 1 is

$$\frac{\partial \pi_A^S}{\partial x_1} = MR_1 + p_{21}x_2 - c = 0, \tag{3.9}$$

where $MR_1 = p_{11}x_1 + p_1$ represents marginal revenue on product 1. Second
order conditions (SOCs) are

$$\frac{\partial^2 \pi_A^S}{\partial x_1^2} \leq 0; \tag{3.10}$$

$$\left( \frac{\partial^2 \pi_A^S}{\partial x_1^2} \cdot \frac{\partial^2 \pi_A^S}{\partial x_2^2} \right) - \left( \frac{\partial^2 \pi_A^S}{\partial x_1 \partial x_2} \cdot \frac{\partial^2 \pi_A^S}{\partial x_2 \partial x_1} \right) > 0. \tag{3.11}$$

The FOC and SOCs for good 2 are obviously analogous to (3.9-3.10), with the
appropriate subscripts. By symmetry, we are also able to state that firm $B$'s
FOC and SOCs are analogous to (3.9) and (3.10-3.11), respectively. Solving
these conditions yields the Cournot-Nash equilibrium pertaining to the third
stage. As the model is symmetric, all quantities and prices must coincide.
Brander and Eaton assume further that $MR_{ij} < 0$, i.e., the marginal revenue
of variety $i$ is decreasing in the output level of variety $j$, for all $i$ and $j$.

Consider now the case where firm $A$ supplies goods $(1, 3)$. The FOC w.r.t.
good 1 becomes

$$\frac{\partial \pi_A^I}{\partial x_1} = MR_1 + p_{31}x_3 - c = 0, \tag{3.12}$$

where superscript $I$ stands for *interlaced*. *Mutatis mutandis*, SOCs are as in
(3.10-3.11).

On these grounds, it can be shown that market regime $S$ yields higher
profits than market regime $I$. To see this, observe that in regime $S$ all goods
must be sold at the same price $p^S$, and likewise in regime $I$ all of them are
sold at price $p^I$. Then, we have three possible situations: either $p^I = p^S$;
or $p^I > p^S$; or, finally, $p^I < p^S$. Both the first and the second case lead to
a contradiction. Consider the first: if the equilibrium prices were the same
in regimes $I$ and $S$, also output levels and consequently marginal revenues
would coincide. However, we have assumed that $p_{21} < p_{31} < 0$; therefore,
the conditions for optima cannot be satisfied by $p^I = p^S$. Consider then the
second case, i.e., $p^I > p^S$. This would imply $x^I < x^S$ and, as $MR_{ij}$ must be
negative, it would also entail that the marginal revenue characterising good
1 is higher in regime $I$ than in regime $S$. Again, under the assumption that
$p_{21} < p_{31} < 0$, conditions (3.9) and (3.12) cannot be satisfied. Thus, the only
plausible case is $p^I < p^S$.

Examine now industry profits $\Pi = \sum_{i=1}^{4} p_i x_i - c \sum_{i=1}^{4} x_i - 4k$. Their variation following a change in $x_1$ is

$$\frac{\partial \Pi}{\partial x_1} = p_1 + \sum_{i=1}^{4} p_{i1} x_i - c. \tag{3.13}$$

In regime $S$, we have

$$\frac{\partial \Pi^S}{\partial x_1} = p_{31} x_3 + p_{41} \dot{x}_4 < 0, \tag{3.14}$$

as, by (3.9), $MR_1 + p_{21} x_2 - c = 0$. Likewise, $\partial \Pi / \partial x_1 < 0$ also in regime $I$, where (3.12) holds. It appears that industry profits decrease as any $x_i$ increases. It follows that, given the concavity of profits w.r.t. output levels, industry profits (as well as individual profits) must decrease in switching from $S$ to $I$, as outputs increase.

It is possible to check the validity of these results by using demand functions (3.6) introduced in the previous subsection. To this aim, we compare setting $S$ where firm $A$ produces the pair $(1, 2)$ and firm $B$ produces the pair $(3, 4)$, with setting $I$ where firm $A$ produces the pair $(1, 3)$ and firm $B$ produces the pair $(2, 4)$. Calculations are quite straightforward and are left to the curiosity of the reader. Since the model is completely symmetric, we confine our attention to the incentive for firm $i$ towards a segmented market structure, measured by

$$\pi_i^S - \pi_i^I \propto d\,(d + 2g)\,(1 + d) - g^2\,(3 - d + 4g)\,. \tag{3.15}$$

The difference $\pi_i^S - \pi_i^I \equiv dsi$ is plotted against $d$ and $g$ in figure 3.1. Since $g < d$, figure 3.1 reveals that structure $S$ is preferred to structure $I$ in the whole admissible range of parameters.[7] Hence, by the symmetry of the model, both firms prefer $S$ over $I$. The validity of the results concerning industry profits obviously follows from this observation.

We are now in a position to investigate product line decisions. In this stage, firms take the number of products as given and choose the composition of the product range to be supplied, anticipating Cournot competition at the market stage. Examine first the case where these choices are simultaneous. We follow Brander and Eaton (1984, pp. 327-30) in focusing upon situations where a firm's best reply to the choice of two particular varieties by the rival

---

[7]The roots of $dsi = 0$ are $g_1 = d$, $g_2 = \left[ -3\,(1 + d) + \sqrt{(1 + d)\,(9 - 7d)} \right] / 8$ and $g_3 = \left[ -3\,(1 + d) - \sqrt{(1 + d)\,(9 - 7d)} \right] / 8$, with $g_3 < g_2 < 0$.

consists simply in offering the remaining two,[8] and any $2 \times 2$ partition of the four-product set is a Nash equilibrium of this stage, under both regimes. Otherwise, if one firm has a first-mover advantage, it will surely choose to produce two close substitutes, inducing the rival to take an analogous decision. Hence, segmentation univocally arises when the solution concept is the Stackelberg equilibrium. As to the selection between Nash and Stackelberg equilibria, the fact that the Stackelberg equilibrium Pareto-dominates all possible Nash equilibria makes it appear as the natural solution of this stage, in that both leader and follower find it preferable to a Nash equilibrium.[9]

**Figure 3.1:** $dsi \equiv \pi_i^S - \pi_i^I$

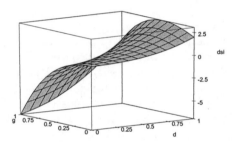

The decision pertaining to the width of the product line can now be briefly characterised. In the most unfortunate circumstances, market demand would be so low that, if a firm finds it convenient to offer just one product, the rival does not enter the market at all. In the opposite situation, market demand might be so high that both firms would find it optimal to offer four products each. Notice that this is made possible by the assumption of

---

[8]This is obviously not true in general. To see this, consider the case where varieties $(1, 2)$ are perfect substitutes, so are $(3, 4)$, while $(1, 3)$, $(1, 4)$, $(2, 3)$, $(2, 4)$ are not substitutable at all. If firm $A$ picks 1 and 2, firm $B$ could pick 1 and 3 to obtain a duopoly profit from the market for goods $(1, 2)$ *and* a monopoly profit from the market for goods $(3, 4)$, instead of picking products $(3, 4)$ to raise monopoly profits from that market, but nothing else.

[9]This approach to equilibrium selection reflects the state of the art characterising game theory in the early 1980s. The concept of a Stackelberg-solvable game, i.e., that a game can be solved à la Stackelberg if there is at least one such equilibrium dominating the Nash ones, is due to d'Aspremont and Gérard-Varet (1980). The endogenisation of timing has been further formalised by Hamilton and Slutsky (1990).

Cournot competition. Under price-setting behaviour, this would entail zero profits. Above we focused on the equilibria arising when best replies at this stage are symmetric, implying the supply of a product line consisting of two varieties by each firm. This situation can be expected to obtain when demand is neither so low to prevent firms from entering, nor so high to induce them to compete head-to-head over the whole product range.

In summary, Brander and Eaton provide a set of fairly general conditions under which segmentation obtains at equilibrium. Relaxing the assumption that each firm supplies two differentiated varieties, Wernerfelt (1986) considers the possibility for each firm to offer a single standardised good satisfying (imperfectly) all consumers. Wernerfelt finds that, if consumer tastes are homogeneous and the level of per product sunk costs is above a critical threshold, the optimal choice is indeed to offer a single variety. Otherwise product proliferation is more attractive (see section 3.6).

We have focused on the interplay between scale economies, product substitutability and demand-side incentives towards product proliferation, overlooking the role of scope economies in production. De Fraja (1992) tackles this problem, in a duopoly model where each firm can supply at most two products, under either quantity or price competition. He proves that, in general, the equilibrium number of products is larger than the socially optimal one, which would allow full exploitation of scale economies. This is due to the incentive for firms to exploit scope economies, whenever available, which have no significant bearing on consumer surplus.

In the remainder, we deal with endogenous differentiation models. We start, in the next section, by considering the behaviour of a horizontally differentiated monopoly.

## 3.3   Spatial monopoly

The behaviour of a spatially differentiated monopolist is studied by Bonanno (1987) in the quadratic transportation cost version (d'Aspremont *et al.*, 1979) of Hotelling's (1929) linear city. To illustrate his contribution, we proceed by induction, starting with the case where the monopolist supplies a single variety.

Unit production cost is assumed to be constant and is normalised to zero. Consumers are uniformly distributed, with density equal to one, along a segment of unit length which can alternatively be interpreted as a geographical space or the consumers' preference space. Each individual purchases a unit of the good, so that the market is fully served. The indirect utility function is

$$V = u - t(x - m)^2 - p; \quad t > 0, \tag{3.16}$$

where $u$ is gross surplus, $t$ is the unit transportation cost rate, $x$ is the location chosen by the monopolist, $m$ is the location of a generic consumer and $p$ is the mill price. Given full market coverage, profit and price coincide, and one needs to find the profit-maximising price when $x = 1/2$. By substitution, we get $V = s - t(1/2 - m)^2 - p$, from which, taking into account that the optimal price must drive to zero the net surplus of marginal consumers in 0 and 1, we obtain $p^M(1) = u - t/4 = \pi^M(1)$.

Consider now the case where the monopolist offers two varieties. Clearly, optimal locations are $x_1 = 1/4$ and $x_2 = 3/4$, i.e., the monopolist segments the market in two sub-markets of the same size, with marginal consumers at 0, 1/2 and 1, the consumer at 1/2 being indifferent between the two varieties.[10] The monopolist will then set the maximum price compatible with the hypothesis of full market coverage, implying that consumers at 0, 1/2 and 1 enjoy zero surplus in equilibrium. Hence, in both sub-markets, $p^M(2) = u - t/16$. Increasing the number of varieties, it is quickly verified that optimal price is $p^M(n) = u - t/(2n)^2$.

This model can be used to analyse strategic product proliferation by a monopolist, as a barrier to entry by outside competitors. Suppose the introduction of each variety entails a sunk cost $k$, independent of location. However, once the latter is chosen, the sunk cost prevents the incumbent from modifying location to react to entry. In the simplest setting, monopoly profits become $\pi^M(1) = u - t/4 - k$. If an outside firm decides to enter, it obviously locates either in 0 or in 1. Then, given locations, suppose firms play a Nash equilibrium in prices. Their profits are $\pi^I = 49t/144 - k$ and $\pi^E = 25t/144 - k$, with superscripts $I$ and $E$ standing for *incumbent* and *entrant*, respectively. It appears that the incumbent remains a monopolist if $k \in (25t/144, 49t/144]$, in that for all values of $k$ within such interval the entrant's profits are negative. Otherwise, if $k \in (0, 25t/144]$, the outsider enters at 0 or 1 with non-negative profits. To avoid this, the incumbent could enlarge her product line, lowering the profitability of any market niche available to the outsider[11] (see Schmalensee, 1978, for a case study supporting

---

[10]Note that 1/4 and 3/4 are also the socially optimal locations, i.e., those which maximise social welfare (and minimise total transportation costs). Hence, a peculiar characteristic of the Hotelling model consists in yielding the same equilibrium under both monopoly and social planning. Under the first regime, the monopolist minimises the maximum distance between the generic consumer and the generic variety in order to raise the price and maximise profits, while under the second regime the social planner does the same in order to minimise the overall disutility from transportation costs, $TC = t \sum_i (x_i - m)^2$.

[11]Notice that, in case of product proliferation, entry deterrence may entail that the $n$-

this view).

## 3.4  Monopoly and product quality

The behaviour of the vertically differentiated multiproduct monopolist has received wide attention in the theoretical literature. The basic issues raised in this field are two. The first concerns the choice by a profit-maximising monopolist between quality and quantity distortions, for a given number of varieties. The second regards the difference between the optimal monopoly behaviour and the socially efficient one. A third issue is that of describing the conditions under which we expect to observe a monopoly rather than a competitive market structure (Gabszewicz *et al.*, 1986). This topic nests into the debate on natural oligopoly and the so-called *finiteness property*, establishing that if quality improvements mainly affect fixed (R&D) costs while marginal costs are flat, a market for vertically differentiated products may accomodate a finite number of firms gaining strictly positive profits at equilibrium (Shaked and Sutton, 1983; see also Gabszewicz and Thisse, 1979; Shaked and Sutton, 1982).[12] Here, we focus on the two issues mentioned above. We will briefly dwell upon the third in section 3.6.

The first results on quality and quantity distortion in monopoly trace back to Spence (1975) and Sheshinski (1976). They establish that a monopolist can, alternatively, restrict the output level for a given quality, or distort quality for a given output. This entails that the quality supplied at the monopoly optimum is lower than the quality supplied at the social optimum if the marginal quality evaluation characterising the average consumer is higher than the marginal evaluation of quality characterising the marginal consumer, and conversely. This is due to the fact that, in setting quality, the monopolist considers the marginal consumer while the social planner considers the average consumer. This conclusion can be reached in a single-good setting.

The possibility that the monopolist expands the product line in order to induce a self-selection mechanism on the part of consumers is considered in several later contributions (Mussa and Rosen, 1978; Itoh, 1983; Maskin and Riley, 1984; Besanko *et al.*, 1987, 1988; Lambertini, 1997). In this stream of

good monopolist chooses locations differing from the socially optimal ones, $1/(2n)$, $3/(2n)$, ..., $(2n-1)/(2n)$, while such locations would certainly be chosen *without entry threat* (see Bonanno, 1987).

[12]In the early contributions on the finiteness property, the number of firms surviving in equilibrium with positive profits coincides with the number of products, all firms being single-product units.

literature, it is usually assumed that unit production cost is constant w.r.t. quantity but is increasing in the quality level, so that the finiteness property does not hold, i.e., this model cannot give rise to a natural oligopoly (or monopoly).

The basic idea underlying all these contributions is that the monopolist expands the product line so as to discriminate between consumers with different incomes. In the next subsections, we follow Lambertini (1997).

## 3.4.1  Full market coverage

Suppose consumers are uniformly distributed, with unit density, over $[\underline{\theta}, \overline{\theta}]$, with $\underline{\theta} = \overline{\theta} - 1$ and $\overline{\theta} \geq 1$.[13] Parameter $\theta$ denotes marginal willingness to pay for quality, which can be thought of as the reciprocal of marginal utility of money (see Tirole, 1988, chapter 2). As income increases, a consumer's willingness to pay for higher quality increases as well. Under full market coverage, each consumer buys one unit of the differentiated good, provided that the net surplus from purchase is non-negative:

$$V = \theta q_i - p_i \geq 0, \quad i = 1, 2, ..., n, \tag{3.17}$$

where $q_i$ and $p_i$ are the quality level and price of variety $i$. On the supply side, total production costs for variety $i$ are $C_i = tq_i^2 x_i$, where $x_i$ is the output level and $t$ is a positive parameter affecting marginal cost.

In what follows, we compare the behaviour of the monopolist with the behaviour of a social planner (or perfect competition), for a given number of products. Before doing that, it is useful to characterise briefly the interval of socially preferred qualities (Cremer and Thisse, 1994). When price equals marginal cost, i.e., $p_i = tq_i^2$, the utility-maximising quality level for a consumer indexed by $\theta$ is $q_i^* = \theta/(2t)$. Hence, the interval of socially preferred qualities is $[\underline{\theta}/(2t), \overline{\theta}/(2t)]$.

Under full market coverage, (3.17) holds as an equality for the marginal consumer at $\underline{\theta} = \overline{\theta} - 1$, while it holds as a strict inequality for all other consumers. For the sake of simplicity, consider first the case where a single variety is supplied. The objective function of the planner is social welfare, defined as follows:

$$SW(1) = \int_{\underline{\theta}}^{\overline{\theta}} (\theta q - tq^2) d\theta. \tag{3.18}$$

It is evident that price is irrelevant, in that, under full coverage, it only affects the distribution of surplus between producer and consumers, leav-

---

[13]The assumption of a uniform distribution is not restrictive. Spence (1975) shows that most of the results we are about to derive hold for a wide class of distributions.

ing unchanged its overall size. From the FOC w.r.t. quality we obtain $q^{SP} = (\overline{\theta} - 1)/(4t) = \left(\underline{\theta}/(2t) + \overline{\theta}/(2t)\right)/2$, i.e., the social planner produces the variety preferred by the average consumer. This result holds irrespective of the degree of convexity characterising the cost function (as long as unit production costs are constant w.r.t. the output level and increasing in the quality level), as well as the shape of the consumer distribution (see Spence, 1975).

The monopolist's objective is to maximise

$$\pi^M(1) = p - tq^2 . \tag{3.19}$$

The derivative of (3.19) w.r.t. price is everywhere positive. This implies that monopoly price is the highest price which is compatible with the assumption that the consumer at $\underline{\theta}$ will be able to buy, i.e., $p^M = \underline{\theta}q$. Plugging it into (3.19), we obtain $\pi^M(1) = q(\underline{\theta} - tq)$, which is maximised at $q^M = \underline{\theta}/(2t)$, the quality preferred by the marginal consumer. Hence, the monopolist undersupplies quality as compared to the social optimum. Again, this result holds irrespective of the degree of convexity characterising the cost function, while it is sensitive to the shape of the consumer distribution. Whenever the marginal willingness to pay for quality of the marginal consumer is lower than the average consumer's then we observe a downward distortion in quality at the monopoly equilibrium, as compared to the social optimum (see Spence, 1975).

Now suppose two qualities are produced, $q_H > q_L > 0$. Demand functions are $x_H = \overline{\theta} - (p_H - p_L)/(q_H - q_L)$ and $x_L = (p_H - p_L)/(q_H - q_L) - (\overline{\theta} - 1)$. Objective functions become

$$\pi^M(2) = (p_H - tq_H^2)x_H + (p_L - tq_L^2)x_L ; \tag{3.20}$$

$$SW(2) = \int_{\underline{\theta}}^{h} (\theta q_L - tq_L^2)d\theta + \int_{h}^{\overline{\theta}} (\theta q_H - tq_H^2)d\theta , \tag{3.21}$$

where $h = (p_H - p_L)/(q_H - q_L)$ is the marginal willingness to pay of the consumer who is indifferent between $q_H$ and $q_L$. The monopolist sets $p_L = \underline{\theta}q_L$ and, plugging it into $\partial \pi^M(2)/\partial p_H = 0$, she obtains the optimal price for the superior variety. Equilibrium qualities can be obtained by solving the corresponding first and second order conditions, yielding $q_H^M = (2\overline{\theta} - 1)/(4t)$ and $q_L^M = (2\overline{\theta} - 3)/(4t)$. The solution to the planner's problem is given by $q_H^{SP} = (4\overline{\theta} - 1)/(8t)$ and $q_L^{SP} = (4\overline{\theta} - 3)/(8t)$. A quick comparison reveals that

$$q_H^{SP} - q_H^M = \frac{1}{8t} ; \; q_L^{SP} - q_L^M = \frac{3}{8t} , \tag{3.22}$$

that is, quality distortion increases as we move down along the quality spectrum. This phenomenon arises because of the monopolist's attempt at extracting more surplus from sales in the higher segment of the market: the distortion of the low quality is meant to make the switching from the high to the low-quality good unattractive for rich consumers. As the number of varieties increase, the monopolist's behaviour can be characterised likewise. For the sake of brevity, we confine to the case of $n$ goods. The upper and lower limits of the quality ranges supplied by the monopolist and the social planner are, respectively:

$$q_H^M = \frac{n\overline{\theta} - 1}{2nt} \; ; \; q_L^M = \frac{n\overline{\theta} - 2n + 1}{2nt} \; ; \tag{3.23}$$

$$q_H^{SP} = \frac{2n\overline{\theta} - 1}{4nt} \; ; \; q_L^M = \frac{2n\overline{\theta} - 2n + 1}{4nt} \; . \tag{3.24}$$

As a result, with $n$ varieties, the two regimes supply the following degrees of differentiation:

$$q_H^M - q_L^M = \Delta q^M = \frac{n-1}{nt} \; ; \; q_H^{SP} - q_L^{SP} = \Delta q^{SP} = \frac{n-1}{2nt} \; , \tag{3.25}$$

from which $\Delta q^M / \Delta q^{SP} = 2$, i.e., the monopolist's product range is twice as large as the social planner's. Moreover, $\lim_{n \to \infty} \Delta q^M = 1/t$, $\lim_{n \to \infty} \Delta q^{SP} = 1/(2t)$, implying that, as the quality spectrum becomes continuous, the social planner provides each consumer with his own preferred quality, while the monopoly range is twice as large, for all $n$. As stressed by Dupuit as early as 1849, this is not aimed at deteriorating the position of low-income consumers, but rather at forcing high-income consumers to pay the prices at which superior qualities are sold, in that lower qualities are not attractive.

## 3.4.2 Partial market coverage

Under partial coverage of the market, some low-income consumers are not served, and condition (3.17) is violated in the right neighbourhood of $\underline{\theta}$. In this situation, given $n$, the monopolist and the social planner produce the same qualities, although the monopolist restricts the output to half the amount supplied by the planner (or under perfect competition). Again, we consider initially the case of a single variety. The marginal consumer locates at $p/q$, so that market demand is $x = \overline{\theta} - p/q$ and the profit function is $\pi^M(1) = (p - tq^2)x$. The FOCs are

$$\frac{\partial \pi^M(1)}{\partial q} = tp + \frac{p^2}{q^2} - 2\overline{\theta}qt = 0; \tag{3.26}$$

$$\frac{\partial \pi^M(1)}{\partial p} = \overline{\theta} - \frac{2p}{q} + qt = 0, \tag{3.27}$$

from which we get $p^M = 2\overline{\theta}^2/(9t)$; $q^M = \overline{\theta}/(3t)$. Equilibrium output is $x^M = \overline{\theta}/3$, and profits amount to $\pi^M(1) = \overline{\theta}^3/(27t)$. Notice that partial market coverage obtains if and only if $\overline{\theta} \leq 3$; when $\overline{\theta} > 3$, the analysis carried out under full market coverage holds. As to the social planner, his aim is the maximisation of

$$SW(1) = \int_{p/q}^{\overline{\theta}} (\theta q - tq^2) d\theta. \tag{3.28}$$

Solving the social optimum problem entails producing the same quality supplied by the profit-maximising monopolist, although sold at marginal cost, i.e., $p^{SP} = \overline{\theta}^2/(9t)$. Moreover, the output level under social planning is $x^{SP} = 2\overline{\theta}/3$.

Consider now the case of two varieties, whose demand functions are:

$$x_H = \overline{\theta} - \frac{(p_H - p_L)}{q_H - q_L} \; ; \; x_L = \frac{(p_H - p_L)}{q_H - q_L} - \frac{p_L}{q_L} . \tag{3.29}$$

Solving the monopolist's and the social planner's optimum problems yields:

$$q_H^M = q_H^{SP} = \frac{2\overline{\theta}}{5t} \; ; \; q_L^M = q_L^{SP} = \frac{\overline{\theta}}{5t} \; ; \tag{3.30}$$

$$X^M = \frac{2\overline{\theta}}{5} = \frac{X^{SP}}{2} \; ; \; x_i^M = \frac{\overline{\theta}}{5} = \frac{x_i^{SP}}{2} \; , \; i = H, L. \tag{3.31}$$

Equilibrium qualities and quantities (3.30-3.31) reveal that the behaviour of the monopolist coincides with that of the social planner on the quality side, while a distortion is observed on the output side. The extension to the case of $n$ varieties is now rather straightforward:

$$q_i^M = q_i^{SP} = \frac{i\overline{\theta}}{t(2n+1)} \; , \; i = 1, 2, ..., n; \tag{3.32}$$

$$X^M = \frac{n\overline{\theta}}{2n+1} = \frac{X^{SP}}{2} \; ; \; x_i^M = \frac{X^M}{n} = \frac{x_i^{SP}}{2} \; , \; i = 1, 2, ..., n, \tag{3.33}$$

from which one immediately obtains $\lim_{n\to\infty} X^M = 1/2$ and $\lim_{n\to\infty} X^{SP} = 1$. This implies that, as the number of varieties becomes infinitely high, the profit-maximising monopolist serves only the richer half of the market, while a social planner would serve all consumers.

We are now in a position to evaluate the choice of the monopolist between full market coverage (with quality distortion) and partial market coverage (with output distortion), in the parameter range where both are admissible. With this aim, it suffices to consider the case of a single good. The monopolist prefers to distort quantity rather than quality if $\bar{\theta}^3/(27t) > (\bar{\theta}-1)^2/(4t)$. This condition is met for all $\bar{\theta} < 3$; hence, in this range the monopolist will choose to supply the same quality as the social planner (or perfect competition), but restrict the output level by 50%. If $\bar{\theta} = 3$, the monopolist is indifferent between output and quality restrictions, while for all $\bar{\theta} > 3$ full market coverage with quality distortion is the only admissible regime. These considerations carry over to the case of $n$ varieties, for the appropriate values of $\bar{\theta}$.

# 3.5    Endogenous product differentiation

Within the literature on product differentiation, the behaviour of multiproduct firms operating under oligopolistic competition has received rather scanty attention. The main contributions in this field are due to Martinez-Giralt and Neven (1988) and Champsaur and Rochet (1989), who deal with horizontal and vertical differentiation, respectively.

## 3.5.1    Horizontal differentiation

Martinez-Giralt and Neven (1988) examine two versions of the spatial differentiation model. In the first, they assume that consumers are distributed along a linear city, as in Hotelling (1929) and d'Aspremont *et al.* (1979). In the second, they assume instead that consumers are distributed along a circle, as in Salop (1979). In both cases, the main issue addressed by the authors is whether at least one firm has any incentive to supply more than one product, and they get to the conclusion that such an incentive does not exist at the subgame perfect equilibrium. This result can be intuitively explained in the following terms. For the sake of simplicity, consider a duopoly. The choices open to a firm that may consider to proliferate its product range are described by figures 3.2 and 3.3. In figure 3.2, firm 1 is single-product, while firm 2 supplies two goods, both located to the right of firm 1, at $L_{21}$ and $L_{22}$. In figure 3.3, firm 1 is again a single-product unit, but her good is located between the two varieties offered by firm 2. Martinez-Giralt and Neven show that it is convenient for firm 2 to adopt the strategy represented in figure 3.2, since this strategy allows it to isolate one product from the competition exerted by the good supplied by firm 1. In other words, the market configuration depicted in figure 3.2 is less competitive than the configuration represented by figure 3.3, where both firm 2's varieties compete directly with the single one produced by firm 1.

Nevertheless, the bunching of firm 2's products on the same side of firm 1 entails a high degree of competition between themselves, leading firm 2 to supply one product only.[14] Seemingly, this implies that we should not observe multiproduct firms under horizontal differentiation. However, Martinez-Giralt and Neven are aware that this result depends on the absence of scale and scope economies, as well as entry threats by outsiders. Another element which is overlooked here is brand loyalty. We will come back to it in section 3.8.

**Figure 3.2:** Firm 2 chooses product bunching

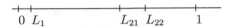

**Figure 3.3:** Firms' products are intertwined

## 3.5.2 Vertical differentiation

Champsaur and Rochet (1989) consider price competition between multi-product firms in the vertical differentiation model with variable costs of quality improvements, originated by Mussa and Rosen (1978). As this model is

---

[14]Or, alternatively, two undifferentiated varieties. As long as we do not consider fixed costs, producing two identical varieties or a single good is the same. With fixed costs attached to every variety the incentive for firm 2 to minimise differentiation between $L_{21}$ and $L_{22}$ would certainly lead it to drop one product.

a generalisation of the spatial differentiation model with convex transportation costs (Cremer and Thisse, 1991), the results obtained by Champsaur and Rochet largely replicate those by Martinez-Giralt and Neven.

Suppose consumers are uniformly distributed over the interval $[\underline{\theta}, \overline{\theta}]$, with $\underline{\theta} > 0$ and $\overline{\theta} = \underline{\theta} + \alpha$. Full market coverage is assumed. Every consumer purchases one unit, his indirect utility function being $U = u(\theta, q_i) - p_i(q_i) \geq 0$, where $q_i$ is the quality level and $p_i$ is the price set by firm $i$. Two firms, $H$ and $L$, operate in the market, each of them supplying a continuous range of qualities, $q_H \in [q_H^-, q_H^+]$ and $q_L \in [q_L^-, q_L^+]$.[15] Unit production costs are convex in quality and constant in quantity, with total costs being $C_i = c_i(q_i, x_i)$; $\partial C_i/\partial q_i > 0$; $\partial^2 C_i/\partial q_i^2 > 0$; $\partial C_i/\partial x_i > 0$; and $\partial^2 C_i/\partial x_i^2 = 0$.

Consider first the case where quality intervals are disjoint, i.e., $q_L^+ < q_H^-$. In this setting, there exists a pure-strategy Nash equilibrium at the price stage, for all conceivable quality intervals such that this inequality is satisfied. All varieties' demand densities, in equilibrium, are strictly positive.[16] Consider then the case of partial overlapping between the quality intervals, where $q_L^+ \geq q_H^-$, i.e., there exists at least one product which is offered by both firms. Also in this situation there always exists a pure-strategy equilibrium in prices. However, a necessary and sufficient condition for both firms to gain strictly positive profits in equilibrium is that both $q_L^+$ and $q_H^-$ belong to the interval of consumers' preferred qualities.[17] If this condition is met, then the price equilibrium is also unique.

We are now in a position to examine what happens in the quality stage, confining our attention to the setting where both firms are active, and they offer connected quality ranges.[18] First of all, it is possible to show that, when $u(\theta, q_i) = \theta q_i$ and $C_i = t q_i^2 x_i$, there exists an equilibrium in pure strategies at the quality stage, where both firms' profits are positive, and firms are single-product. This is a straightforward extension of a result contained in Cremer and Thisse (1994) and Lambertini (1996). Hence, the same incentive towards shrinking the product range into a single variety emerges here as in the horizontal model examined in the previous subsection. Moreover, provided

---

[15] In a recent paper, De Fraja (1996) extends the vertical differentiation model originated by Gabszewicz and Thisse (1979) to show that firms may leave some gaps in their product lines, this choice being independent of fixed costs, while related to the structure of variable costs and consumer preferences.

[16] A simple proof of these claims, in the case where product intervals collapse into a single variety, can be found in Cremer and Thisse (1994) and Lambertini (1996).

[17] When, e.g., $c_i(q_i, x_i) = t q_i^2 x_i$, the interval of socially preferred qualities is $[\underline{\theta}/(2t), \overline{\theta}/(2t)]$. See the previous section.

[18] Observe that equilibria with interleaved quality ranges may exist, e.g., where one firm offers top and bottom qualities while the other offers intermediate qualities. Champsaur and Rochet do not provide a characterisation of such equilibria.

each firm supplies an interval of qualities, its decisions are summarised by the behaviour of the lower and upper bounds of such interval, $q_i^-$ and $q_i^+$. These values affect the profits of firm $i$ in very different ways, respectively. Firms' profits, when quality intervals are disjoint, i.e., when $q_L^+ < q_H^-$, can be written as follows:

$$\Pi_H = \pi_H(q_L^+, q_H^-) + \pi_H(q_H^+, \infty); \quad \Pi_L = \pi_L(q_L^+, q_H^-) + \pi_L(-\infty, q_H^-). \quad (3.34)$$

The first term on the right-hand side of both expressions in (3.34) represents the profit for firm $i$ in the quality range where it competes with the rival, that is, the central part of the market. Such a profit can be defined as a *pure differentiation profit*. This is the same profit each firm would get if it produced a single variety. The second term is independent of the behaviour of the rival and can be labelled as a *pure segmentation profit*. When instead $q_L^+ \geq q_H^-$, at least partial overlapping obtains, and both firms' profits reduce to the pure segmentation profits in the ranges where there is no overlapping, while in the quality interval where both firms operate with the same varieties, profits are driven to zero by a standard Bertrand argument. Hence, in the corresponding Nash equilibrium in qualities, if neither quality interval degenerates into a single product and both firms' profits are positive, it must necessarily be that $q_L^+ < q_H^-$, i.e., quality intervals must be disjoint in that this strategy ensures larger profits as compared to the case of partial overlapping.

The above results have been obtained under the assumption that firms supply connected intervals of varieties. Obviously, the production of an infinite number of varieties is admissible only on purely theoretical grounds. In general, product lines are discrete, and their size can be determined by firms' strategic incentives towards current and potential competition. The incentive towards product innovation and proliferation as a barrier to entry is dealt with in the next section.

## 3.6    Persistence of monopoly

The issue of the incentives towards both process and product innovation under monopoly *vis à vis* oligopoly or perfect competition is a *vexata quaestio* in the literature on industrial organisation, dating back to the seminal contributions by Schumpeter (1942) and Arrow (1962). In the recent literature, the main contributions on the issue of the persistence of monopoly are due to Gilbert and Newbery (1982) and Reinganum (1983). These authors explicitly deal with process innovation, that is, with an R&D activity aimed at reducing the marginal cost associated with the production of an existing good, but their analysis can be easily reformulated in terms of a product innovation. Imagine an auction by an independent lab holding the rights over the innovation. This lab is willing to sell the patent of infinite duration over the innovation to the highest bidder between an incumbent and an outsider that, in case she wins, can enter the market which will thus become a duopoly made up by single-product firms. Otherwise, if the incumbent bids more and gets the patent, monopoly will persist with a two-product firm. Label these two firms as $I$ (*incumbent*) and $E$ (*entrant*). The current profit of firm $I$ as a single-good monopolist is $\pi_I^M(1)$, where superscript $M$, as usual, stands for *monopoly*. The profit it would obtain by winning the auction is $\pi_I^M(2)$. Finally, the firms' duopoly profits, when the outsider obtains the patent, are $\pi_I^D(1)$ and $\pi_E^D(1)$, where superscript $D$ stands for *duopoly*. Suppose both firms have the same intertemporal preferences, represented by a common discount rate $r$. The incentive to innovate exists for the incumbent whenever $\pi_I^M(2) \geq \pi_I^M(1)$, and the incumbents wins the auction if

$$\frac{\pi_I^M(2)}{r} \geq \frac{\pi_I^D(1)}{r} + \frac{\pi_E^D(1)}{r} , \qquad (3.35)$$

or, equivalently, if the price that $I$ is willing to pay for the rights over the innovation is larger than the maximum price that $E$ is willing to pay. Since a two-product monopolist must necessarily be able to gain at least the same profits as two non-colluding firms operating with one product each, condition (3.35) is certainly met and monopoly persists. This condition describes what is known as the *efficiency effect* (Fudenberg and Tirole, 1986; Tirole, 1988) or the *incentive to preempt* (Katz and Shapiro, 1987), summarising the tradeoff between static and dynamic efficiency characterising monopoly. That is, the innovative performance of a monopoly is higher than that of a duopoly, but at each point in time a duopoly would be preferable to a monopoly from a social standpoint.

This result, derived by Gilbert and Newbery (1982), holds under perfect certainty. When the innovation race is uncertain, another effect enters the stage, namely the so-called *replacement effect*, which shows that the innovation might be attained by the outsider because the incumbent "rests on her laurels" (Reinganum, 1983). Overall, the net effect, and the outcome of the innovation race or auction, is ambiguous.

A similar approach is adopted by Shaked and Sutton (1990). They drop the auction metaphor, and their answer to the question of whether monopoly persists or not relies exclusively on factors operating on the demand side, economies of scope being assumed away. Shaked and Sutton examine price competition in a model where each product requires the same amount of fixed costs, and they identify two elements: (i) as to the monopolist, the incentive to introduce a new good depends on the market demand for it, net of the demand loss borne by the existing good because of product proliferation, with part of the demand initially satisfied by the "old" good being relocated to the new one. This *expansion effect* is measured by the increase in monopoly profits as a result of innovation; (ii) as to the potential entrant, the incentive to introduce a new product depends only on the absolute demand level expressed by the market for this good, when it is offered under duopoly, without any externality on the other good. This incentive is weakened by the fact that entry generates a duopoly with price competition. Accordingly, it can be labelled as *competitive effect*. Market structure in equilibrium is then determined by the relative size of these two effects.

We illustrate the problem through a simple example. Assume there are only two firms and two goods, each of them being produced at most by one firm.[19] The (sunk) fixed cost attached to each good is $F$. Define $\pi(j, k)$ the operative profit (i.e., gross of fixed costs) of a firm, when it produces $j$ goods and the rival produces $k$ goods, with $j, k \in \{0, 1, 2\}$. Hence, single-product operative monopoly profit is $\pi(1, 0)$; two-product monopoly profit is $\pi(2, 0)$; and, finally, individual duopoly profit with single-product firms is $\pi(1, 1)$. As a last assumption, suppose $\pi(2, 0) > \pi(1, 0)$ and $\pi(2, 0) > 2\pi(1, 1)$. The expansion effect is measured by:

$$\epsilon = \frac{\pi(2, 0) - \pi(1, 0)}{\pi(1, 0)} > 0, \tag{3.36}$$

i.e., by the rate of increase in the monopolist's profits when she expands the product range. The competitive effect is measured by:

$$\psi = \frac{\pi(2, 0) - 2\pi(1, 1)}{2\pi(1, 1)} > 0. \tag{3.37}$$

That is, $\psi$ describes the incentive towards monopolising the market. Notice that $\psi$ increases as price competition becomes tougher, and conversely. In the limit, if products are perfect substitutes, Bertrand competition implies that $\pi(1, 1) = 0$. Therefore, in such a situation $\psi$ tends to infinity, while $\epsilon$ is nil. Conversely, when the two goods are completely independent, $\epsilon = 1$ and $\psi = 0$. For the sake of simplicity, normalise $\pi(1, 0) = 1$ and consequently $F \in (0, 1)$. Simple calculations show that $\pi(1, 1) = F$ if $\epsilon = 2F\psi + 2F - 1$, and $\pi(2, 0) - \pi(1, 0) = F$ if $\epsilon = F$. This allows us to identify the equilibrium market structure in the space $\{\psi, \epsilon\}$, i.e., as a function of the relative size of

---

[19]Notice that this assumption makes Shaked and Sutton's model similar to those dealing with the persistence of monopoly, and, at the same time, quite different from the view adopted by Brander and Eaton (1984) and De Fraja (1992).

the two effects. By using the relationships $\epsilon = 2F\psi + 2F - 1$ and $\epsilon = F$, we can investigate the equilibrium through figure 3.4, where we consider $F \in (1/2, 1)$.

**Figure 3.4:** Competitive effect and expansion effect

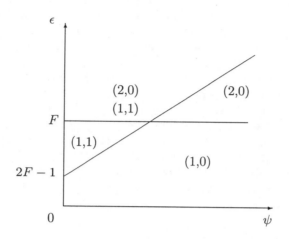

The pairs in brackets indicate the number of products supplied by firms. An interpretation can be given in the following terms. Consider an increase in $\epsilon$, for a given competitive effect $\psi$ along the horizontal axis. If the expansion effect is sufficiently high, both $(1, 1)$ and $(2, 0)$ are pure-strategy Nash equilibria. Consider then the opposite perspective where, for a given expansion effect $\epsilon$, the competitive effect increases. Observe that, if the value of $\psi$ is sufficiently high, the unique equilibrium structure in pure strategies is monopoly, be that either single- or two-product: intuitively, as the intensity of price competition increases, the dominant position initially held by the incumbent becomes safer. Likewise, for a given level of $\psi$, the incentive for the monopolist to enlarge her product range is increasing in the size of the expansion effect.

These results, derived under a fairly general set of assumptions, can obviously be expected to hold in many specific settings as well. A natural example that immediately springs to mind is endogenous differentiation, either horizontal or vertical. As noted by Shaked and Sutton, in such a setting both of the effects considered above become completely endogenous, and will depend upon the extent of market coverage, in particular the expansion effect (i.e., the incumbent's incentive to monopolise the market through product proliferation) may drastically shrink under full market coverage, as assumed, e.g., by Bonanno (1987) in examining entry deterrence in the Hotelling model.

## 3.7 Switching costs

The casual observation of consumption choices in many markets suggests that those individuals who have already bought a certain product from a given firm must bear a cost (whether real or just perceived is relatively irrelevant) if they decide to purchase a good offered by another firm, even if these two goods are completely or at least largely equivalent under many respects. This real or perceived *switching cost* gives firms some degree of monopoly power in a repeated purchase setting, or in the affine setting where consumers purchase a set of complement goods. An example is given by hi-fi equipment: it is frequently observed that a customer buys all components of the same brand, even if there is no need to do so, in that all products supplied by different firms are reciprocally compatible in terms of electrical specifications.[20] In this case, consumers perceive a cost (or a disutility) associated with pure "brand" heterogeneity. A different case is that of computers, where indeed the existence of different standards (Mac vs IBM) generates a tangible switching cost.[21] Be that as it may, what matters is that the influence exerted by such costs on consumer behaviour confronts firms with a tradeoff, at any point in time, between attracting new customers by setting low prices currently and obtaining a return in the future volume of demand, and exploiting the established market position by setting high prices which, in turn, may jeopardise any future increase in demand.

Although relatively recent, the literature on switching costs is wide (see Klemperer, 1995). Here, we confine to the analysis of its main features, by exposing a simplified version of a model by Klemperer (1992). It is convenient to consider first a duopoly with single-product firms. Define as $p_i$ the price set by firm $i$, $q_i$ the output level, $\pi_i$ the profit function and $s_i = q_i/(q_i + q_j)$ the market share of firm $i$. Production entails a constant marginal cost $c$. Firms cannot price-discriminate. The number of consumers is $N$, and each consumer, characterised by a reservation price equal to $R$, purchases one unit

---

[20]There exists an exception to this rule, namely, the fact that MC (moving coil) and MM (moving magnet) phono cartridges need completely different pre-amplification stages due to their different output voltages.

[21]The issue of supplying product lines in the presence of different standards is examined in the literature on compatibility and network externalities. For an introduction and overview, see Shy (1995, chapter 10).

either from firm $i$ or from firm $j$. Assume there is only one marketing period, with an initial condition (inherited possibly from the past history of the market) according to which in the previous period a fraction $s_i$ of consumers patronised firm $i$, and obviously a fraction $s_j = 1 - s_i$ patronised firm $j$. Each consumer has the same switching cost $\sigma$. If this is sufficiently high, the unique non-cooperative equilibrium of the market game is observationally equivalent to a collusive equilibrium, in that equilibrium profits are indeed the same that firms would attain by colluding. The reason for this is that firm $i$ cannot steal customers from firm $j$, unless it decreases its price at least to $p_i = p_j - \sigma$.[22] As price discrimination is ruled out by assumption, such a price reduction entails a uniform profit loss on all customers initially served by firm $i$, i.e., her market share $s_i$. It is easily verified that this loss is larger than the increase in profits generated from stealing the rival's demand. Therefore, the optimal choice for both firms consists in setting the price equal to the reservation price $R$.[23]

Consider now the case where each firm can choose which product to supply out of a pair of goods, labelled 1 and 2, that may be perfect or imperfect substitutes. Each consumer purchases, overall, one unit, combining the two available varieties in proportions $f$ and $(1 - f)$, with $f \in (0, 1)$. As a consequence, if $f = 1/2$, maximum differentiation is observed in the consumption basket. The utility accruing to a generic consumer, gross of price(s) and switching costs, if any, is

$$U = R + \nu - \mu \left( \frac{1}{2} - f \right)^2 > R \quad \forall \quad f \in (0, 1). \tag{3.38}$$

Parameter $\nu$ measures a consumer's evaluation of the relative value of maximum variety ($f = 1/2$) vs complete standardisation (either $f = 0$ or $f = 1$) in consumption, while parameter $\mu$ measures the disutility incurred by the consumer if he buys the two goods in different proportions. To simplify further the exposition, assume $s_i = s_j = 1/2$ and $\nu > 2\sigma > R - c > \mu > 0$.[24] Under these conditions, it can be shown that firms get larger profits when

---

[22]The same result obtains if firm $i$ expands output so as to reduce $p_i$ below such a threshold. Hence, intuitively the equilibrium outcome mimics collusion independently of the strategic variable considered.

[23]Here, it is worth noting the analogy of this result to Diamond's (1971), where consumer search costs, be they as small as they can, may lead to monopoly prices.

[24]In this example, utility from consumption is discontinuous at $f = 0$ and $f = 1$, which have been appropriately excluded from the admissible interval. However, the results we are about to derive hold for utility functions $U(f)$ where $U(0) = U(1) = R$; $U(f) = R + \nu - \mu(1/2 - f)^2$, with $f \in [\xi, 1 - \xi]$; and, for any other $f$, $U(f) \leq U(\xi)$, where $\xi$ is a positive constant appropriately chosen.

they supply perfect substitutes, that is, when both firms sell either good 1 or good 2. To verify this result, observe that when they do so, their individual profits are $\pi_i = \pi_j = N(R-c)/2$, as in the previous example. When instead they produce imperfect substitutes, a consumer previously served by firm $i$ obtains $R - p_i$ if he continues to buy from firm $i$, while he gets $R - p_j - \sigma$ if he switches to firm $j$; and he obtains

$$R + \nu - \mu \left(\frac{1}{2} - f\right)^2 - fp_i - (1-f)p_j - \sigma \qquad (3.39)$$

if he combines the two products, in which case his utility is maximised at $f = 1/2 + (p_j - p_i)/(2\mu)$. If $\nu$ is sufficiently large, all consumers choose to combine the two goods, and therefore profits are defined as follows:

$$\pi_i = (p_i - c) \left[\frac{1}{2} + \frac{p_j - p_i}{2\mu}\right] N. \qquad (3.40)$$

It is now easy to check that, if $\nu > \sigma + \mu/4$, the market subgame obtaining when firms have chosen to supply imperfect substitutes has a unique equilibrium in which $p_i = p_j = c + \mu$ and $\pi_i = \pi_j = N\mu/2$. This proves that, in the presence of switching costs, differentiation is not profitable. By extension, it can be shown that this result carries over to the case where firms indeed offer product lines rather than single goods.

This implies that switching costs play a crucial role in explaining firms' behaviour in differentiated markets, where firms may use product proliferation strategically. The reason for this is intuitive: if preferences induce consumers to purchase more than one good, then a single-product firm is worse off when faced with the competition of a multiproduct firm, because it forces its own consumers to choose between bearing a switching cost or giving up differentiation, i.e., the consumption of a product line.[25] This fact induces each firm to offer the same number of products as the rival firms. However, the softer price competition due to the switching costs reduces firms' incentives towards differentiation in the product space. If product lines were differentiated, consumers might indeed purchase a combination of lines notwithstanding the switching cost, provided that the beneficial effect of differentiation were sufficiently large. Being aware of this, firms prefer to offer product lines which are perfect substitutes for each other and exploit fully the anti-competitive effect of switching costs. This is what leads Klemperer to state that "competing head-to-head may be less competitive". The

---

[25] Notice the analogy between this model and that of Brander and Eaton (1984), summarised in section 3.2. Of course, as switching costs tend to zero, Brander and Eaton's results obtain.

existence of switching costs implies that prices are higher when products are close (in the limit, perfect) substitutes than in the opposite case, and this contrasts with the standard literature on product differentiation where the opposite happens. Another relevant implication of this model is that the search for market niches still not preempted by rivals might drastically lose relevance, with imitation becoming more relevant than innovation.

The latter issue, however, is controversial. Indeed, as far as social welfare is concerned, switching costs imply the possibility for firms to offer excess product variety as compared to social optimum (Klemperer and Padilla, 1997). The intuition behind this is that, if consumers prefer to patronise a single producer, the firm offering a wider range of products might attract all consumers. Therefore, innovation within a line, and thus product proliferation, would have the well known effect of strengthening the position of a firm in the market. Yet, expanding product lines may be inefficient from the firms' viewpoint as well. Gilbert and Matutes (1993) show that the choice of offering a product line by all firms operating in a certain market can be the consequence of a prisoner's dilemma. Each firm is aware that it would be preferable to produce a single good, if this strategy were associated with a credible commitment on the part of every firm. In the absence of such a commitment, product proliferation is a dominant strategy and the outcome is inefficient for all firms within the industry.

## 3.8   Concluding remarks

The theory of product differentiation allows us to understand how firms may acquire some market power by decreasing substitutability between products, and how firms can deter entry by widening their product ranges (Schmalensee, 1978; Brander and Eaton, 1984). In doing so, they face a tradeoff between economies of scale in a single product and economies of scope over a product line (De Fraja, 1992). This is particularly true in the case of the address approach to product differentiation (be that horizontal or vertical), where pure profit incentives, in the absence of entry threats, drive firms to reduce the width of their product lines (Bonanno, 1987; Martinez-Giralt and Neven, 1988; Champsaur and Rochet, 1989).

This holds as long as we take the producer's viewpoint. As soon as the consequences on consumer surplus and social welfare are accounted for, it emerges that firms' choices are obviously socially inefficient, with very few exceptions. The degree of differentiation which is optimal for firms is usually excessive from a social standpoint. Moreover, the need to create barriers to entry leads firms to underexploit scale economies and favour instead scope economies disproportionately. This also implies that firms can be expected to be inefficient in producing each single good, in that they will tend not to minimise average costs. This fact is driven by market forces, and it is but another example of the well known tradeoff between static and dynamic efficiency stressed initially by Schumpeter (1942).

To some extent, the introduction of switching costs (Klemperer, 1992) into the picture restores consumers' sovereignty, in that firms' decisions over their respective product lines are conditional upon these costs, which are equivalent, on the demand side, to the sunk costs that may operate on the supply side. Consumer sovereignty ends, though, as soon as the presence of switching costs produces a quasi-collusive market outcome. These considerations open an interesting perspective on the possibility for firms to exploit the success of a certain brand, i.e., brand loyalty on the part of consumers, in extending their activity in other markets. The strategic use of brand loyalty through *umbrella brands* allows firms to enter new markets by bearing the informational costs otherwise borne by consumers, who, in turn, may condition the global success of such firms. In this light, Klemperer's contribution recasts in modern terms a debate opened by Chamberlin (1933).

# References

1] Anderson, S. and A. de Palma (1992), "Multiproduct Firms: A Nested Logit Approach", *Journal of Industrial Economics*, **40**, 261-76.

2] Anderson, S., A. de Palma and J.-F. Thisse (1992), *Discrete Choice Theory of Product Differentiation*, Cambridge, MA, MIT Press.

3] Arrow, K. (1962), "Economic Welfare and the Allocation of Resources for Invention", in R. Nelson (ed.), *The Rate and Direction of Innovative Activity*, Princeton, Princeton University Press.

4] Bailey, E. and A. Friedlander (1982), "Market Structures and Multiproduct Industries", *Journal of Economic Literature*, **20**, 1024-48.

5] Baumol, W., J. Panzar and R. Willig (1982), *Contestable Markets and the Theory of Industry Structure*, New York, Harcourt Brace Jovanovich.

6] Besanko, D., S. Donnenfeld and L. White (1987), "Monopoly and Quality Distortion: Effects and Remedies", *Quarterly Journal of Economics*, **102**, 743-67.

7] Besanko, D., S. Donnenfeld and L. White (1988), "The Multiproduct Firm, Quality Choice, and Regulation", *Journal of Industrial Economics*, **36**, 411-29.

8] Bonanno, G. (1987), "Location Choice, Product Proliferation and Entry Deterrence", *Review of Economic Studies*, **54**, 37-46.

9] Brander, J. and J. Eaton (1984), "Product Line Rivalry", *American Economic Review*, **74**, 323-34.

10] Brock, J. (1983), "Contestable Markets and the Theory of Industry Structure: A Review Article", *Journal of Political Economy*, **91**, 1055-66.

11] Chamberlin, E.H. (1933), *The Theory of Monopolistic Competition*, Cambridge, MA, MIT Press.

12] Champsaur, P. and J.-C. Rochet (1989), "Multiproduct Duopolists", *Econometrica*, **57**, 533-57.

13] Cremer, H. and J.-F. Thisse (1991), "Location Models of Horizontal Differentiation: A Special Case of Vertical Differentiation Models", *Journal of Industrial Economics*, **39**, 383-90.

14] Cremer, H. and J.-F. Thisse (1994), "Commodity Taxation in a Differentiated Oligopoly", *International Economic Review*, **35**, 613-33.

15] d'Aspremont, C., J.J. Gabszewicz and J.-F. Thisse (1979), "On Hotelling's 'Stability in Competition'", *Econometrica*, **47**, 1045-50.

16] d'Aspremont, C. and L.-A. Gérard-Varet (1980), "Stackelberg-Solvable Games and Pre-Play Communication", *Journal of Economic Theory*, **23**, 201-17.

17] De Fraja, G. (1992), "Product Line Competition and Market Structure", *Economic Notes*, **21**, 511-25.

18] De Fraja, G. (1994), "A General Characterization of Multiproduct Cournot Competition", *Bulletin of Economic Research*, **46**, 171-83.

19] De Fraja, G. (1996), "Product Line Competition in Vertically Differentiated Markets", *International Journal of Industrial Organization*, **14**, 389-414.

20] Diamond, P. (1971), "A Model of Price Adjustment", *Journal of Economic Theory*, **3**, 156-68.

21] Dupuit, J. (1849), "On Tolls and Transport Charges", *International Economic Papers*, London, Macmillan, 1952; translated from the French original, *Annales des Ponts et des Chaussées*, **17**.

22] Eaton, B.C. and R.G. Lipsey (1978), "Freedom of Entry and the Existence of Pure Profit", *Economic Journal*, **88**, 455-69.

23] Fudenberg, D. and J. Tirole (1986), *Dynamic Models of Oligopoly*, London, Harwood.

24] Gabszewicz, J.J. and J.-F. Thisse (1979), "Price Competition, Quality and Income Disparities", *Journal of Economic Theory*, **20**, 340-59.

25] Gabszewicz, J.J., A. Shaked, J. Sutton and J.-F. Thisse (1986), "Segmenting the Market: the Monopolist Optimal product Mix", *Journal of Economic Theory*, **39**, 273-89.

26] Gilbert, R. and C. Matutes (1993), "Product Line Rivalry with Brand Differentiation", *Journal of Industrial Economics*, **41**, 223-40.

27] Gilbert, R. and D. Newbery (1982), "Preemptive Patenting and the Persistence of Monopoly", *American Economic Review*, **72**, 514-26.

28] Hamilton, J. and S. Slutsky (1990), "Endogenous Timing in Duopoly Games: Stackelberg or Cournot Equilibria", *Games and Economic Behavior*, **2**, 29-47.

29] Hay, D. (1976), "Sequential Entry and Entry-Deterring Strategies in Spatial Competition", *Oxford Economic Papers*, **28**, 240-57.

30] Hotelling, H. (1929), "Stability in Competition", *Economic Journal*, **39**, 41-57.

31] Itoh, M. (1983), "Monopoly, Product Differentiation and Economic Welfare", *Journal of Economic Theory*, **31**, 88-104.

32] Judd, K. (1985), "Credible Spatial Preemption", *RAND Journal of Economics*, **16**, 153-66.

33] Katz, M. and C. Shapiro (1987), "R&D Rivalry with Licensing or Imitation", *American Economic Review*, **77**, 402-20.

34] Klemperer, P. (1992), "Equilibrium Product Lines: Competing Head-to-Head May Be Less Competitive", *American Economic Review*, **82**, 740-55.

35] Klemperer, P. (1995), "Competition when Consumers Have Switching Costs: An Overview with Applications to Industrial Organization, Macroeconomics, and International Trade", *Review of Economic Studies*, **62**, 515-39.

36] Klemperer, P. and A.J. Padilla (1997), "Do Firms' Product Lines Include Too Many Varieties?", *RAND Journal of Economics*, **28**, 472-88.

37] Lambertini, L. (1996), "Choosing Roles in a Duopoly for Endogenously Differentiated Products", *Australian Economic Papers*, **35**, 205-24.

38] Lambertini, L. (1997), "The Multiproduct Monopolist under Vertical Differentiation: An Inductive Approach", *Recherches Economiques de Louvain*, **63**, 109-22.

39] Lane, W.J. (1980), "Product Differentiation in a Market with Endogenous Sequential Entry", *Bell Journal of Economics*, **11**, 237-60.

40] MacDonald, G.M. and A. Slivinsky (1987), "The Simple Analytics of Competitive Equilibrium with Multiproduct Firms", *American Economic Review*, **77**, 941-53.

41] Martinez-Giralt, X. and D. Neven (1988), "Can Price Competition Dominate Market Segmentation?", *Journal of Industrial Economics*, **36**, 431-42.

42] Maskin, E. and J. Riley (1984), "Monopoly with Incomplete Information", *RAND Journal of Economics*, **15**, 171-96.

43] Mussa, M. and S. Rosen (1978), "Monopoly and Product Quality", *Journal of Economic Theory*, **18**, 301-17.

44] Okuguchi, K. and F. Szidarovsky (1990), *The Theory of Oligopoly with Multiproduct Firms*, Lecture Notes in Economics and Mathematical Systems, vol. 342, Heidelberg, Springer-Verlag.

45] Panzar, J. and R. Willig (1981), "Economies of Scope", *American Economic Review*, **71**, 268-72.

46] Prescott, E.J. and M. Visscher (1977), "Sequential Location among Firms with Foresight", *Bell Journal of Economics*, **8**, 378-93.

47] Reinganum, J. (1983), "Uncertain Innovation and the Persistence of Monopoly", *American Economic Review*, **73**, 741-8.

48] Robinson, J. (1953), "Imperfect Competition Revisited", *Economic Journal*, **63**, 575-93.

49] Rosenlicht, M. (1968), *Introduction to Analysis*, Glenview, Scott, Foresman & Company.

50] Salop, S. (1979), "Monopolistic Competition with Outside Goods", *Bell Journal of Economics*, **10**, 141-56.

51] Schmalensee, R. (1978), "Entry Deterrence in the Ready-to-Eat Breakfast Industry", *Bell Journal of Economics*, **9**, 305-27.

52] Schumpeter, J. (1942), *Capitalism, Socialism and Democracy*, London, Allen & Unwin.

53] Selten, R. (1975), "Re-Examination of the Perfectness Concept for Equilibrium Points in Extensive Games", *International Journal of Game Theory*, **4**, 25-55.

54] Shaked, A. and J. Sutton (1982), "Relaxing Price Competition through Product Differentiation", *Review of Economic Studies*, **49**, 3-13.

55] Shaked, A. and J. Sutton (1983), "Natural Oligopolies", *Econometrica*, **51**, 1469-83.

56] Shaked, A. and J. Sutton (1990), "Multiproduct Firms and Market Structure", *RAND Journal of Economics*, **21**, 45-62.

57] Sheshinski, E. (1976), "Price, Quality and Quantity Regulation in Monopoly", *Economica*, **43**, 127-37.

58] Shy, O. (1995), *Industrial Organization*, Cambridge, MA, MIT Press.

59] Singh, N. and X. Vives (1984), "Price and Quantity Competition in a Differentiated Duopoly", *RAND Journal of Economics*, **15**, 546-54.

60] Spence, A.M. (1975), "Monopoly, Quality and Regulation", *Bell Journal of Economics*, **6**, 417-29.

61] Spence, A.M. (1983), "Contestable Markets and the Theory of Industry Structure: A Review Article", *Journal of Economic Literature*, **21**, 981-90.

62] Tirole, J. (1988), *The Theory of Industrial Organization*, Cambridge, MA, MIT Press.

63] Wernerfelt, B. (1986), "Product Line Rivalry: A Note", *American Economic Review*, **76**, 842-4.

# Chapter 4

# Labour participation

Michele Moretto and Gianpaolo Rossini

## 4.1 Introduction

During the last fifty years or more, the theory of the firm behaviour has been extended to see how the market behaviour and the performances of a firm are affected by: 1) the objective function; 2) the ownership structure; 3) the degree of labour participation to decisions; 4) the structure of internal incentives. The first three issues belong to the literature on firm organizations departing from pure profit maximizing (PM). The fourth concerns the internal organization of any kind of firm, including the PM. As far as the ownership structure of the firm is concerned the PM and the labour managed firm or cooperative firm (LM) represent the two polar cases. In the latter employees own the firm and take decisions via a democratic voting mechanism. Between the two polar cases there exists a rich typology of firms sharing features of either one pole or the other.

Why has one type prevailed over the other? Causal and statistical observation point to a prevalence of the PM firm over the LM or even over the heterogeneous firms in between. The result is the absence of "economic democracy" within firms. Then why don't we observe much economic democracy in market economies? To this question we devote part of this work, referring to existing literature. A second question concerns the efficiency of firms' organizations according to the degree of employees' participation. Decisions taken by shareholders are sometimes inefficient. Of course we do not address the question "who should control the firm" (see Zingales, 1997, p. 11) in terms of the financial assets.[1]

---

[1] For a survey on this topic, see Shleifer and Vishny (1997).

We'll start with LM enterprises. We consider extensions of the traditional model of value added maximization and tradable memberships. Some empirical comparisons between LM firms and PM firms are mentioned. In the third section, we dwell on the Aoki firm where employees take part in some decisions. In the fourth section, employees share the economic rent of a firm facing uncertain market conditions. Some of the above questions touch corporate governance, or how to distribute a rent among specific factors. This happens when factors can command in the firm more than they would reap outside.

## 4.2   The LM firm

The first LM firms appeared in the nineteenth century. Alfred Marshall (Marshall, 1920, pp. 110, 191, 545) refers to them as associations of workers based on the principles of mutuality and solidarity. Most of them dedicate mainly to agricultural production and to commercial activities (Ireland and Law, 1981, 1982; Bonin and Putterman, 1987; Bonin et al., 1993).

Despite its democratic and socialist bias the LM firm succeeds only in market economies, i.e., in western countries, like Spain, the Basque provinces, Germany, England, Italy, even with a marginal share. The former semisocialist Jugoslavia is the only instance of a non-capitalist country where the LM firm prospers. In Europe LM firms grew during the 1970s, reaching a share of employment of some 2.5% (Ben Ner, 1988a). After that they started to contract slightly. There is still a notable presence of LM firms in the USA in the plywood industry and in some services (Craig and Pencavel, 1992, 1995). In former socialist countries LM firms were mostly absent because of the inconsistency between self-management and central planning. The LM firm develops as an economic institution generated by socialist aims in economic systems which are not, by and large, socialist. Despite that, in many cases, socialist collective firms are run "on behalf of workers". The scanty attention paid by the students of socialism is due to a general neglect of the theory of the firm. This vacuum is partially filled by the contributions of Ward (1958), Domar (1966), Vanek (1970), Meade (1972), to mention just the most outstanding ones. In all these contributions the question of the optimal ownership structure and of the optimal allocation of decisions is taken as given. The LM firm represents a benchmark case for labour participation in the decisions of the firm. However, its scarce diffusion is a signal of intrinsic difficulties. This is one of the reasons why the LM firm has not become the enterprise organization preferred by the fans of economic democracy.

## 4.2.1 The basic model of the LM firm

An LM firm is owned and managed by employees. The objective function of the LM firm is the individual value added, i.e.:

$$\max y = \frac{p\left(f(K,L)\right)f(K,L) - rK}{L} \geq w\,, \tag{4.1}$$

where $f(K,L)$ is a concave production function with arguments the capital services and number of employees; $p$ is the market price of output, $r$ the price of capital services and $w$ the market labour wage. We assume that $K, L \geq 0$, $f_K, f_L \geq 0$, $f_{KK}, f_{LL} \leq 0$ and linear homogeneous technology. The corresponding PM objective function is:

$$\max \pi = p\left(f(K,L)\right)f(K,L) - rK - wL. \tag{4.2}$$

First order conditions (FOCs) for the two firms operating in perfect competition are:

$$\frac{\partial y}{\partial K} = p\left(1 + \frac{dp}{df}\frac{f}{p}\right)f_K - r = 0, \tag{4.3}$$

$$\frac{\partial y}{\partial L} = p\left(1 + \frac{dp}{df}\frac{f}{p}\right)f_L - \frac{pf - rK}{L} = 0, \tag{4.4}$$

and:

$$\frac{\partial \pi}{\partial K} = p\left(1 + \frac{dp}{df}\frac{f}{p}\right)f_K - r = 0, \tag{4.5}$$

$$\frac{\partial \pi}{\partial L} = p\left(1 + \frac{dp}{df}\frac{f}{p}\right)f_L - w = 0. \tag{4.6}$$

The first two FOCs concern the LM firm, the other two the PM firm. As it can be seen (4.4) and (4.6) differ, while the other two look alike. The difference depends on individual value added instead of the market wage. In a perfectly competitive market, i.e., with zero price elasticity, free entry and zero profits, (4.4) and (4.6) coincide. Under these conditions, the individual value added attainable within the LM firm equals the market wage, which amouts to saying that any rent from LM membership disappears.

On the basis of this result, we may highlight a first affinity between a PM and an LM firm in the long run equilibrium. In this circumstance, it becomes irrelevant to establish who hires whom, i.e., whether it is capital who hires labour or the other way round (see Samuelson, 1957). Nonetheless, when we consider either the short run or imperfect competition, the equilibrium configurations change considerably and we observe either positive profits or a positive difference between individual value added within the LM firm and the market wage. Then the behaviour of the LM firm shows some "perversion".

Let us consider first how the LM firm responds to market changes in the short run. The LM firm reacts to a price increase in the opposite way with respect to a PM firm. While the PM firm sells more, the LM firm restricts supply. Then, we observe the downward sloping supply curve. This may be shown from the application of the implicit function theorem to (4.4):

$$\frac{dL}{dp} \propto - \left( f_L - \frac{f}{L} \right), \qquad (4.7)$$

where $\propto$ indicates proportionality. With concave technology, the average productivity is always larger than the marginal productivity. Then, as the market price increases, $L$ decreases and, consequently, the short run supply curve of the LM has a negative slope.

With imperfect competition the LM firm employs a smaller number of members-employees as compared to the PM firm. Accordingly, second best comparison places the LM on an inferior step. The LM firm reacts to the variation of fixed costs, unlike the PM firm. By substituting fixed costs to $rK$, using a term $F$, in (4.4) and resorting again to the implicit function theorem, we can calculate $dL/dF$. When fixed costs increase, the LM firm adds new members in order to let them bear the larger fixed cost.

There are also other "perversities". With imperfect competition and non-increasing returns to scale, in the long run, the level of optimal production tends to zero (Meade, 1974; Pestieau and Thisse, 1979; Landsberger and Subotnik, 1981). This tendency becomes stronger when the LM firm strategically interacts in a static framework with PM firms (Delbono and Rossini, 1992; Rossini and Scarpa, 1992). It becomes even stronger when the LM firm competes dynamically using capacity as a control variable (Lambertini and Rossini, 1998). When we consider the choice of product quality, it appears that the LM is downward biased also in this dimension (Lambertini, 1997). As to the incentive to carry our R&D for process innovation, the LM suffers from underinvestment *vis à vis* its PM counterpart (Lambertini, 1998).

This set of anomalies raises some relevant questions. The first concerns the effective theoretical plausibility of the downward sloping supply curve. The second concerns the empirical validity of some of the theoretical conclusions above, especially as to the short run reactions of the LM firm *vis à vis* its PM counterpart. The third question relates to the marginality and small dimension of most LM firms, since their PM competitors are usually bigger. These issues are dealt with in the next sections.

## 4.2.2  Short run downward sloping supply curve: other explanations

The adjustment to a change of the market price could take a different route, instead of the variation of the number of members, for instance, considering the number of hours worked per member. In that case, the perversity of the LM firm response to market disappears (Ireland and Law, 1982). Otherwise the perversity comes back with its entire plausibility. Then, let us provide an intuitive explanation. The increase in the market price, if it were to increase supply, leads to a value of marginal productivity and profit per employee growing less, by concavity, than when profit per employee goes up due to a decrease of the quantity supplied.

However, this perversity is ambiguous, since $L$ is treated as the labour input in a PM firm. But $L$, in this case, is the decision maker in the firm. Then we cannot consider it as an ordinary input since labour is simultaneously the decision maker and the input. This double coincidence lets the LM decision scheme fall apart. To be clearer, it would be as if, in the comparative statics exercises on the PM firm, we were to associate with any variation of the input $K$ a change in the executive board appointed by shareholders. The "perversion" of the LM firm lies in the ambiguous definition of the labour input, which cannot be treated the same way as in the PM firm. If we consider labour as the decision maker we must clearly look for other forms of reactions of the LM firm. The variable factor should be capital, even though this cannot be the case in the short run. If capital can be leased and therefore become a variable factor with no firm specificity we should be able to find some less perverse response of the LM firm. Consider equation (4.3). Applying the implicit function theorem, by concavity, we can get:

$$\frac{dK}{dp} = -\frac{f_K}{p f_{KK}} \geq 0. \tag{4.8}$$

This means that, if we consider that in the short run the membership is fixed and capital can be leased and made quantitatively flexible, any sort of perversion disappears and the short run supply curve becomes positively sloped.

Following an extended literature, if the LM firm operates in a market with random shocks, there could be a random reduction of the number of members. Otherwise the LM firm operates without any random variation of the number of members. Then it will display a rigid supply curve, even though it does not appear quite clear how that is consistent with the existence of a competitive market (Steinherr and Thisse, 1979). An alternative route is the introduction of compensations for those who decide voluntarily (why?)

to leave the firm, for instance, through the market for membership, as we shall see later.

In some LM firms the labour force of the LM firm is made partly of members and partly of non-members (hired workers). In that case short run flexibility of the variable input is on the shoulders of hired workers and the LM firm has a non-perverse behaviour. It becomes very similar to a PM firm, with the shareholders working in the firm, reducing the principal-agent inefficiency because of easier and cheaper monitoring of the production activity.

### 4.2.3   The market for membership: the new theory of workers' enterprise

During the first half of the 1980s the theory of the LM firm received a further boost. The innovation came from the modelling of the market for member-ships made exchangeable and no longer personally specific. This marked the beginning of the new theory of the LM firm. However, some think that it is fairly unrealistic and therefore, they reject the extension. When a market for memberships exists (Dow, 1986; Sertel, 1982, 1987, 1991) the LM firm may become very similar to its PM counterpart. The new definition "work-ers enterprise" (WE) was coined by Sertel (1982, 1987) and Fehr and Sertel (1993). Paretian efficiency is restored and the WE firm behaves like a PM firm also in the case of imperfect competition (Sertel, 1991, 1993). Every individual worker can enter (and exit) a WE enterprise buying (selling) an individual right to take part in the production activity and share the rents deriving from it. This right has an equilibrium price equal to the discounted sum of individual profits that the firm is expected to get. This scheme ap-plies also to the reduction or expansion of the number of members. However, in an LM firm, any variation of the number of members must be approved by incumbent members. The voluntary quit of a member is possible only if the firm pays the quitter an amount equal to the income flow he would be getting if he stayed in the firm. The equilibrium deed price makes an employee indifferent between staying and quitting. A potential entrant will have to pay the same amount the quitter receives. Let us review the Sertel (1982, 1987) model. We consider entry and exit in a static environment. The reservation price of the entering member is given by:

$$P_D(L) = y(L+1) - w, \qquad (4.9)$$

where $y(L+1)$ is the individual value added with $L+1$ members. On the other hand, the loss of any incumbent member because of the new entry is given by:

$$y(L) - y(L+1).\tag{4.10}$$

The council of incumbents is willing to let a new member join the party if the entrant pays at least:

$$P_S(L) = [y(L) - y(L+1)]L.\tag{4.11}$$

The LM firm does not expand (*condition of non-expansion*) if:

$$P_D < P_S.\tag{4.12}$$

If we assume that the firm has capital $\widehat{K}$, which is fixed in the short run, then, substituting in (4.12), we get:

$$\frac{pf(L+1,\widehat{K}) - r\widehat{K}}{L+1} + L\frac{pf(L+1,\widehat{K}) - r\widehat{K}}{L+1} - L\frac{pf(L,\widehat{K}) - r\widehat{K}}{L} < w,\tag{4.13}$$

or,

$$f(L+1,\widehat{K}) - f(L,\widehat{K}) < \frac{w}{p}.\tag{4.14}$$

In a similar manner we consider the *condition of non contraction*, which appears as:

$$P_D(L-1) > P_S(L-1).\tag{4.15}$$

From which, by using the same procedure, owing to the non-expansion condition, we get:

$$f(K,L) - f(K,L-1) > \frac{w}{p}.\tag{4.16}$$

The left side of (4.14) may be considered an integer approximation of marginal productivity of labour. The left side of (4.16) has the same meaning.

These two conditions of *non-expansion* and *non-contraction* provide an answer as to the non-perversion of the LM firm when new members have to pay to obtain the rent that the LM firm distributes to its members. We actually see that, if the price $p$ increases, the constraint in (4.14) gets more severe, while in (4.16) it gets looser. In (4.14) marginal productivity, on the left, may decrease, in (4.16) it may decrease. This can be obtained by increasing the level of activity via a higher $L$. The two conditions ensure that the LM firm behaves non-perversely, i.e. like a PM firm. A more sophisticated version of this model is due to Dow (1986, 1993a). In a subsequent paper Fehr and Sertel (1993) considered the behaviour of two workers' enterprises (WE) with a different internal structure: the discriminatory workers' enterprise (DWE) and the non-discriminatory workers' enterprise (NDWE), to endogenize the number of members. In the DWE founding members let new members enter sequentially by price discriminating the membership right. In the NDWE, on the contrary, founding members admit fresh members in one shot and let them pay the same entry price. Fehr and Sertel (1993) show that, with imperfect labour markets, the two different WE display distinct behaviours. The DWE, like its PM counterpart, employs an efficient amount of labour. On the contrary, the NDWE not only behaves inefficiently, but hires an amount of labour larger than that used by its PM counterpart. However, since this quantity does not correspond to any equilibrium situation, an entry process starts with groups of potential members and discriminates over the membership price. This process comes to an end in the long run when the efficient dimension is reached.[2]

### 4.2.4 The market for memberships: some objections

Markets for memberships are not just a theoretical artifact. In Italy and France it is possible to enter and exit LM firms by trading memberships. However, these markets are not well developed and are scarcely competitive. They are mostly managed by the firms themselves with a moderate participation of financial intermediaries. Craig and Pencavel (1992) report that in the American LM firms memberships prices vary between some 40,000 and 90,000 US dollars. The level of these prices points to a non-competitive market for memberships, letting LM firms appear as a sort of closed shop. However, despite the existence of markets for memberships, the prevailing tendency appears to be one of transforming the LM ownership structure into a PM one. The reason is that it is quite burdensome for a worker to finance joining an LM firm. Therefore both the LM firm and the entrant workers prefer to expand production through employees who are not eligible to become members. The LM firm tends to become less cooperative and more similar to a joint stock company organized around a core of initial members who tend to become the next shareholders while working in the firm. This tendency can be observed also in LM firms which are not particularly successful, simply because it is awkward for a worker to obtain from a financial

---

[2]In the behaviour of the NDWE, as described by Fehr and Sertel, time does not play any role. It just has a logical meaning, since all decisions collapse in a unique instant of time. Therefore, the entry process is instantaneous even though it considers many blocks of potential entrants.

intermediary the funds to buy a membership, while it is much easier for an entrepreneur to get credit to acquire shares of a firm either to let it grow faster or simply for a buyout.

We list at least seven reasons why the market for membership turns out to be quite imperfect or, simply does not work.

- First. It is awkward for a worker to provide collateral to the lender of the funds needed for the membership acquisition. For an entrepreneur the collateral is provided by what he buys. In an LM firm what a worker buys is the right to work in the firm. This is an asset contingent on his effectively working.

- Second. Workers buying a membership of the firm where they work end up with a portfolio which is not diversified. This is not consistent with risk aversion of workers. Inefficient diversification is thought to be (Dreze, 1976) one of the major obstacles for the growth of the firm based on participation.

- Third. The reasoning of an LM member is the following: "If I borrow money to become a member the collateral asset is my membership. However if I decide to quit I give my membership to an investment bank who will sell it to somebody willing to take over my job". In this case the firm loses a worker and replaces him with somebody else. However, the entrant is not chosen by the firm but is the result of a buying choice by an individual acquiring the right to work in a particular firm. This situation corresponds to a labour market quite far apart from the usual ones. The competitive market works only for the buying and selling of memberships, but not for labour to be hired by the firm. Once you have acquired the membership you have a right to work, regardless of any ability or willingness to work. Then, it is not possible to write down standardized contracts. Memberships are, after all, personal, unlike shares, which are never so.

- Fourth. Financing a membership acquisition in an LM firm is an investment in human capital, mainly if that happens in firms with a low capital intensity or which have just begun their activity. Financial intermediaries are often unable to finance human capital 1) because it is not entirely appropriable and, therefore, not wholly exchangeable, and 2) because it is often highly firm specific. The degree of irreversibility of human capital investment may be fairly high.

- Fifth. Workers who want to become members of an LM firm have to gather information as to the future value added the firm is able to secure. A lot of asymmetric information may prevent an efficient result in the market for memberships. The insiders or the sellers of the memberships have a better knowledge of future earnings than the entrants. A worker who is hired by a PM firm does not face a similar problem. The worker accepts a fixed wage that does not require him to know much about the firm.

- Sixth. If entrants pay the membership at its market price only the founders of the firm will be able to reap a rent or an extra over the market wage (Meade, 1972; Dow, 1986). So why should an entrant risk investing in the same firm in which he works if he just gets the market wage? This is also one of the reasons why memberships are sold at a discount.

- Seventh. Severe hurdles are faced by the firm when it tries to grow by increasing the number of members. In that case, the effect on the incumbents may be a downward shift of the market price of memberships, the same way as happens for a PM firm when it tries to raise capital on the stock exchange. As a consequence there is a preference for credit markets.

As a partial conclusion it seems that the market for memberships, whenever it works, is far from being an efficient market. In some countries legislation limits the degree of exchangeability of membership shares (S. Zan, 1982; L. Zan, 1990).

Empirical observation shows that LM firms tend to resort more to the credit market than their PM counterparts (S. Zan, 1982). The LM firm is the outcome of an agreement among founding workers, who are not supposed to own much capital. Then it needs, from the beginning of its life, quite a lot of borrowed funds. The LM firm then results almost always overleveraged. Undercapitalization and excessive borrowed funds make the LM firm more exposed to the risk of bankruptcy. A higher moral hazard is likely to appear among LM members as compared to shareholders of a PM firm. An additional explanation may be that the consequences of a bankruptcy are less burdensome for LM members than for shareholders (Eswaran and Kotwal, 1989).

Despite these considerations the condition of a worker in an LM firm is much different compared to a PM firm. In the latter firm he cannot affect the management decisions and he has no stake in the property of the firm. In the LM firm there is no hierarchy and the rule, one member-one vote, ensures a democratic management of the firm. However, democratic voting systems incur inefficiency, as the literature on voting has emphasized. It remains to be seen whether the more comfortable conditions for workers in the LM firm have a positive effect on internal efficiency or, else, if LM firms have similar problems of incentives to the PM firm. In that case inefficiency would be the likely result since, in the LM firm, we have to add a more lengthy and complicated decision process.

Even though the management of the LM firm is in the hands of workers through a voting system, there are exceptions to this rule since sometimes the management is delegated to an outsider.

## 4.2.5   Static and dynamic efficiency of the LM firm: theory and empirical evidence

We compare statically an LM firm and a PM firm, following Dow (1993a). Take a firm using two inputs $K$ and $L$ in fixed proportions obtaining an output $f(K, L) \geq 0$, for every unit of capital ($L = K$). Assume that production is decided after the realization of a technological shock $h$ and that there is no risk aversion.

An employee producing output $f$ gets a disutility $c_L(f, h)$ which is increasing and convex in the first argument. The unitary cost of capital is $r(f, h)$ increasing and convex in $f$. The price of output is normalized to 1. The surplus function appears as:

$$s(f, h) \equiv f - r(f, h) - c_L(f, h). \qquad (4.17)$$

In the case of a PM firm the owner is the *residual claimant*, i.e., he gets all that remains after having paid workers a fixed wage $w$ that does not vary from state to state, since it is not contingent on the realization of any shock $h$. Once the shock has been realized $f$ is chosen by the owner according to the rule:

$$\max_{f \geq 0} f - r(f, h) - w, \qquad (4.18)$$

with the participation constraint for the worker:

$$w - c_L(f, h) \geq 0. \qquad (4.19)$$

We can then define different levels of production for any pair of state/wage $f(w, h)$. The owner will choose *ex ante* the optimal wage as a result of the maximization of the *expected profit*:

$$\pi_K \equiv \max_{w \geq 0} E\{f(w, h) - r[f(w, h), h] - w\}. \qquad (4.20)$$

When the participation constraint is binding, the wage determines output, otherwise it determines the surplus going to labour.

The payoff from maximizing, ex-post, the *social surplus* ($W^*$) over all states is:

$$W^* \equiv \max_{f \geq 0} E_h \left\{ f^*(h) - r[f^*(h), h] - c_L[f^*(h), h] \right\}. \qquad (4.21)$$

Dow (1993b, p. 181) shows that $\pi_K < W^*$ if the disutility $c_L$ varies from state to state. Since $w$ does not depend on the state and therefore on the output, the owner does not internalize the disutility of the employee when he chooses the level of production. Therefore the PM firm does not produce the socially optimal output that maximizes (4.21). Once the fixed wage constrains labour participation it ends up also limiting total firm profits. This does not happen in the LM firm as workers share the residual in any state of the world, since they are not paid a fixed wage independent of the state. The participation constraint never bites and the surplus can be maximized. As a consequence, there is no choice of the wage ex-ante, only of the output which is chosen in each state according to the rule:

$$\max_{f > 0} f - r(f, h) - c_L(f, h). \qquad (4.22)$$

The LM firm is therefore statically efficient, while the PM firm is not, because of the inflexibility of the wage over the states that does not allow a proper consideration of work effort.

Things change in a dynamic framework. If we consider the investment of an LM firm, we find an insufficient incentive due to the reason seen when considering the market for memberships. The tendency of memberships to be sold with a discount, in a sort of "*backwardation*" is one of the main reasons for underinvestment and the marginalization of the LM firm in the long run. The long run race between the PM firm and the LM firm is definitely won by the PM firm.

### 4.2.6   Some conclusions on the LM firm

We are now ready to draw some conclusions as to the marginality of the LM firm in our economies. The LM firm satisfies the need for economic democracy as to the decision making process, despite complications arising in the implementation of a voting system and because of the heterogeneity of employees (white collars versus blue collars) that may spoil the one member-one vote system (Hansmann, 1990). However, the LM firm is at a disadvantage in growth, since two sets of factors hinder it. On the one side its tendency to hire non-member workers establishes a tendency of the LM firm to become a PM firm organized around the core of founding members. On the other hand the quasi-impossibility to set up an efficient and competitive market for memberships makes it impossible for members to have a time horizon similar to the one of a PM firm shareholder. Taking part in the property and in decision making within the LM changes the individual incentive structure. Monitoring of individual effort is easier than in a PM firm. However, free riding is around the corner, making hierachical control necessary. In that case it may be more difficult to set up than in a PM firm (Guesnerie and Laffont, 1984) because the controllers are the controlled. Nonetheless, opportunism does not seem to have the same role as in a PM firm (Alchian and Demsetz, 1972). The recurrent confrontation, that emerges within the PM firm, as to the distribution of the rent produced by factor specificities does not replicate within an LM firm. Social conflict is almost completely absent within the LM firm.

Empirical evidence on LM firm performances is not very rich. Nonetheless, some answers have been given recently as to the presumed perversions of the LM firm and its market performances (Craig and Pencavel, 1992, 1995; Pencavel and Craig, 1994). Some results are worth noting. First of all, there is no evidence of the downward sloping supply curve, in the short run. The LM firm has a supply curve which is more rigid than its counterpart PM firm because the LM firm tends to increase wages when the price of the output goes up. The effect of this is definitely an allocative inefficiency but also a greater stability of employment over the cycle, since, when prices go down, adjustment is born by workers' incomes. We may therefore maintain that the LM firm has the objective of both maximizing the individual value added and keeping a stable level of employment. This is the result of the decision process in which the candidates to be fired also participate. Their participation makes their dismissal less likely. This has a consequence also on the mortality and ability to survive of LM firms *vis à vis* the PM firms. The few empirical analyses show that LM firms tend to live longer (Ben Ner, 1988b) regardless of market structure.

As far as the effect of the LM internal organization on productivity is concerned, other empirical investigations (Craig and Pencavel, 1995; Estrin *et al.*, 1987; Lee, 1988) provide a differentiated answer. Most of the analyses estimate production functions with a disembodied effect of labour participation. As a matter of fact there seems to be a gap, even though not so large, between the productivity of LM firms and their PM counterparts, with some advantage for the LM firms. An analysis confined to Italian LM firms (Estrin, 1991) appears quite inconclusive. A similar result is reported in Lee (1988), who studied Swedish LM firms. Berman and Berman (1989) examined marginal productivity in PM and LM firms in the plywood industry in the USA, without finding any significant difference. An inconclusive, yet interesting result can be found in Conte and Svejnar (1988) on the effects of different participation schemes of employees in the USA. They find positive allocative effects when labour participation is less radical than in the LM firms. Two contributions (Piesse *et al.*, 1996; Smith *et al.*, 1997) cast a shadow on the desirability of LM enterprises mostly when compared with firms privatized and sold to foreigners in Eastern European countries. Sometimes it appears that LM firms in the agriculture sector are more efficient just because they are bigger and enjoy economies of scale which cannot be reached by small private farms which are the result of reforms.

Empirical literature finds a tiny advantage for the LM firm in terms of productivity due to better internal incentives. However, this advantage does not compensate for the disadvantage the LM firms have in the long run because of their inability to grow, without becoming a PM firm. The chronic undercapitalization of the LM firm is not adequately studied in empirical studies. The productivity advantage explains why in some cases the LM organization is seen as the *extrema ratio* of firms near to shut-down. Unfortunately, most of these "experiments" end up with the demise of the firm, since the higher labour productivity is not a guarantee for better market performance of a firm.

The crucial problem for an LM firm appears in the long run, when the financial aspects of growth, the existence and/or the efficiency of the market for memberships seem to push the LM firm towards its transformation into a PM firm (Vanek, 1970).

A great bundle of literature has analysed, since the early 1980s the performance of collective and state Chinese firms. Collective firms can be partially assimilated to the LM firms even though memberships are not tradable. Despite that, they seem to have contributed quite a lot to the rocketing growth rates of China in the last twenty years. These firms do not seem to be quite constrained in their capital and liquidity needs since they get loans and privileged credit facilities from state enterprises and state banks (Chow and Fung, 1998) and appear therefore quite apart from the LM firms we are concerned with.

## 4.3   Profit and decision sharing

One of the firm organizations between the PM and the LM firm is the so called J firm, or Japanese firm, or Aoki firm. In this firm workers participate in many decisions of the management and share profits, but they do not have any stake in the property of the firm, which belongs to shareholders. Despite the ownership structure of the Aoki firm, there are many similarities with ESOPs (employee stock ownership plans) in which workers possess some or the capital of the firm but not in the same proportion as in the LM firm. A similar firm, studied by Komiya (1987) behaves almost like an LM firm. It decides the labour input, the investment policy to maximize the value added per employee, after having paid a fixed share of profits to shareholders. This firm faces some of the problems of the LM firms seen above. However, it keeps most of the opportunities of the PM firm since shareholders receive a profit which is fixed in terms of share but is state contingent.

There remains to be seen how the share of profits going to shareholders is set. This is the question on which the Aoki model seems more interesting. Here the share of profits going respectively to shareholders and workers is bargained upon simultaneously with growth and other variables.

Aoki's firm is a joint organization of employees and shareholders who give rise, through their reciprocal collaboration, to a surplus over what they would be able to command by operating separately. This surplus is denominated by Aoki *organizational rent* and is generated because of specialization acquired within the firm by workers and managers. Human capital accumulated by workers and financed by the firm makes them firm specific. As a consequence, within the firm there arises a market for specific factors. This market is highly imperfect and prices are set by a bargaining process through which an equilibrium can be reached when neither of the contenders can expect to be able to increase their utility without incurring any risk of breakdown. In the PM firm the distribution of the rent takes place by referring to what the market dictates in terms of collective (nationwide, countrywide, areawide and so on) contracts. But the external market sets only the reference level of the wage which does not include any rent. With supplementary contracts signed at firm level we introduce some rent sharing if the extra wage is contingent upon the performance of the firm. In the Aoki model the bargaining process involves also strategic decisions, i.e., market and growth policies. In this sense the labour participation is far broader than the one considered in Weitzman's contributions (Weitzman, 1984).

Let us consider briefly the Aoki model (Aoki, 1980, 1984; Aoki and Dore, 1994). Assume we have a firm whose idiosyncratic market demand is:

$$x = \alpha p^{-(1/\eta)} \quad \text{with } 0 < \eta < 1 \text{ and } \alpha > 0, \tag{4.23}$$

where $\alpha$ represents the state of the economy and $x$ the quantity sold. A higher $\alpha$ indicates a larger demand for the firm product. $\eta$ indicates the inverse price elasticity of demand or the degree of monopoly and/or the specificity of the firm *vis à vis* the competitors. The growth expenditure function is defined as:

$$G = \varphi(g), \qquad (4.24)$$

where $G$ represents the average unitary expenditure per unit of good sold necessary to support the growth rate $g$. This function is monotone, convex and increasing.[3]

Employees are homogeneous and receive a benefit:

$$w = \overline{w} + \Delta w, \qquad (4.25)$$

where $\overline{w}$ is the market wage and $\Delta w$ represents the *premium earning* linked to the labour participation in the firm's profits. This premium, part of the *organizational rent*, is endogenous. Then, the profit, or *organizational rent* after the payment of growth expenditure, is:

$$\pi = (p - c - G)x, \qquad (4.26)$$

where the unitary labour cost is $c = \overline{w}$ and no further operating cost appears. Defining $\theta$ the share of profits going to shareholders, the average premium earning per employee is:

$$\Delta w = \frac{(1 - \theta)\pi}{Lx}, \quad \text{for } 0 \le \theta \le 1, \qquad (4.27)$$

where $L$ indicates the labour units needed for a unit of product. We confine ourselves to a fixed number of employees, larger than the number of workers necessary to produce the quantity of output demanded, i.e. $N \ge L$, and we assume that, in the short run, there are *no layoffs*. Then the price set by the firm will be:

$$(x_{\max}^{\alpha})^{-\eta} \le p \le \left(\frac{N}{\alpha L}\right)^{-\eta}, \qquad (4.28)$$

or, in terms of the produced quantity:

$$\frac{N}{L} \le x \le x_{\max}. \qquad (4.29)$$

Employees are interested in their *lifetime earning at the employing firm*. Assuming stationarity for the firm and indicating with $H$ the expected duration of the time spent by an employee at the firm, the extra wage or the lifetime earning an employee can get is given by:

---

[3] Aoki also assumes that growth expenditure is completely financed by current sales revenue without issuing new equity.

$$\Delta w \left\{ 1 - \left( \frac{1}{1+\rho} \right)^H \right\} / \rho \,, \qquad (4.30)$$

where $\rho$ is the discount rate equal to the cost of capital. From (4.30), the levels of lifetime well-being of employees may be ordered according to current premium earning $\Delta w$. Total premium earning for the existing employees can be indicated as:

$$W = \Delta w N. \qquad (4.31)$$

Shareholders maximize the value of the firm. Assuming away market uncertainty, the arbitrage condition on the financial market requires that the competitive value of the firm $S$ satisfies the following condition:

$$gS + \theta \pi = \rho S \,, \qquad (4.32)$$

where $\theta \pi$ are the dividends at the end of the current period, and $gS$ indicates the expected share-value appreciation.[4] Rearranging we obtain:

$$S = \frac{\theta \pi}{\rho - g}. \qquad (4.33)$$

The shareholders are interested in having the largest value of $S$. The firm has to set the market price $p$ implicit in the employment level, the growth rate $g$ and the profit share parameter $\theta$. For given values of $p$ and $g$ there is a level of $\pi$ which can be allocated between the shareholders and the employees.

Using (4.27), (4.31) and (4.33), this allocation can be represented by a straight line trade-off relation between $S$ and $W$. For all possible pairs of $g$ and $p$ satisfying previous constraints on output (4.28), we get several trade-off relations in the space $(S, W)$. The envelope of these straight lines represents the *bargaining possibility frontier*:

$$S = \psi(W). \qquad (4.34)$$

In figure 4.1 we have many frontiers in the space $(S, W)$, each relative to a particular pair $(p, g)$. The envelope curve says that for each pair $(p, g)$ we have only one efficient combination of $(S, W)$, i.e. only one $\theta$. Referring to the definition of average premium (4.27), the two intercepts in figure 4.1 provide the two extreme situations: the LM firm on the horizontal axis and the PM on the vertical axis.

---

[4] Aoki assumes that investors replace their uncertainty about future evolutions of dividends by a simple rule of stationarity. That is, they believe that, on average, the current firm's performances will continue indefinitely. With this assumption, the expected rate of share-value appreciation will be equal to the current rate of growth $g$.

**Figure 4.1:** The bargaining possibility frontier

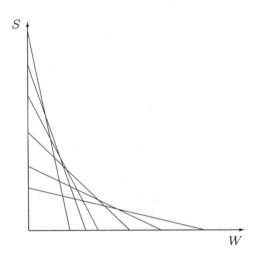

The shape of the frontier depends on the asymmetry between shareholders and workers as to the growth of the firm. Shareholders gain from the growth of the firm financed by the cash flow, because this implies a higher value of the firm and therefore a net benefit. The growth of the firm requires new workers hired by the firm and therefore a reduction or at least no increase in workers' profit share. Again we face the question of durability of shareholders' property *vis à vis* that of workers. Shareholders' property can be extended to an infinite horizon, while workers have a right to get a share of profits depending upon the number of workers and the time each worker will spend at the firm. The share of profits going to an individual worker is limited by the time of his staying at the firm while for a shareholder there is no limit of this kind. Then workers would like a suboptimal investment. Then employees fail to reap the entire benefits that are brought up by the investment over future periods (Grossman and Hart, 1986; Hart and Moore, 1990). As we know, the remedy for this failure is the pure PM firm, which, on the other hand, does not represent a first best, due to the static inefficiency seen above.

### 4.3.1   The bargaining process in Aoki

Workers and shareholders have a reciprocal interest to write a contract. Otherwise they both cannot reap the rent they get by joining their efforts. Aoki's model is based on which specificity of factors of production can also enact threats. Workers may let the value of the firm decrease if no agreement is reached. Shareholders may let workers miss the opportunity of sharing a rent not available elsewhere. The neoclassic sequence is reversed. At the beginning the strategies of the firm are chosen (price and growth rate). Then the distributive parameter is bargained upon. In the PM firm the sequence changes, since distribution rules are given by the market through a fixed wage. Strategic decisions are taken once the distribution of value added coming from the market is known.

Using the *Nash Bargaining Solution* (NBS) concept as formulated by Harsanyi (1956, 1977) and extended by Rubinstein (1987), a joint objective function of workers and shareholders is maximized with respect to the distributive parameter $\theta$, instead of renegotiating every time market conditions change. The organizational equilibrium of the firm is characterized by a stationary condition of the weighted sum of $W$ and $S$, where the weights are the respective *boldness* of the two contenders (Aumann and Kurz, 1977, p. 1147), defined as follows:[5]

$$\frac{u'(W)}{u(W) - \widehat{u}} \equiv B_u(W) \quad \text{and} \quad \frac{v'(S)}{v(S) - \widehat{v}} \equiv B_v(S), \tag{4.35}$$

where $u$ and $v$ are the utility functions respectively of workers and shareholders and $\widehat{u} = u(\hat{W})$ and $\widehat{v} = v(\hat{S})$ are the levels of utility the two contenders would get in case of no agreement. The total premium earning as well as the value of the firm in a situation of conflict could be zero at worst. Aoki does not restrict possibilities to this extreme case and allows $\hat{W} > 0$ and $\hat{S} > 0$.

Then the simplest way to proceed is to use the weighting method where "*the manager of the firm mediates internal distributional claims and formulates managerial policies in the direction of increasing:*

$$B_u(W)W + B_v(S)S \tag{4.36}$$

i.e., *increasing the weighted sum of total earnings of the existing employees and the share value of the firm, with the respective measures of parties' boldness $B_u(W)$ and $B_v(S)$ as parametric weights*" (Aoki, 1984, pp. 72-3). Using the definitions of $\Delta w, W, S$ and differentiating with respect to $\theta$, we get:

---

[5]In words, $B_u(W)$ is the reciprocal of the marginal risk premium needed to compensate the employees for risking an infinitesimally small probability of internal conflict when the total earnings are $W$. The same interpretation holds for $B_v(S)$ (Harsanyi, 1956).

$$\frac{B_u(W^*)W^*}{1-\theta^*} - \frac{B_v(S^*)S^*}{\theta^*} \left\{ \begin{array}{c} > \\ = \\ < \end{array} \right\} 0 \quad \text{for} \quad \left\{ \begin{array}{c} \theta^* = 0 \\ 0 < \theta^* < 1 \\ \theta^* = 1 \end{array} \right. \tag{4.37}$$

or, for $0 < \theta^* < 1$:

$$\frac{1-\theta^*}{\theta^*} = \frac{B_u(W^*)W^*}{B_v(S^*)S^*}, \tag{4.38}$$

where asterisks indicate the equilibrium values. The implication is that the share of profits going to each contender is directly proportional to her respective boldness.

When is the solution (4.38) adopted? What is the market behaviour of the firm?

Consider the first question. Relation (4.38) determines the equilibrium value of profit distribution between shareholders and employees, without determining before equilibrium values of $p$ and $g$. These can be set after having chosen the optimal $\theta$. This operation is justified only in a particular case, i.e., if the *pure boldness of contenders* is constant (CPB). The *pure boldness* is a transformation of the *boldness*. It can be obtained by dividing it by the index of absolute risk aversion of Arrow-Pratt, $-u''/u'$, i.e.:

$$\xi_u = \max\left\{\frac{-(u')^2}{u''(u-\hat{u})}, 0\right\}, \tag{4.39}$$

and by sequentially integrating (see Aoki, 1984, p. 76):

$$\log u(W) = \frac{\xi_u}{1+\xi_u}\log(W-\hat{W}) + C_u, \tag{4.40}$$

with $C_u$ as the integration constant. Symmetrically, for the shareholders we get:

$$\log v(S) = \frac{\xi_v}{1+\xi_v}\log(S-\hat{S}) + C_v. \tag{4.41}$$

The two utility functions of (4.40) and (4.41) are functions with constant *pure boldness*. By substituting them in (4.38) we can write the optimal distribution as:

$$\frac{(1-\theta^*)\pi^* - (1-\hat{\theta})\hat{\pi}}{\theta^*\pi^* - \hat{\theta}\hat{\pi}} = \frac{1+\xi_v^{-1}}{1+\xi_u^{-1}} \equiv \xi, \tag{4.42}$$

where $(1 - \hat{\theta})\hat{\pi} = (Lx^*/N)\hat{W}$ and $\hat{\theta}\hat{\pi} = (r - g^*)\hat{S}$ are, respectively, the employees' and shareholders' share of the organizational rent in case of no agreement. From (4.42) we see that the distribution of profits depends on the contenders' boldness. Solving for $\Delta w$ we get:

$$\Delta w = \frac{\hat{W}}{N} + \frac{\xi}{1 + \xi}\left(\frac{\pi^*}{Lx^*} - \frac{\hat{\pi}}{Lx^*}\right). \tag{4.43}$$

The extra wage is equal to the gain workers get without the agreement, plus $\xi/(1 + \xi)$ times the productivity gain that is brought about by cooperation. If $\hat{W}$ and $\hat{S}$ are equal to zero it means that the lack of agreement leads to zero gain for the two contenders. Then we have the solution:

$$\frac{1 - \theta^*}{\theta^*} = \frac{1 + \xi_v^{-1}}{1 + \xi_u^{-1}} \equiv \xi. \tag{4.44}$$

The shares going to workers and to shareholders do not change as the decisions of the firm on market price and growth vary, if we have CPB and outside options equal to zero. The CPB functions are a subset of constant relative risk aversion functions (CRRA) for which the Arrow-Pratt index of relative risk aversion is constant. In particular, assuming $u(W) = W^{1-R}$ as the workers' utility function and $v(S) = S^q$, as the shareholders's one, with $0 \leq R < 1$ and $0 \leq q < 1$, the *pure boldness* becomes respectively $(1 - R)/R$ and $q/(1 - q)$, and the solution (4.44) reduces to:

$$\frac{1 - \theta^*}{\theta^*} = \frac{1 - R}{q}. \tag{4.45}$$

What happens if shareholders are neutral to the risk of internal conflict? In this case $\xi_v$ tends to $\infty$ and (4.44) becomes:

$$\frac{1 - \theta^*}{\theta^*} = \frac{1}{(1 + \xi_u^{-1})}. \tag{4.46}$$

Workers enjoy a rent. However, if workers are very much risk averse $(\xi_v < 0)$ the entire gain of cooperation goes to shareholders (*neoclassic firm*).

The *second* question concerns the market behaviour of the Aoki firm, i.e. the choice of $p$ and $g$. From their behaviour there emerges some question about the efficiency of labour participation in firms' decisions. It can be shown (Aoki, 1984, pp. 78-81) that an increase in the boldness of workers tends to increase the market price set by a monopolist. At the dynamic level the Aoki firm responds to an exogenous price increase by growing faster than the corresponding PM firm, only if growth does not require an increase in the number of workers. If the growth of the firm requires more workers, growth has a perverse effect since it makes Aoki's firm grow slower than the PM firm. This parallels the dynamic inefficiency of the LM firm.

Another inefficiency arises when the cost of capital increases. When there are fixed costs, the Aoki firm tends to transfer the higher cost to consumers. The price shows a sort of downward rigidity each time either the workers boldness or the cost of capital increases.

## 4.3.2 Profit sharing: empirical results

The set of empirical analyses undertaken on profit sharing is quite large. There are many studies which try to assess the crucial question about profit sharing, i.e., whether it improves productivity or not (OECD, 1995). Biagioli (1995) investigates the productivity issue in Italy and finds a positive effect enhancing firm performances. An awkward question concerns the causality link, i.e., whether good firm performances lead to profit sharing or the other way round. Fitzroy and Kraft (1987) try to establish the direction of causality, but no conclusive answer seems to come out. On the contrary, Kruse (1992) is even able to measure the productivity gains of profit sharing. He finds that, in the USA, for manufacturing firms, the advantage is about 7-9% in productivity terms, while in non-manufacturing sectors it is about 10-11%, if profit sharing involves 100% of the employees. Partial profit sharing, i.e. not extended to the entire labour force, is not considered, even though it is quite common. On a group of Japanese firms, Brunello (1991) finds no evidence of the positive effect of profit sharing on firm performances. By and large it must be recognized that the empirical literature attributes a positive role to profit sharing. However, we lack systematic analysis of profit sharing and typology of firms and industries where profit sharing is adopted more frequently. For instance whether it applies more to capital intensive firms or to labour intensive ones, to less or more competitive product markets, to large or small firms. The gap in these themes is also on theoretical grounds. Before closing this section we have to mention some results of participation of workers in the firm property, as in ESOPs. These schemes may enhance productivity, like profit sharing, with productivity gains between 2% and 5%. In a cross-sectional analysis of Japanese firms, Jones and Kato (1995) find that the effects on productivity take some 3-4 years to show up. The implication is that ESOPs may be convenient when the labour mobility is limited and the association of workers with the firm has a quasi-permanent character as in Japan until the mid-1990s.

A comparative analysis of the effects of different kinds of participation has been conducted by Conte and Svejnar (1988). By comparing firms where participation takes place at different levels, i.e. management, profits, stocks, best firm performances come when participation does not take radical shapes. In other words, *there seems to be an optimal level of participation of workers, beyond which the firm loses efficiency.*

# 4.4   Participation under uncertainty

The Aoki model represents, from a theoretical standpoint, the most complete interpretation of profit sharing schemes. The importance of profit sharing grows as factors become more specific. In these cases the market value of a firm is higher than the value of physical and intangible assets taken separately (Mailath and Postlewaite, 1990). In some cases workers give rise to networks or teams which cannot be substituted by labour force from the market. If they are paid just the market wage workers are not rewarded for their portion of human capital which is firm specific. In these cases it is difficult to figure out firm organizations differing from profit sharing.

In a series of papers (Moretto and Rossini, 1995, 1996, 1997, 2002; Moretto and Pastorello, 1998) this question is dealt with in an uncertain environment and the firm is defined as a continuous series of options to produce.

Market uncertainty modifies the organization of the participated firm. Three distinct aspects are considered.

a) Market uncertainty affects the distribution of the rent when the firm has some flexibility, for instance if it can shut down when market conditions are very adverse.

b) There are imperfections in the internal market for labour, in case of firm specific factors. In that case a factor may assume a dominant position, mainly if it owns a set of "non-contractible" decisions. These imperfections can be reduced by regulation of the bargaining timing.

c) The traditional allocation of decisions linked to the shareholders' property rights is not optimal in all circumstances. Some decision redistribution is needed to restore efficiency.

We consider these three topics in more detail.

## 4.4.1   Market uncertainty, inertia and profit sharing

The recent literature, surveyed by Pindyck (1991), Dixit (1992), Dixit and Pindyck (1994, 1998), emphasizes the role of uncertainty in two aspects of investment and firm decisions: 1) the irreversibility of decisions, especially those concerning the size of the firm, and 2) The possibility of postponing decisions keeping the opportunity of adopting them later under more favourable circumstances. Irreversible investments and uncertainty explain many hysteresis cases, i.e., the persistence of a phenomenon when its cause has disappeared or even reversed. Firms, for instance, do not exit at the Marshallian points, but only when the price goes far below the average variable cost, at a "trigger" level which is endogenously set. In this context, Moretto and Rossini (1995) examine the effect of uncertainty on the profit sharing parameter. Profit sharing modifies the trigger price at which the firm exits with respect to the PM firm. Then the optimal level of the sharing parameter is jointly determined by employees and shareholders as a Nash bargaining solution. Shareholders have an advantage since they possess a decision set which is larger than that of workers. In particular, they can close the firm. The shareholders use this opportunity as a threat, whose credibility is effective, since it is the result of an optimal programme. Both contenders have the same set of information as to market uncertainty. They have the same degree of aversion towards the risk of open conflict. Workers maximize an expected utility of discounted flow of the extra wage they get over their time period spent at the firm. Shareholders maximize the expected present value of the firm, defined taking into account the option value of the opportunity to shut down. The optimal exit price, or trigger price, depends inversely on the parameter defining the willingness by workers to share, not only profits, but also losses. The higher this parameter the longer the firm lives. An additional parameter defining loss sharing is considered. When it increases, in certain circumstances, lifetime earnings are larger. There is an optimal value for the parameter of loss sharing, not coinciding for the two contenders, even though low levels of the loss sharing parameter may be beneficial for both contenders.

The option to close by the shareholders shifts the share parameter to their advantage. This happens independently of the magnitude of the parameter of loss sharing. If loss sharing is reduced, the power of shareholders increases and the closure threat gains momentum. Then market uncertainty modifies the distributive result of Aoki. Profit shares are no longer proportional to the boldness of contenders. The advantage shareholders have, since they can decide the shut down, introduces an asymmetry.

Here are the main features of the model. An incumbent firm exhibits a constant-returns-to-scale technology and is endowed with a capital stock of infinite life. Each period it produces one unit of output. Marginal and average costs are equal to $c$. The labour force is normalized to one. Profit sharing between workers and shareholders is the result of a bargaining.

There are two kinds of uncertainty. One relates to the risk of *internal conflict*, whilst the other concerns the *market price*, driven by a geometric Brownian motion (random walk in continuous time):

$$dp_t = \alpha p_t dt + \sigma p_t dz_t, \qquad \text{with } p_0 = p \text{ and } \sigma > 0, \tag{4.47}$$

where $dz_t$ is the increment of a standard Wiener process, uncorrelated over time and satisfying the conditions that $E(dz_t) = 0$ and $E(dz_t^2) = dt$ (Harrison, 1985; Dixit and Pindyck, 1994).

The organizational rent, or operating profit, at time $t$ is:

$$\pi(p_t) = p_t - c, \tag{4.48}$$

when the firm is working, zero otherwise. This is the first departure from the original Aoki model, where the firm is assumed to face no market uncertainty but only an internal organizational uncertainty.

The second departure relates to shut down, if market conditions require it, by paying laid off workers a bonus equal to $K$. This represents the *closure cost*.[6] As there is an opportunity cost of abandoning now rather than waiting for new information, the firm does not exit if today's price is just below the average variable cost. It is optimal to exit only if the price falls below a trigger level $p_L < c$, which has to be endogenously determined by considering future expected opportunities *vis à vis* the exit cost (Dixit, 1989). Workers are associated with the firm and do not quit because outside opportunities are less appealing.

Payments are conditional on current profits and workers share profits and losses symmetrically.[7] Therefore as in (4.25):

$$w_t = \overline{w} + \Delta w_t, \tag{4.49}$$

where $\overline{w}$ is the market wage and $\Delta w_t$ is a premium earning which represents the employees' share of profits accruing to the firm. Let $0 \le \theta \le 1$ be the share parameter indicating the proportion of profits and losses going to shareholders, then:

$$\Delta w_t(p_t; \theta) = (1 - \theta)\pi(p_t), \tag{4.50}$$

with $\pi(p_t) \ge p_L - c$.

---

[6]In many industrialized countries severance payment for laid off workers is determined (and enforced) by law. For this reason we consider it as an institutional parameter that cannot be negotiated upon. We could also think of different bonus schemes, for instance by linking the amount of $K$ to the time spent by workers at the firm or assuming that only a part of the entire exit cost $K$ is paid as a bonus to the laid off workers.

[7]Employees may receive negative extra wages when the firm makes losses. This is the case of "solidarity contracts". A variable degree of loss sharing between shareholders and workers is discussed in Moretto and Rossini (1995).

**Workers' and shareholders' objective functions**

The firm is a value maximizer operating in perfectly competitive markets for its product and assets. Then the expected present value of the stream of profits is:

$$S(p; \theta) = E_0 \left\{ \int_0^T \theta(p_t - c)e^{-\rho t}dt \mid p_0 = p \right\} \qquad \text{for } p \in [p_L, \infty). \quad (4.51)$$

The firm's value $S$ is a function of $\theta$ representing the share of profits going to shareholders; $\rho$ is the discount rate ($> \alpha$) and $T = \inf(t > 0 \mid p_t = p_L)$ is the stochastic stopping time at which the firm exits.

As long as workers completely share the firm's losses and $\bar{w} = c$ is constant, the level of their well-being, up to the shut down, may be ordered according to the expected discounted sum of the premium earnings at the firm. That is:

$$W(p; \theta) = E_0 \left\{ \int_0^T \Delta w_t(p_t; \theta)e^{-\rho t}dt \mid p_t = p \right\} \qquad \text{for } p \in [p_L, \infty). \quad (4.52)$$

The bargaining process takes place at the beginning of the planning period. As the solution concept adopted is the NBS, the joint objective function of workers and shareholders, to be maximized with respect to $\theta$, is:

$$\nabla = \lg[u(W) - \hat{u}] + \lg[v(S) - \hat{v}], \qquad (4.53)$$

subject to (4.51) and (4.52). There are specificities for both parties. Workers are not able to find a similar job if the contract is not signed. Shareholders lose the opportunity of producing with skilled workers who cannot be easily found in the labour market. If negotiations fail the reservation levels of utility (the *threat points* of the bargaining) are equal to zero, i.e. $\hat{u} = \hat{v} = 0$. This does not impose any loss of generality.

**The efficient bargaining set**

Shareholders independently decide the exit policy. For any given $\theta$, when the firm is in operation, $S(p; \theta)$ must satisfy the no-arbitrage condition (4.32). Then the sum of the return on the investment, given by the dividend flow plus the capital gain $E(dS/dt)$, equals the market cost of capital $\rho S$. Since $p_t$ is driven by (4.47), applying Itô's lemma to $S$, the expected capital gain is given by $E(dS) = [S'\alpha p_t + \frac{1}{2}S''\sigma^2 p_t^2]dt$; then the asset market equilibrium condition leads to the following differential equation (Dixit and Pindyck, 1994, pp. 114-17):

$$\frac{1}{2}\sigma^2 p_t^2 S'' + \alpha p_t S' - \rho S = -\theta(p_t - c) \quad \text{for } p_t \in [p_L, \infty), \tag{4.54}$$

with boundary conditions:

$$S(\infty; \theta) = 0, \tag{4.55}$$
$$S(p_L; \theta) = -K, \tag{4.56}$$
$$S'(p_L; \theta) = 0. \tag{4.57}$$

Equation (4.55) states that the value of the firm must be bounded when the market price goes to infinity. The *value matching condition* (4.56) holds that, when the firm exits, its value must be equal to its liabilities represented by the bonus paid to laid off workers. The *smooth pasting condition* (4.57) rules out arbitrary exercise of the option to exit. By linearity with respect to $S$ and making use of (4.55), the general solution of (4.54), evaluated at $p$, takes the form:

$$S(p; \theta) = Ap^\beta + \theta\left(\frac{p}{\rho - \alpha} - \frac{c}{\rho}\right) \quad \text{for } p \in [p_L, \infty), \tag{4.58}$$

where $\beta$ is the negative root of the quadratic equation: $\Psi(\beta) \equiv \frac{1}{2}\sigma^2\beta^2 + (\alpha - \frac{1}{2}\sigma^2)\beta - \rho = 0$. The last term on the r.h.s. of (4.58) represents the discounted value of expected profits when the firm is active for ever, while $Ap^\beta$ indicates the option value of shutting down, in terms of avoidance of expected losses.[8] The constant $A$ and the optimal trigger price $p_L$ are jointly determined by using (4.56) and (4.57):[9]

$$p_L = \frac{\beta}{\beta - 1}\frac{\rho - \alpha}{\rho}\left(c - \frac{\rho}{\theta}K\right), \tag{4.59}$$
$$A = -\theta\frac{1}{\beta}\frac{1}{\rho - \alpha}p_L^{1-\beta} > 0.$$

---

[8] The last term on the r.h.s. of (4.58) is given by (see Harrison, 1985, p. 44):

$$E\left\{\int_0^\infty \theta(p_t - c)e^{-\rho t}dt \mid p_t = p\right\} = \theta\left(\frac{p}{\rho - \alpha} - \frac{c}{\rho}\right)$$

[9] Observe that $c\theta > \rho K$ suffices to guarantee that $p_L > 0$.

Substituting (4.59) into (4.58) the firm's value in the simplified form is:

$$S(p; \theta) = \theta V(p; \theta), \tag{4.60}$$

where $V(p; \theta) = \frac{A}{\theta} p^\beta + (\frac{p}{\rho - \alpha} - \frac{c}{\rho})$ is the value of the stream of profits before distribution.

By using a similar procedure for workers it can be shown that:

$$W(p; \theta) = B p^\beta + (1 - \theta) \left( \frac{p}{\rho - \alpha} - \frac{c}{\rho} \right) \quad \text{for } p \in [p_L, \infty), \tag{4.61}$$

with a *matching value condition* saying that at the exit trigger price the value for a worker of being employed at the firm is equal to the bonus. That is:

$$W(p_L; \theta) = K. \tag{4.62}$$

No *smooth pasting condition* is introduced in this case since the exit decision is controlled by shareholders and workers have no influence on it.[10] The workers' well-being, attributable to the firm's option to stop producing, $B p^\beta$ depends, *ceteris paribus*, on the size of the bonus $K$. Considering the firm's market value before distribution $V$ and taking account of (4.61) and (4.62):[11]

$$W(p; \theta) = (1 - \theta) V(p; \theta) + G(p; \theta, K), \tag{4.63}$$

where $G(p; \theta, K) = \frac{1}{\theta} K (\frac{p}{p_L})^\beta > 0$ is the increase of the lifetime well-being accruing to the workers, induced by the asymmetry between shareholders and employees, due to the bonus $K$ (Moretto and Rossini, 1997).[12]

**The bargaining**

Solution comes from maximization of (4.53) with respect to $\theta$. The workers' utility function is $u(W) = W^{1-R}$ and that of the shareholders is $v(S) = S^q$,

---

[10]Applying (4.62), the constant $B$ is equal to:

$$B = -(1 - \theta) \left( \frac{1}{\beta} \frac{1}{\rho - \alpha} p_L^{1-\beta} \right) \left( \frac{c\theta - \beta \rho K}{c\theta - \rho K} \right) + K p_L^{-\beta} > 0.$$

[11]Omission of the dependence of $S$ and $W$ on $K$ is only for notational convenience.

[12]As the bonus $K$ introduces an asymmetry between the two contenders, the workers would like to exit earlier. Indeed, if they could set the exit trigger price, $p_L^w$, independently, it would be:

$$p_L^w = \frac{\beta}{\beta - 1} \frac{\rho - \alpha}{\rho} \left( c + \frac{\rho}{1 - \theta} K \right) > p_L.$$

where $0 \leq R < 1$ and $0 \leq q < 1$ are the respective degrees of relative risk aversion. In Moretto and Rossini (1995, 1997) the joint maximization of $\nabla$ leads to the following results:

- (a) If $K > 0$ and $\pi(p_t) \geq p_L - c$ the optimal relative share of shareholders and employees in a firm's profits is state-dependent and given by the necessary condition:

$$\frac{W^{**}(p;\theta^{**})}{S^{**}(p;\theta^{**})}(1 - \Phi^{**}(p;\theta^{**},K))^{-1} = \frac{B_u(W^{**})W^{**}}{B_v(S^{**})S^{**}} \equiv \frac{1-R}{q}, \quad (4.64)$$

where:

$$\Phi^{**}(p;\theta^{**},K) = \frac{\dfrac{dV^{**}}{d\theta} + \dfrac{dG^{**}}{d\theta}}{\dfrac{dS^{**}}{d\theta}} > 0.$$

- (b) When the option to shut down is viable (i.e., $p_L > 0$), the shareholders' bargained share of profit is greater than Aoki's share $\theta^*$. That is:

$$\frac{1-\theta^{**}}{\theta^{**}} < \frac{1-\theta^*}{\theta^*} = \frac{1-R}{q}.$$

Part (a) indicates how the condition (4.38), for the share of profits going to each contender, changes when an option to shut down is introduced. Part (b) means that the bargaining over $\theta$ leads to a profit distribution which is more favourable to shareholders than Aoki's original result, $\theta^*$, represented by the ratio of the respective degrees of risk aversion (i.e. equation (4.45)).

As the threat point is zero for both actors, the only asymmetry between workers and shareholders is due to the exit cost. Then, if $K$ tends to zero, this asymmetry disappears and the profit share parameter is no longer state-dependent. That is, if $K = 0$ (or $\sigma = 0$) and $\alpha > 0$, the profit share parameter reduces to Aoki's one (Moretto and Rossini, 2002):

$$\frac{1-\theta^{**}}{\theta^{**}} = \frac{1-\theta^*}{\theta^*} = \frac{1-R}{q}.$$

This result has two implications. First: as long as exit is costless, shareholders and workers would choose the same exit policy, and therefore the same distribution policy as in Aoki. Second: uncertainty affects profit distribution only if there is irreversibility. On the other hand, if $\alpha > 0$ and $\sigma = 0$, the value of the option of shutting down goes to zero and the result above is straightforward. A different outcome follows if $\alpha \leq 0$ and $\sigma = 0$. Under certainty the firm knows exactly when it will quit: i.e., $p_L = c - \rho K / \theta$ and the option is still alive.

It can be proved (Moretto and Rossini, 1997) that, when the option to shut down is viable (i.e., $p_L > 0$), the profit share going to shareholders decreases as $p$ increases:

$$\frac{d\theta^{**}}{dp} < 0.$$

The effectiveness of the shut down threat weakens as market profitability grows since exit becomes less likely. As $p$ tends to infinity, the Aoki's solution is back.

## 4.4.2   Profit sharing and the regulation of the recontracting time

Profit sharing may redistribute the risk among factors and improve firm performances. Efficiency requires that contracts over the profit share parameter must be renegotiated, when market conditions change. But there is no state of the world and no time that can be agreed upon by both parties to give rise to renegotiation, just because the profit is state-dependent. Then an external arbitrator or regulator may decide when and whether to renegotiate. The alternative is to subside to open conflict. The regulator may impose a recontracting of the distribution parameter when market conditions are buoyant. If the regulator's objective is lower variability of employment in the firm so as to minimize losses of specific human capital, he will summon parties for recontracting when market conditions are depressed. In this case, the regulator may appear too favourable to the labour factor. As a matter of fact, he is quite neutral when considered on a long run horizon, since in that circumstance it may also be in the interest of the firm not to dispose of the specific human capital the firm has contributed to grow. Therefore, the arbitrator-regulator tries to optimally distribute the risks deriving from market uncertainty when there are sunk costs borne by both contenders. In Moretto and Rossini (1997) two negotiations are considered. At the beginning and after the realization of a predetermined level of the market price. This may be done in two different ways: 1) it can be announced by the regulator at the beginning of the activity period of the firm and made known to both contenders; 2) it can be set by the regulator and not made known in advance. The result of both arrangements is the setting of two distribution parameters, one for each period.

When the regulator adopts a preannounced rule, recontracting with a price higher than the initial one shifts the distribution of profits in favour of employees. The shut down threat is less effective. If contracting takes place at prices lower than the initial ones the opposite happens. Less trivial is the case of a regulator operating in a discretional way. The result is a more stable distribution of profits. There seem to be many arguments in favour of recontracting. When profits, i.e. market prices, become very volatile the firm would prefer a much more flexible wage setting. Profit sharing and recontracting allow this. With downward contracting employees are more keen on renegotiating. However, both prefer the regulator to intervene discretionally because this leads to a lower variability of the distribution parameter. Then, a discretional regulator appears socially superior.

### 4.4.3   The efficient allocation of the shut down decision

Why does the opportunity to close provide the shareholders with an advantage? Why is assigning the shut down decision to shareholders is not always Pareto optimal? Some of these questions touch the field of law, some remain within the borders of economics. The legal question concerns the trade-off between the property of the firm and the complete disposition of its activity by the owners. In the extreme, this implies the governance of shareholders on firm specific human capital. Any decision taken within an economic entity has to be efficient. Otherwise the Coase theorem (Coase, 1960) fails to apply. According to Coase, it is irrelevant, within any economic institution or organization, who has the responsibility of a decision, whenever there is perfect information and the decision can be traded without bearing any transaction cost. If legal entitlements are perfectly exchangeable they can be allocated in an efficient way. However, uncertainty and specificities make the Coasian theorem hard to apply. From that the need for generalizations, in this case, to find an optimal allocation for the shut down decision of a firm in which there is profit sharing, market uncertainty and firm specificities. Then, to whom to assign the shut down decision in order to achieve optimality? And which mechanism may be adopted to allocate it efficiently?

Why and when, taking for granted that shareholders decide to close, may it be suboptimal?

Closing inflicts a loss to dismissed workers since they will lose the entire firm specific human capital accumulated while working at the firm. Or it will cost them a lot in terms of search to find a firm that is able to use their specific capital. Therefore, if they are immediately employed elsewhere they are not able to obtain the same income because of their specificity. Efficiency is restored if the loss borne by employees is lower than the benefit shareholders receive when they close. Otherwise, if the loss of workers is larger than the benefit of shareholders, a deadweight loss emerges as a result of inefficiency. How to get out of this stalemate? In Moretto and Rossini (2002), the victim of the decision taker (workers) may be willing to pay an amount lower than the loss suffered to "buyout" the right to close or to condition the decision, that is now attributed to shareholders. If employees are able to grab the closure decision, will they do it efficiently or not? Or, in other words, what is the opportunity cost of closure for shareholders and employees when there are specificities? To this purpose individual gain functions are devised, to capture the gain that a contender gets with the decision to close as compared to the case in which she does not own it. The two gain functions are simply given by the difference between the values of the option to close in the hands of shareholders and the option to close in the hands of workers. Three cases are considered.

1. Capital and labour have the same degree of specificity, or they have to face the same costs to be redeployed elsewhere. In this case, there is an interval of the parameters in which the total payoff accruing to both contenders would be larger if the shut down decision were attributed to workers, since they have a time horizon longer than the one of shareholders. In this case the traditional firm organization leads to inefficiency.

2. Non-specific capital, specific labour. In this case, the traditional conduct is not efficient if workers receive a small portion of profits and get a small bonus when dismissed.

3. Specific capital, non-specific labour. Here, the traditional conduct of shareholders deciding whether to close or not is efficient.

It seems that there are many circumstances in which traditional governance is not efficient. Moretto and Rossini (2002) suggest an arrangement, whereby the losers "subsidize" the gainers. A binding commitment supplied by the subsidizer is needed. The alternative, i.e., a lump sum subsidy is neither feasible nor efficient. If workers resort to a lump sum subsidy, shareholders have the incentive to close immediately after they receive it. Only with a continuously binding committed subsidy can closure by shareholders be avoided. The subsidy must go on until either the sum paid by workers hits their extra wage flow or the workers' optimal exit price is touched.

What is the nature of the subsidy? It is a further form of profit sharing whereby workers bear some more risk to elongate the life of the firm. Participation is contingent upon the realization of a particular value of the state variable and it mimics an internal market for the closure decision which can then be efficiently allocated in a Coasian fashion.

# 4.5 Conclusions

The PM firm suffers from static inefficiency since it is not able to provide the proper incentives to workers. The LM firm displays many inefficiencies and some perversion, even though not proved empirically. It appears that in the LM firm workers-members do not have the incentives to sustain an optimal growth path. A membership market may provide an escape way, as suggested in the literature on WE. However it is very difficult to set up workable and efficient markets for memberships. The main reason is that a membership is simultaneously a right to work and an asset. In case of factor specificities the LM firm appears superior with specific labour and non-specific capital. While with specific capital and non-specific labour the PM appears preferable.

Profit sharing and the Aoki firm stand in between the two polar cases represented by the LM firm and the PM firm. They provide useful hindsight into issues on internal organization. The Aoki firm is hindered by some rigidities once it has to react to market shocks. When there are factor specificities profit sharing seems to be quite a good shock absorber for shareholders and for the life expectancy of a firm. However, profit sharing coupled with market uncertainty and factor specificities requires a fresh definition of the optimal allocation of some decision within the firm. In such circumstances the traditional conduct, assigning to shareholders all choices, is no longer optimal in all contingencies. The decision to close is a credible threat which shifts distribution in favour of shareholders. This makes contracting about the profit share parameter quite asymmetric. To avoid dominant and/or asymmetric positions an arbitrator-regulator may call for recontracting in some particular circumstances. Nonetheless this may not allow an efficient solution. When the benefit shareholders get from closing is smaller than the damage they inflict on workers an additional internal market for the closing decision should be established to avoid the deadweight loss. If that market works the decision entitlement becomes immaterial.

Specificities and uncertainty reopen many questions about the optimal internal organization of a firm between the two polar cases of the pure PM and LM settings. This means opportunities for future research.

# References

1] Alchian, A. and H. Demsetz (1972), "Production, Information Costs, and Economic Organization", *American Economic Review*, **62**, 777-95.

2] Aoki, M. (1980), "A Model of the Firm as a Stockholder-Employee Cooperative Game", *American Economic Review*, **70**, 600-610.

3] Aoki, M. (1984), *The Co-operative Game Theory of the Firm*, Oxford, Clarendon Press.

4] Aoki, M. and R. Dore (1994, eds), *The Japanese Firm: Sources of Competitive Strength*, Oxford, Oxford University Press.

5] Aumann, R. and M. Kurz (1977), "Power and Taxes", *Econometrica*, **45**, 1137-60.

6] Ben Ner, A. (1988a), "Comparative Empirical Observations on Worker-Owned and Capitalist Firm", *International Journal of Industrial Organization*, **6**, 7-32.

7] Ben Ner, A. (1988b), "The Life Cycle of Worker-Owned Firms in Market Economies", *Journal of Economic Behavior and Organization*, **10**, 287-313.

8] Berman, K. and M. Berman (1989), "An Empirical Test of the Theory of the LM Firm", *Journal of Comparative Economics*, **13**, 281-300.

9] Biagioli, M. (1995), "Italy: Decentralization of Wage Bargaining and Financial Participation", in D. Vaughan Whitehead (ed.), *Workers Financial Participation: East-West Experiences*, Geneva, ILO, 85-105.

10] Bonin, J. and L. Putterman (1987), *Economics of Cooperation and the Labor-Managed Economy*, New York, Harwood Academic Publishers.

11] Bonin, J., D. Jones and L. Putterman (1993), "Theoretical and Empirical Studies of Producer Cooperatives: Will Ever the Twain Meet?", *Journal of Economic Literature*, **31**, 1290-320.

12] Brunello, G. (1991), "Bonuses, Wages and Performances in Japan: Evidence from Micro Data", *Ricerche Economiche*, **45**, 377-96.

13] Chow, C.K.W. and M.K.Y. Fung (1998), "Ownership Structure, Lending Bias, and Liquidity Constraints: Evidence from Shanghai's Manufacturing Sector", *Journal of Comparative Economics*, **26**, 301-16.

14] Coase, R. (1960), "The Problem of Social Cost", *Journal of Law and Economics*, **1**, 1-44.

15] Conte, M. and J. Svejnar (1988), "Productivity Effects of Workers' Participation in Management Profit-Sharing, Worker Ownership of Assets and Unionization in US Firms", *International Journal of Industrial Organization*, **6**, 139-51.

16] Craig, B. and J. Pencavel (1992), "The Behavior of Worker Cooperatives: the Plywood Companies of the Pacific Northwest", *American Economic Review*, **82**, 1083-105.

17] Craig, B. and J. Pencavel (1995), "Participation and Productivity: A Comparison of Worker Cooperatives and Conventional Firms in the Plywood Industry", *Brookings Papers on Economic Activity, Microeconomics*, 121-74.

18] Delbono, F. and G. Rossini (1992), "Competition Policy vs. Horizontal Merger with Public, Entrepreneurial and Labor-Managed Firms", *Journal of Comparative Economics*, **16**, 226-40.

19] Dixit, A.K. (1989), "Entry and Exit Decisions under Uncertainty", *Journal of Political Economy*, **97**, 620-38.

20] Dixit, A.K. (1992), "Investment and Hysteresis", *Journal of Economic Perspectives*, **6**, 107-32.

21] Dixit, A.K. and R.S. Pindyck (1994), *Investment Under Uncertainty*, Princeton, Princeton University Press.

22] Dixit, A.K. and R.S. Pindyck (1998), "Expandability, Reversibility, and Optimal Allocation Choice", *NBER Working Paper* n. 6373.

23] Domar, E. (1966), "The Soviet Collective Farm as a Producers' Cooperative", *American Economic Review*, **56**, 734-57.

24] Dow, G. (1986), "Control Rights, Competitive Markets and Labor Management Debate", *Journal of Comparative Economics*, **10**, 48-61.

25] Dow, G. (1993a), "Democracy versus Appropriability: Can Labor-Managed Firms Flourish in a Capitalist World?", in S. Bowles, H. Gintis and B. Gustafsson (eds), *Markets and Democracy: Participation, Accountability and Efficiency*, Cambridge, Cambridge University Press.

26] Dow, G. (1993b), "Why Capital Hires Labor: A Bargaining Perspective", *American Economic Review*, **83**, 118-34.

27] Dreze, J. (1976), "Some Theory of Labor Management and Participation", *Econometrica*, **44**, 1125-39.

28] Estrin, S. (1991), "Some Reflections on Self Management, Social Choice, and Reform in Eastern Europe", *Journal of Comparative Economics*, **15**, 349-66.

29] Estrin, S., D. Jones and J. Svejnar (1987), "The Productivity Effects of Worker Participation: Producer Cooperatives in Western Economies", *Journal of Comparative Economics*, **11**, 40-61.

30] Eswaran, M. and A. Kotwal (1989), "Why are Capitalists the Bosses?", *Economic Journal*, **99**, 162-76.

31] Fehr, E. and M. Sertel (1993), "Two Forms of Workers Enterprises Facing Imperfect Labor Markets", *Economic Letters*, **41**, 121-7.

32] Fitzroy, F. and K. Kraft (1987), "Cooperation, Productivity and Profit Sharing", *Quarterly Journal of Economics*, **102**, 23-35.

33] Grossman, S. and O. Hart (1986), "The Costs and Benefits of Ownership: a Theory of Vertical and Lateral Integration", *Journal of Political Economy*, **94**, 691-719.

34] Guesnerie, R. and J. Laffont (1984), "A Complete Solution to a Class of Principal Agent Problems with an Application to the Control of a Self-Managed Firm", *Journal of Public Economics*, **25**, 329-69.

35] Hansmann, H. (1990), "When Does Worker Ownership Work? ESOPs, Law Firms, Codetermination and Economic Democracy", *Yale Law Journal*, **99**, 1749-816.

36] Harrison, J.M. (1985), *Brownian Motion and Stochastic Flow Systems*, New York, Wiley & Sons.

37] Harsanyi, J. (1956), "Approaches to the Bargaining Problem Before and After the Theory of Games: a Critical Discussion of Zeuthen's, Hicks's and Nash's Theories", *Econometrica*, **24**, 144-57.

38] Harsanyi, J. (1977), *Rational Behaviour and Bargaining Equilibrium in Games and Social Situations*, Cambridge, Cambridge University Press.

39] Hart, O. and J. Moore (1990), "Property Rights and The Nature of The Firm", *Journal of Political Economy*, **98**, 1119-58.

40] Ireland, N. and P. Law (1981), "Efficiency Incentives and Individual Labor Supply in the Labor Managed Firm", *Journal of Comparative Economics*, **5**, 1-23.

41] Ireland, N. and P. Law (1982), *The Economics of Labor Managed Enterprises*, London, Croom Helm.

42] Jones, D. and T. Kato (1995), "The Productivity Effects of Employers Stock Ownership Plans and Bonuses: Evidence from Japanese Panel Data", *American Economic Review*, **85**, 391-414.

43] Komiya, R. (1987), "Japanese Firms, Chinese Firms: Problems for Economic Reform in China, Part II", *Journal of the Japanese and International Economies*, **1**, 229-47.

44] Kruse, D. (1992), "Profit-Sharing and Productivity: Microeconomic Evidence from the United States", *Economic Journal*, **102**, 24-36.

45] Lambertini, L. (1997), "On the Provision of Product Quality by a Labor-Managed Monopolist", *Economic Letters*, **55**, 279-83.

46] Lambertini, L. (1998), "Process Innovation and the Persistence of Monopoly with Labor-Managed Firms", *Review of Economic Design*, **3-4**, 359-69.

47] Lambertini, L. and G. Rossini (1998), "Capital Commitment and Cournot Competition with Labor Managed and Profit-Maximizing Firms", *Australian Economic Papers*, **37**, 14-21.

48] Landsberger, M. and A. Subotnik (1981), "Some Anomalies in the Production Strategy of a Labor-Managed Firm", *Economica*, **48**, 195-7.

49] Lee, B. (1988), *Productivity and Employee Ownership: The Case of Sweden*, Stockholm, Trade Union Institute for Economic Research.

50] Mailath, G. and A. Postlewaite (1990), "Workers versus Firms: Bargaining Over a Firm's Value", *Review of Economic Studies*, **57**, 369-80.

51] Marshall, A. (1920), *Principles of Economics*, 8th Edition, London, Macmillan.

52] Meade, J. (1972), "The Theory of Labor Managed Firms and of Profit Sharing", *Economic Journal, 82*, 402-28.

53] Meade, J. (1974), "Labor-Managed Firms in Condition of Imperfect Competition", *Economic Journal, 84*, 817-24.

54] Moretto, M. and S. Pastorello (1998), "Entry-Exit Timing and Profit Sharing", *Rivista Internazionale di Scienze Sociali, 106*, 67-88.

55] Moretto, M. and G. Rossini (1995), "The Shut-down Option and Profit Sharing", *Journal of Comparative Economics, 21*, 93-124.

56] Moretto, M. and G. Rossini (1996), "Prevarranno sempre le imprese capitalistiche? Le risposte della letteratura", *L'Industria, 17*, 647-77.

57] Moretto, M. and G. Rossini (1997), "Profit Sharing Regulation, Repeated Bargaining and the Shut-down Option", *Economic Design, 43*, 1-31.

58] Moretto, M. and G. Rossini (2002), "Designing Severance Payments and Decision Rights for Efficient Closure under Profit-Sharing", in M. Sertel (ed.), *Advances in Economic Design*, Heidelberg, Springer-Verlag, forthcoming.

59] OECD (1995), "Profit Sharing in OECD Countries", *Employment Outlook, 139-66*.

60] Pencavel, J. and B. Craig (1994), "The Empirical Performance of Orthodox Models of the Firm Conventional Firms and Workers Cooperatives", *Journal of Political Economy, 102*, 718-44.

61] Pestieau, P. and J.-F. Thisse (1979), "On Market Imperfections and Labor Management", *Economic Letters, 3*, 353-6.

62] Piesse, J., T. Colin and J. Turk (1996), "Efficiency and Ownership in Slovene Dairying: A Comparison of Econometric and Programming Techniques", *Journal of Comparative Economics, 22*, 1-22.

63] Pindyck, R.S. (1991), "Irreversibility, Uncertainty and Investment", *Journal of Economic Literature, 29*, 1110-52.

64] Rossini, G. and C. Scarpa (1992), "The Transformation of a LM Monopoly: Competition Policy vs Mixed Firms", *Journal of International and Comparative Economics, 2*, 191-206.

65] Rubinstein, A. (1987), "A Sequential Strategic Theory of Bargaining", in T. Bewley (ed.), *Advances in Economic Theory*, 5th World Congress of the Econometric Society, monograph n. 12, Cambridge, Cambridge University Press.

66] Samuelson, P. (1957), "Wages and Interest: a Modern Dissection of Marxian Economic Models", *American Economic Review, 47*, 884-912.

67] Sertel, M. (1982), *Workers and Incentives*, Amsterdam, North Holland.

68] Sertel, M. (1987), "Workers' Enterprises Are Not Perverse", *European Economic Review, 31*, 1619-25.

69] Sertel, M. (1991), "Workers' Enterprises in Imperfect Competition", *Journal of Comparative Economics, 15*, 698-710.

70] Sertel, M. (1993), "Workers' Enterprises in Price Competition", *Managerial and Decision Economics,* **14**, 445-9.

71] Shleifer, A. and R. Vishny (1997), "A Survey of Corporate Governance", *Journal of Finance,* **52**, 737-83.

72] Smith, S., C. Beom-Cheon and M. Vodopivec (1997), "Privatization Incidence, Ownership Forms, and Firm Performance: Evidence from Slovenia", *Journal of Comparative Economics,* **25**, 158-79.

73] Steinherr, A. and J.-F. Thisse (1979), "Are Labor Managers Really Perverse?", *Economic Letters,* **2**, 137-42.

74] Vanek, J. (1970), *The General Theory of Labor Managed Market Economies,* Ithaca, NY, Cornell University Press.

75] Ward, B. (1958), "The Firm in Illyria: Market Syndicalism", *American Economic Review,* **48**, 566-89.

76] Weitzman, M. (1984), *The Share Economy: Conquering Stagflation,* Cambridge, MA, Harvard University Press.

77] Zan, S. (1982), *La cooperazione in Italia,* Bari, DeDonato.

78] Zan, L. (1990), *Economia dell'impresa cooperativa: peculiarità e rilievi critici,* Torino, Utet.

79] Zingales, L. (1997), "Corporate Governance", *NBER Working Paper* n. 6309.

# Chapter 5

# Financial reporting

Marco Trombetta

## 5.1 Introduction

A common view about financial reporting sees it as a set of mechanical rules and standards which one has to master in order to be able to produce financial statements. Consequently, financial reporting is often judged to be boring and intellectually non-stimulating. Why is it then, that so many economists, especially in the field of information economics and game theory, have decided to focus their research on the study of financial reporting problems? The purpose of this chapter is to present some of the reasons why financial reporting is an interesting field of research for an economist and why the interaction between economics and financial reporting is not only fruitful, but surely necessary. Over the last three decades, a considerable part of the interaction between accounting and economics has taken place at the level of empirical research. However, no empirical research will be reviewed in this chapter.[1] The focus will be on normative economic and financial reporting theory only.

This chapter is organised as follows. The next section presents some of the reasons why financial reporting is an interesting economic activity and not simply a mechanical routine. The following two sections present some of the details of two of the economic models of financial reporting: the signalling model of accounting policy choice and the disclosure model. The last section draws some conclusions.

---

[1] For further discussion, see Scott (1997, ch. 5) and Beaver (1998, ch. 5).

# 5.2   The nature of financial reporting

## 5.2.1   The economic nature of accounting choices

In a very influential article, Beaver and Demski (1979) stated how, under ideal conditions, accounting is, from a theoretical standpoint, useless. The argument is as follows. Suppose there exists a perfect market for each possible good and that these markets are in equilibrium. Assume either that there is no uncertainty or that there exists a complete set of state-contingent markets. Suppose also that each agent is a price-taker.

Consider now a firm which buys inputs to produce outputs, and examine the problem of giving a measure of the performance of the firm within a certain period of time (e.g., a year). A value-free measure of this performance, that we could call the income generated by the firm, is easily defined in this setting as the sum of the value of the outputs minus the sum of the value of the inputs. By introducing the standard assumptions on preference orderings, we could also easily rank different levels of this performance measure in the sense that more income is always preferred to less income, and hence that one production plan is better than another if it generates a higher income.

In this setting, accounting is easily defined as the calculation of this income measure, but it is useless because the information it eventually provides is already freely available to everybody. The only role accounting could have would be to spare some calculation to the general public, but nothing else.

Obviously, the ideal conditions under which accounting is both extremely easy and valueless are not to be found in reality. Markets are neither complete nor perfect and risk cannot always be perfectly priced through state-contingent markets. Then, there is scope for an accounting function within the market, but its role remains to be decided upon. In order to attempt and define this role, the nature of accounting rules and principles needs to be clarified.

Sunder (1997, ch. 9) provides a useful classification. He draws a distinction between *conventions* and *economic features*. They are both patterns of behaviour which are used as coordinating devices. However, in order to distinguish between them, the following question has to be answered: if we move from one pattern of behaviour to an alternative one, leaving aside the cost of adjusting, will the interests of any agent be affected in equilibrium?

If the answer is negative, then the pattern of behaviour we are considering is a convention. As an example, Sunder considers the choice between driving on the left or on the right of the road. The economic value to the agents involved rests in the ability to avoid road accidents, but it is unaltered by the particular choice made (left or right).

If the answer to the above question is positive, then the pattern of behaviour can be considered an economic feature. Consider the well known coordination game traditionally labelled as *the battle of the sexes*, where a man and his partner have to decide where to spend a Saturday afternoon. They both prefer to be together, but the man would prefer to go to a football game whereas the woman would prefer to go to a museum. Two Nash equilibria exist, prescribing that the players go to the same place together. Equilibrium payoffs are of course asymmetric. Independently of the players' decisions, a switch to the alternative would affect the interests of the two agents. In this case, the choice between the football game and the museum is an economic feature of the relationship between the man and his partner.

After having introduced this distinction, Sunder moves on to consider a list of accounting patterns of behaviour (rules, principles and the like) and tries to divide them between conventions and economic features. Very few of them can actually be classified as conventions. Consequently, the accounting system as a whole is certainly not a convention.

If accounting rules are not neutral conventions, but economic features of accounting, then we could ask why they have to be developed in the first place. In answering this question, a crucial role is played by what is technically called the *accruals* principle. Its logic is as follows. Usually, there exists a temporal mismatch between the economic effects and the cash flow effects of business transactions. Classic examples are sales and purchases on credit and investment activities. In these cases, the cash outflow or inflow takes place either before or after the economic effects of the activity.

According to the accruals principle, what determines the economic situation of the firm are the economic effects and not the cash flow effects. Hence, financial statements should follow an economic logic rather than a cash flow logic. This is the reason why we find non-cash flow entries like depreciation or provisions for future losses in a standard profit and loss account. However, accrual entries are often arbitrary and based on estimates. This is the reason why they are crucial in making accounting policy choice a discretionary activity. If, instead, accounting is a discretionary activity, then rules are needed in order to define the boundaries of this discretion.

The arguments provided by Beaver and Demski (1979) and Sunder (1997) together with the acceptance of the accruals principle lead us to the conclusion that accounting is neither simply a mechanical reorganisation of raw data nor a problem-free activity.

Accounting can play a relevant role as an activity within an economic system and accounting choices are economic choices in the sense that they affect the final payoffs of the agents involved. It is then perfectly reasonable and indeed necessary to analyse them through the lenses of economic theory.

## 5.2.2   From accounting to financial reporting

The process of communicating information about the economic result and the total wealth of a business enterprise goes beyond the simple provision of a set of figures organised in different statements and under different headings.

If we analyse the annual report of a business enterprise we will find that proper accounting numbers occupy only a small proportion of the total number of pages. For example, in the 1997 annual report of Whirlpool Corporation (USA) only 3 pages out of 52 (5.7%) are occupied by the proper financial statements (i.e. profit and loss account, balance sheet and cash flow statement). We could also add the explanatory tables and count up to 10 pages of accounting numbers. What is the content of the other 42 pages?

These additional pages are usually occupied by a combination of text and numbers that tries to explain, certify, supplement the accounting numbers. Here we can find, for example, the description of the accruals adjustment made by the enterprise and create the difference between the cash flow statement and the profit and loss account. But we can also find additional value relevant information. In the case of Whirlpool Corporation, in the remaining 42 pages of the annual report we find information about the restructuring process of the organisation of the whole business, a description of key products, management's discussion of the operations for 1997, notes explaining the accounting numbers, the auditor report and so on.

If a new product is being developed and launched, this information will be found in this additional section of the annual report. Forecasts on the future evolution of the relevant markets will also be found in these additional sections. Moreover the communication of value relevant information does not take place only through the annual report. News can be released to the press at any time. The top management can produce and decide to disclose earnings forecasts during the year. Half year results are also usually communicated to the general public.

The term *financial reporting* encompasses all these additional forms of communicating information to key investors and the general public. The top management of a company possesses a considerable amount of information over and above strict accounting numbers. This information can be useful for all the economic agents that have an interest in valuing the company.

## 5.2.3   The financial reporting game

We have seen that the application of the accruals principle makes accounting an economic activity, because the choice of the accounting policy to be chosen is discretionary. Moreover, the top management of a company also has discretion in choosing which pieces of information to disclose over and above the accounting numbers contained in the main financial statements.

Both the decision of which accounting policy choice to follow and the decision on which pieces of information to disclose, other than the accounting numbers, are strategic decisions. The financial reporting strategy of the company influences the perception that investors, competitors and the general public have of the company. Hence, it will have an effect on the actions taken by these economic agents while dealing with the company. It is for this reason that the financial reporting activity of a company can be analysed as a game between an informed agent (the company and/or its top management) and one or more uninformed agents (investors, competitors, the general public etc.).

In the following sections, two of the more popular versions of this game will be presented in some detail.

## 5.3 The signalling approach to the design of accounting policy

### 5.3.1 Harnischfeger Corporation

Harnischfeger Corporation[2] is a machinery company based in Milwaukee, producing construction equipment, mining and electrical equipment, handling equipment and engineering services. In 1982, the corporation experienced a financial crisis and had to default on certain covenants of its debt agreements. In 1984, it decided to change its accounting policies as follows. Part of its business consisted in the resale of products purchased by Kobe Steel Ltd. Up to 1984 only the gross margin of these resales was included in the Harnischfeger net sales figure. In 1984, the corporation decided to include the full value of these resales. This increased the reported net sales figure by 5.4 million US dollars. The corporation also decided to switch from accelerated depreciation to straight-line depreciation and to extend the economic life of fixed assets. The effect of these changes was to increase the reported net income by 14.3 million US dollars. A few questions can be raised by a case like Harnischfeger Corporation:

- Why do companies choose a particular accounting method?
- How does the stock market react to accounting policy choice?
- How do we regulate accounting policy choice?

---

[2]This case is taken from Palepu *et al.* (1996).

## 5.3.2   A signalling game

Examine the following game with two players: a manager-owner $O$ and a group of prospective buyers (the market) $T$.

Consider a company run by a manager-owner. We are at the end of an accounting period and the company has to choose the accounting policy to adopt for its annual report. After the report is released, the manager has to sell a quota of the company in order to raise an amount of funds $K$ to finance a new business venture. With probability $(1-p)$ this business venture can be either highly successful and make the true worth of the company $(x)$ equal to $G$. On the other hand, with probability $p$ the venture will be fairly unsuccessful and make the true worth of the company equal to $B$. However, even in the worst case, the venture has still some positive value, i.e., $G > B > 0$. The share of the ownership of the company that has to be sold in order to finance this venture depends on the value $V$ given to the company by the market. Suppose that the total number of shares is $n$. The number of shares $s$ to be sold in order to finance the venture will have to satisfy the following relationship:

$$\frac{V}{n}s = K \tag{5.1}$$

Hence, the share of the ownership that has to be sold in order to finance the venture is equal to

$$\frac{s}{n} = \alpha = \frac{K}{V} \qquad K < V \tag{5.2}$$

At the moment of choosing the accounting policy the manager knows the outcome of the venture (i.e. he/she knows the true worth $x$), but the potential buyers do not. However, the buyers can observe the accounting policy chosen before quoting their price.

Focus now on the choice of the accounting policy. Suppose that the discretion in choosing this accounting policy is such that, depending on the policy chosen, a discretionary component of reported income $(y)$ can be any value in the interval $[m, M]$. The discretionary component of reported income affects the final wealth of the owner according to the parameter $\delta$. If $\delta < 0$, the net effect of reporting higher levels of income is a decrease in the company's net wealth as well as in the final payoff of the owner, and conversely if $\delta > 0$. Call $I$ the part of the net wealth of the company that does not depend on the discretionary accounting policy choice. The final payoff for the owner is

$$\pi^O = I + \delta y + (1 - \alpha)x \tag{5.3}$$

Assume there are sufficiently many buyers so that the market valuation when the shares are offered is always equal to the expected value of the company's true worth, given the information available, which, in this case, is the accounting policy chosen, i.e. the level of discretionary income.[3] Hence, the share of the ownership sold in order to finance the project depends on the discretionary income reported through the effect that this has on the market valuation of the company, $\alpha(V(y))$.

Check first what is the effect of a change in the market value on the final payoff of the owner:

$$\frac{d\pi^O}{dy} = \frac{\partial\pi^O}{\partial y} + \frac{\partial\pi^O}{\partial\alpha}\frac{d\alpha}{dV}\frac{dV}{dy} = \frac{\partial\pi^O}{\partial y} + \frac{\partial\pi^O}{\partial V}\frac{dV}{dy} \tag{5.4}$$

where

$$\frac{\partial\pi^O}{\partial y} = \delta \; ; \; \frac{\partial\pi^O}{\partial V} = x\frac{K}{V^2} > 0 \qquad x = B, G \tag{5.5}$$

**Remark 1** *There is always an incentive to induce a market valuation as high as possible* $(\partial\pi^O/\partial V > 0)$. *Hence, there is an incentive to use the choice of the accounting policy to convince the market that good news has been received.*

We will call this effect of accounting policy choice the *signalling effect*. Formally it is captured by the second term in (5.4).[4] However,

**Remark 2** *If the accounting policy choice has no effect on valuation (i.e., if* $dV/dy = 0$*), then accounting policy choice is driven solely by the effect on the discretionary reported income.*

We will label this effect as the *reported income effect*. This is captured by the first term in (5.4).

**Remark 3** *The total effect of a change in accounting policy choice on the final payoff of the owner depends on the true worth of the company* $x$.

In other words, the benefits of inducing a higher market valuation are greater for an owner with good news than for an owner with bad news.

Suppose $\delta > 0$. This means that there is an incentive to report discretionary income as high as possible. Suppose now that the level of reported

---

[3] We are assuming that $I$ is not informative about the true worth $x$.

[4] To be correct, this second term should be discounted. Given that this extension of the model does not add anything to the general flavour of the results, it is neglected here.

income influences positively the market valuation, i.e., $dV/dy > 0$. In order to reach a certain payoff $\bar{\pi}$, a manager with good news needs to report less income than the owner with bad news. That is, the incentive to over-report income in the short term in order to reach a certain level of valuation is less for a good company than for a bad company. This is the crucial point of any signalling model.[5]

## Pooling equilibria

Consider the equilibria where both types of owners (with good news and with bad news) choose the same accounting policy.

Now focus on the case of $\delta > 0$. If they know that they are going to make the same choice, then it is intuitive to think that they will choose the accounting policy that reports the highest possible level of income $M$.

The intuition is as follows. If the manager knows that there is no way he/she can succeed at signalling good news, then he/she knows that, no matter what signal is chosen, the valuation obtained will always be the expected value of the true worth $x$, i.e. $V = E(x)$ and $dV/dy = 0$. Hence, the signalling effect is zero and it is optimal to choose the maximum level of reported income because of the reported profit effect.

The equilibrium strategies will be as follows:

$$
\begin{aligned}
y^G &= y^B = M & (5.6) \\
V &= E(x) & (5.7)
\end{aligned}
$$

However, we also have to specify the beliefs of the uninformed party about the type of informed party (given the choice observed). They are as follows:

$$
\eta(x = B \,|y) = p \quad \text{for any } y \tag{5.8}
$$

It is easily checked that, given (5.8), strategy (5.6) is indeed optimal for both types. On the other hand, given strategy (5.6), the beliefs (5.8) are acceptable. Therefore, (5.6) and (5.8) form a Bayesian Nash equilibrium. However, it can be shown that this is not the only pooling equilibrium produced by this game.

---

[5]In technical terms, this is what is called the *single-crossing property* of the preference mapping for the informed player.

**Figure 5.1:** Pooling equilibria in the signalling game

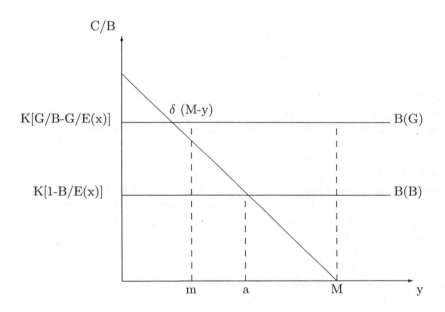

With this aim, examine the following situation:

$$y^G = y^B = y^P < M \; ; \; V = E(x) \tag{5.9}$$

$$\eta(x = B \,|y) = \begin{cases} p & \text{if } y \le y^P \\ 1 & \text{if } y > y^P \end{cases} \tag{5.10}$$

It can be shown that this is also an acceptable pooling equilibrium. Infinitely many equilibria of this sort exist. It is also possible to show that, if

$$K\left(1 - \frac{B}{E(x)}\right) \ge \delta(M - m) \tag{5.11}$$

then there exists a pooling equilibrium for any acceptable $y$. On the other hand, if

$$K \left( 1 - \frac{B}{E(x)} \right) < \delta(M - m) \tag{5.12}$$

separating equilibria exist only with $y^P > a$, where $a$ is determined by

$$K \left( 1 - \frac{B}{E(x)} \right) = \delta(M - a) \tag{5.13}$$

and $a > m$. A graphic explanation of this argument is given by figure 5.1.

## Separating equilibria

Keep on focusing on $\delta > 0$. We will now try to see if there is also an equilibrium where a manager with good news signals that through an accounting policy choice other than the policy chosen by the manager with bad news. How do we build this equilibrium?

Consider first the manager with bad news. It seems sensible to assume that, in a separating equilibrium, if he/she knows that his/her type will be revealed to the market (no signalling effect), then he/she will choose the policy that maximises the reported profit effect, i.e. $y^B = M$.

Consider now the manager with good news. He/she could choose to maximise the reported profit effect and choose $y^G = M$. But in this case, in a separating equilibrium, he/she will be assumed to have bad news. On the other hand, he/she could decide to sacrifice some of the reported income gains in order to distinguish his/her policy choice from the choice made by the manager with bad news. In order to do so he/she could choose a policy $y^G < M$, be recognised as a good company and enjoy a higher market valuation. Will this happen? It depends on the balance between the cost and the benefits of such a policy choice.

The maximum payoff that a manager with good news can obtain if he/she accepts being taken as a bad type is

$$\pi^O(M) = I + \delta M + \left( 1 - \frac{K}{B} \right) G \tag{5.14}$$

On the other hand, if he/she chooses to report a lower income $y^G < M$, but manages to be recognised as a good type he/she gets

$$\pi^O(y) = I + \delta y^G + \left( 1 - \frac{K}{G} \right) G \tag{5.15}$$

The cost in terms of smaller reported income is equal to

$$Cost \left( y^G \right) = \delta \left( M - y^G \right) \tag{5.16}$$

The benefit in terms of signalling effect is

$$Benefit^G = \left(1 - \frac{K}{G}\right) G - \left(1 - \frac{K}{B}\right) G = K \left(\frac{G}{B} - 1\right) \qquad (5.17)$$

There always exists a range of $y$ such that the manager with good news finds it profitable to signal. If

$$\delta(M - m) \leq K \left(\frac{G}{B} - 1\right) \qquad (5.18)$$

then all accounting policies other than $M$ are preferred by the good news manager, as long as he/she is successful in being recognised as such. If

$$\delta(M - m) > K \left(\frac{G}{B} - 1\right) \qquad (5.19)$$

there is a range of policies such that the signalling cost (5.16) is too high with respect to the signalling benefit (5.17).

However, this is not enough to guarantee the existence of a separating equilibrium. We also have to make sure that the manager with bad news does not have an incentive to mimic the manager with good news and choose the same reported income. The cost of doing so in terms of reported profit is the same as for the manager for good news, i.e.

$$Cost\left(y^B\right) = \delta\left(M - y^B\right) \qquad (5.20)$$

The benefit however is different from (5.17):

$$Benefit^B = \left(1 - \frac{K}{G}\right) B - \left(1 - \frac{K}{B}\right) B = K \left(1 - \frac{B}{G}\right) < Benefit^G \quad (5.21)$$

**Figure 5.2:** Separating equilibria in the signalling game

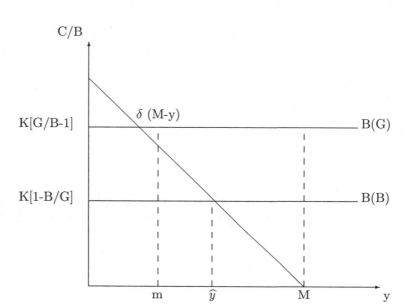

Figure 5.2 provides the graphical argument to prove that a separating equilibrium exists if and only if

$$Cost(m) = \delta(M - m) > K \left(1 - \frac{B}{G}\right) = Benefit^B \qquad (5.22)$$

If (5.22) holds, then there exists an accounting policy choice $\widetilde{y}$ (with $m < \widetilde{y} < M$) such that for $y < \widetilde{y}$ the manager with bad news does not have an incentive to try to cheat and be taken as a manager with good news. $\widetilde{y}$ is defined by

$$\delta (M - \widetilde{y}) = K \left(1 - \frac{B}{G}\right) \qquad (5.23)$$

Hence, if an accounting policy choice $y < \widetilde{y}$ is observed, then it can only have been chosen by a manager with good news. If (5.22) holds, we can build an infinity of separating equilibria of the following sort:

$$y^G < M; y^B = M \tag{5.24}$$

$$V = \begin{cases} G & \text{if } y \leq y^G \\ B & \text{if } y > y^G \end{cases} \tag{5.25}$$

$$\eta(x = B \,|y) = \begin{cases} 0 & \text{if } y \leq y^G \\ 1 & \text{if } y > y^G \end{cases} \tag{5.26}$$

where $m \leq y^G \leq \tilde{y}$.

## Comments

The above discussion shows that there are infinitely many pooling equilibria and there can be infinitely many separating equilibria. This is an unfortunate feature of signalling models. The search for a criterion that allows us to select only one of these equilibria has kept busy some of the most famous game theorists during the 1980s. The description of *equilibrium refinements* is beyond the scope of this chapter (see Fudenberg and Tirole, 1991, *inter alia*). Accordingly, we confine our attention to the following observations.

When we considered pooling equilibria, we started by considering the equilibrium where both companies choose the least costly accounting policy ($M$ if $\delta > 0$ or $m$ if $\delta < 0$). Then we saw that there are other pooling equilibria, but this particular equilibrium is always one of them. It seems *sensible* to choose this equilibrium among all the possible pooling equilibria because it is the equilibrium that gives the highest payoff to the companies. However to put this intuition into a formal argument is far from being immediate, even if, at least in this case, it is actually possible.

Let us now consider the set of separating equilibria, if they exist. Again, if $\delta > 0$, it seems sensible to choose the equilibrium where $y^G = \tilde{y}$; $y^B = M$. Again, it is as difficult as with pooling equilibria to provide a formal argument to do so, but in this case it could be done. This is the reason why we can focus on these two equilibria in this discussion.

Turn now to the informational properties of the model. Suppose we adopt the perspective of a financial analyst, his/her objective being to infer the true type of the company. In this case, pooling equilibria are not desirable but are always there. Separating equilibria are preferred but they exist only occasionally when some particular conditions are verified. The good news is that if different accounting policy choices are observed, then we should be in a separating equilibrium, where the most costly accounting policy is chosen by good companies and the "easy" accounting policy is chosen by bad companies.

**Proposition 1** *If an accounting policy is too popular, i.e., every company follows it, then its choice cannot be informative. Only the situation where a variety of accounting policies is observed can be informative.*

Remember, however, that we have focused on the case $\delta > 0$, i.e., more reported income is good for the company. This is not always the case. If $\delta < 0$, then the direction of our conclusions should be reversed. Good news is signalled through income increasing accounting policies and bad news is signalled by income decreasing accounting policies.

**Proposition 2** *The interpretation that has to be given to accounting policy choice depends on the net effect of a change in reported income on the short term payoff of the company. Accounting policy choices that increase reported income can be either a signal of good news or a signal of bad news.*

### 5.3.3  The Harnischfeger Corporation reconsidered

This corporation decided to change its accounting policy mix. All the changes went in the direction of increasing reported income. We asked the following question: why did the company change its accounting policies?

There is no straightforward answer to this question. If we want to interpret this choice within a signalling framework, we need to establish the direction of the reported income effect (i.e., the sign of $\delta$).

Some of the changes (the change in the way net sales are calculated) will have an effect on the tax bill of the company. In this sense $\delta$ should be less than zero. However, the changes in the depreciation policy will probably not be acceptable for tax purposes (and in fact did not affect pre-tax income and tax calculations). Hence, their effect is simply to increase the reported income and present a better picture of the performance of the company, i.e., $\delta > 0$. This effect was considerable because without these changes only 4 of the 15 million dollars net income would have been reported! Moreover in 1982 and 1983 substantial losses were reported and the corporation had to default on some of its debt agreement. Overall, it seems plausible to assume that the second effect dominates the first and to interpret the changes in accounting policies under the assumption that $\delta > 0$.

The second question we asked was: how will the market react? Again, it is difficult to answer this question. We should compare the policies chosen by the Harnischfeger Corporation with the policies chosen by some similar company. Only if they are different can we try to interpret them as *signals*. If we observe that the Harnischfeger Corporation is the only one choosing such a set of income-increasing policies, then we could suspect that perhaps some bad news had been received and this made a set of more conservative policies not sustainable.

Following this line, market reaction should not have been particularly favourable at least until the uncertainty about the future of the company was resolved. In other words, such a substantial change in the accounting policy mix in the direction of increasing accounting income should have created some concern in the market, because good companies should not need to do that.

However, during January 1985 the stock price of Harnischfeger went up by 25% whereas the S&P 400 Industrial Index went up only by 9.7%, i.e., the immediate reaction was certainly positive. This raises a very deep question: do investors see through accounting policy changes?

### 5.3.4 Regulation of accounting choices in a signalling model

Finally, let's have a look at the effect of regulation of the accounting choice within a signalling framework. Again, we focus on the case of $\delta > 0$. Suppose that only two accounting policies are allowed: $y_l$ and $M$ with $m \leq y_l < M$.

It is fairly easy to accept that a separating equilibrium can exist only if $m \leq y_l \leq \widetilde{y}$, where $\widetilde{y}$ is defined as in the general model (i.e., it is the highest level of reported income that allows separation to occur).

In other words, when the choice of accounting policies is restricted, it is relatively more difficult to observe separation because the set of admitted accounting policies cannot be rich enough (there is no room to signal). If this is the case then no signalling interpretation can be given to the choice of accounting policy and each company chooses the policy that maximises the reported income effect. Hence, all the companies are *forced* to make the same choice.

**Proposition 3** *The regulation of accounting choices has a strong effect on the information content of such choices. If the set of permitted choices is too narrow, then it is very unlikely that information on the quality of the company can be extracted from such a choice.*

### 5.3.5 Implications for financial reporting

If no formal contractual relationship is attached to reported income, we can assume that $\delta = 0$. If some formal contractual relationship is linked (directly or indirectly) to reported income and accounting policy choice, then we have seen how important it is to distinguish the direction of this effect.

A real example analysed by Frantz (1997) is the case of debt covenants. With respect to this family of contracts a higher level of reported income is beneficial, i.e. $\delta > 0$. Another real example analysed by Hughes and Schwartz (1988) is the case of taxation. If the accounting policy change is acceptable for tax reporting, then it will affect directly the tax bill. In this case $\delta < 0$. A few real world accounting choices that have been analysed through the lenses of signalling theory are the following.

**Inventory (stock) accounting method**

This is the most popular example. The reason why it is so popular is because in the USA, LIFO is admitted for tax purposes. However, a lot of companies keep on using FIFO, foregoing potentially huge tax savings. So the natural questions asked by many researchers is: why is it so?

The theoretical explanation based on a signalling model was given by Hughes and Schwartz (1988). The empirical literature on the subject is vast and dates back to the 1970's. Still, the article by Cushing and LeClere (1992) is a good example of this literature. Their questionnaire found the following:

- the main reason why LIFO is adopted is because it allows tax savings;

- the reasons why FIFO is adopted instead of LIFO are less clear cut. Yet, one of the reasons mentioned was the fear of negative stock price reactions. This is consistent with the signalling theory.

**Stock dividends**

Another accounting related choice that has been studied under the lenses of signalling theory is the choice between stock dividends that involve less than 25% increase in outstanding shares and more than 25% increase in outstanding shares. In the first case US standards require a transfer from retained earnings of the *market* value of the new shares issued. In the second case (25% or more) the transfer required is equal to the *par* value of the share issued. Hence, less than 25% stock dividends are more costly than 25% or more stock dividends.

Rankine and Stice (1997) test the hypothesis that companies that choose less than 25% stock dividends are confident that future income will be high. They find that abnormal returns after the announcement of these stock dividends confirm this hypothesis because less than 25% stock dividends generate much higher returns than stock dividends of 25% or more.

# 5.4 Information disclosure

## 5.4.1 BOC plc

BOC plc is a UK chemical group that provides industrial gas supplies, health care products and operates a cryogenic plant. In its 1997 annual report, it decided to voluntarily disclose a set of information about financial instruments. In particular it disclosed:

- the fair value of financial instruments,
- the effects of currency swaps on net debt,
- the repayment profile of interest rate swaps and borrowing and financian lease,
- the major financial risks it was facing and how financial instruments are used to manage this risk.

Examples of voluntary disclosure of value relevant information can be found in many annual reports. We can ask the following questions:

- Why do voluntary disclosures take place?
- What is the effect of voluntary disclosures?
- Should disclosure be mandated?

## 5.4.2 The basic disclosure game

In this section the basic disclosure game that takes place between an informed manager-owner and a set of competitive buyers will be presented. This will be done by analysing a series of variations of this game starting from the case when no disclosures are allowed and then introducing free disclosures, credible disclosures, costly disclosures and disclosures when there is uncertainty about the flow of information.

### Game 1: No disclosure

Consider the following adverse selection game (Akerlof, 1970). Suppose again that we have two players. A manager-owner $O$ who is willing to sell his firm and a group of investors who are the potential buyers (traders) $T$. Both players are risk neutral. Let us call $P$ the price at which the firm (i.e., its shares) are sold. The actual worth of the firm $x$ can take only two values: $B$ with probability $p$ and $G$ with probability $(1 - p)$; $G > B$.

In this first version of the disclosure game we will assume as in the previous section that the manager always observes the true worth $x$, but the buyers do not know this worth before they offer a price. The payoff of the manager will be either the price obtained if the sale takes place or the worth of the firm if there is no sale, i.e.

$$\pi^O = \begin{cases} P \text{ if sale} \\ x \text{ if no sale} \end{cases} \tag{5.27}$$

The buyers' collective payoff is given by the actual worth of the firm, $x$, minus the price paid for it or 0 if the transaction does not take place, i.e.

$$\pi^T = \begin{cases} x - P \text{ if sale} \\ 0 \quad \text{ if no sale} \end{cases} \tag{5.28}$$

Assume that, if indifferent, they both prefer to make the transaction. Suppose that the buyers have to quote a price without having any knowledge of the actual value of the firm. In this case, they have three pricing strategies. Either they quote $P = B$, or they quote $P = G$, or they quote something in between. In the latter case, we can assume they will quote the expected worth $P = E(x)$.

The manager has four possible strategies: always sell, never sell, sell if $G$ and don't if $B$, sell if $B$ and don't if $G$. Given our assumption on the willingness to trade the only Nash equilibrium is $[(S\,|B, NS\,|G); B\,]$, i.e. only bad firms would sell and the buyers would correctly infer that and would offer only $B$ as the price. This is a simple case of *adverse selection*.

Assume now the manager is forced to sell the firm anyway. This is a convenient way of modelling the fact that the market valuation of a company always matters. If we assume that there are sufficiently many buyers who compete for the purchase of the firm, then they must offer at least the expected value of the worth of the company given the available information (i.e. $P = E\,(x|I)$) in order to be able to buy it. Moreover, if no additional information is provided, they would not offer anything more. In this case in equilibrium we will have $B < P = E\,(x) < G$. But if this is the case, then a firm with good news cannot be happy because it is obtaining a valuation that is below its true worth. This is another version of the adverse selection problem: *the market rewards bad firms and penalises good firms.* Hence a firm with good news would look for some way to convey this information to the market.

We have an answer to the first question raised at the beginning of the section:

**Proposition 4** *A company that is convinced of having good news about some value relevant information will try to communicate this information to the market, even if it is not forced to do so.*

From now on we will always assume that the manager is forced to sell.

## Game 2: Free disclosure

Suppose the manager can make an announcement and disclose his/her information. However, this announcement cannot be certified and/or verified (Crawford and Sobel, 1982). Hence, anybody can make any announcement. Could this opportunity solve the adverse selection problem? The answer is no. If a firm having bad news can also announce that news is good, then it will do so. Hence, in equilibrium both good and bad firms will make the same announcement and the situation will be exactly as before. The price is the expected value of the worth, bad firms are rewarded and good firms are penalised. So, we can start answering the second question raised at the beginning of the section:

**Proposition 5** *Disclosures can have an effect on the adverse selection problem only if they are credible.*

## Game 3: Truthful disclosures

Suppose now the manager can make an announcement and this announcement is credible, i.e. it is the truth. We can think of a situation where disclosure has to be audited or the liability for false disclosure is so high that it is not possible to make false announcement (Milgrom, 1981).[6]

If this is the case the manager can choose between two strategies: disclosure $(D)$ or no disclosure $(ND)$. Competition among buyers forces them to pay the true worth if disclosure takes place. If no disclosure is observed, we still assume that so many buyers are competing for the purchase of the firm that the price has to be equal to the expected value of the worth given no disclosure. Obviously we will have $B \leq P = E(x|ND) \leq G$. The payoffs of the possible strategies for the manager can be expressed through the following matrix:

|  |  | Strategy | |
|---|---|---|---|
|  |  | $ND$ | $D$ |
| News | $B$ | $P = E(x|ND) \geq B$ | $B$ |
|  | $G$ | $P = E(x|ND) \leq G$ | $G$ |

---

[6]The requirement that disclosures have to be completely truthful is obviously very strong. However, when we have more than simply two possible values for the worth, then this requirement can actually be relaxed into the less demanding requirement that the true worth is to be part of the disclosure, but the disclosure can be a "range" disclosure that includes the true worth.

In the binary case, the disclosure of the two states is equivalent to no disclosure, hence the two requirements are equivalent.

The manager with bad news has a weak incentive to hide it and the manager with good news has a weak incentive to disclose it. If we eliminate weakly dominated strategies, then the Nash equilibrium of the game is $[(ND|B, D|G); B]$. The buyers will anticipate the optimal disclosure strategies and set $P = E(x|ND) = B$. Hence, even if the bad firm tries to hide, it is successfully detected as a bad firm in equilibrium. This is a simple version of what is called the *unravelling argument*.

Notice how the adverse selection problem is solved in this case. The market works and prices fairly both types of firm. So, we can give an answer to the second question raised by the BOC plc case:

**Proposition 6** *If disclosures are credible, then they can solve the adverse selection problem and assure a fair market valuation.*

The unravelling result depends crucially on three assumptions:

1) Disclosures are costless.

2) The manager-owner is perfectly informed (he/she knows the true worth of the company) and investors know it.

3) The manager-owner always prefers to disclose good news than bad news or *vice versa*, i.e. his/her preference ordering is monotone in the induced valuation of the company.

We will discuss in some detail only the first two assumptions.[7]

### Game 4: Costly disclosures

Now, following Verrecchia (1983), suppose the manager can make credible announcements, but making an announcement involves a cost equal to $C > 0$. The situation facing the manager becomes:

|  |  | Strategy | |
|---|---|---|---|
|  |  | $ND$ | $D$ |
| News | $B$ | $P = E(x|ND) > B - C$ | $B - C$ |
|  | $G$ | $P = E(x|ND)$ | $G - C$ |

For a manager with bad news $ND$ is always a dominant strategy. The optimal strategy for a manager with good news is less obvious in this case and it depends crucially on the size of the disclosure costs. If the manager with good news does not disclose, the price will be equal to the *ex ante* expected

---

[7]Disclosure with a strategic opponent, i.e., with non-monotone objective functions, has been studied, for example, by Wagenhofer (1990) and Gigler (1994).

value of the worth of the firm,[8] i.e., $P = E(x)$. Consequently, the manager with good news will prefer strategy $D$ if

$$C \leq G - E(x) \qquad (5.29)$$

However, when (5.29) does not hold, the cost of disclosure is higher than the gain $(G - E(x))$ from disclosure and we go back to the adverse selection situation with no disclosure observed and good companies are undervalued. The difference is that, in this case, they *prefer* to be undervalued if the alternative is to pay the disclosure costs. So, we have to qualify our previous answer to the question about the effects of disclosures:

**Proposition 7** *Disclosures can take place and assure a fair market valuation, if*

1. *they are credible;*

2. *their cost is sufficiently small with respect to the benefit expected from the disclosure.*

### Game 5: Uncertainty about the flow of information

Following Dye (1985) and Jung and Kwong (1988), we add another complication to our model. Suppose the manager does not necessarily know the true worth of the company, $x$. With probability $q$ the manager is not informed whereas with probability $(1 - q)$ the manager is informed and knows $x$. Disclosure costs do not play any significant role in this simple version of the model. We still assume that disclosures have to be credible. Hence, non-informed managers cannot disclose anything. If the manager is informed, then the game is the same as the game of the previous section. Hence, we have only two situations:

a) $C > G - E(x|ND)$. In this case, we know that disclosure never takes place, hence the fact that the manager can be uninformed does not matter.

b) $C \leq G - E(x|ND)$. This is the only interesting situation, because the cost of disclosure does not prevent disclosure.

For the sake of simplicity we can focus on the case of $C = 0$. When the manager is informed, the disclosure decision depends on the expected price when no disclosure takes place.

---

[8] Because a manager with bad news will never disclose anyway. Hence if the manager with good news also does not disclose, then the buyers cannot distinguish between the two types.

| News | Strategy | |
|---|---|---|
| | ND | D |
| B | $P = E(x\|ND) > B$ | B |
| G | $P = E(x\|ND) < G$ | G |

Consider first the choice of a manager who is informed and receives good news. If the manager discloses, given credibility, the price will be $G$. If the manager does not disclose the price will be somewhere between $B$ and $G$. Hence for the manager with good news $D$ is a weakly dominant strategy.

If we delete the weakly dominated strategy for the manager with good news, then no disclosure can only be the strategy either of informed manager with bad news or of uninformed managers (*but not of informed managers with good news*). But if this is the case the price offered by the buyers when no disclosure is observed cannot be just $B$. The expected value of the worth of the firm in this case is above $B$ because there is always a (maybe small) positive probability that the non-disclosing firm is good and simply the manager does not know it. Specifically the expected value of the worth (and consequently the price) given no disclosure verifies the following:

$$G > P = E(x|ND) = \Pr(B|ND)B + \Pr(G|ND)G$$
$$= \frac{p}{p + q(1-p)}B + \frac{q(1-p)}{p + q(1-p)}G > B \tag{5.30}$$

because using Bayes rule we have that $\Pr(B|ND)$ is given by:

$$\frac{\Pr(ND|B)\Pr(B)}{\Pr(ND|B)\Pr(B) + \Pr(ND|G)\Pr(G)} = \frac{p}{p + q(1-p)} \tag{5.31}$$

and $\Pr(G|ND)$ is given by:

$$\frac{\Pr(ND|G)\Pr(G)}{\Pr(ND|B)\Pr(B) + \Pr(ND|G)\Pr(G)} = \frac{q(1-p)}{p + q(1-p)} \tag{5.32}$$

Given that the price with no disclosure is always greater than $B$, $ND$ is a dominant strategy for the manager with bad news. In this case a manager with bad news will be partially successful in hiding the bad news and the adverse selection problem will still be at least partially in place, with some good companies being undervalued and bad companies being overvalued.

**Remark 4** *Notice however that, in this case, the good companies that are affected by the adverse selection problem do not know that ex ante, because they are the companies where the manager does not know that the news is good.*

Going back to our original questions we have to add another qualification to our answer:

**Proposition 8** *Disclosures can take place and assure a fair market valuation, if*

1. *they are credible;*

2. *their cost is sufficiently small with respect to the benefit expected from the disclosure;*

3. *the market can be confident that the managers know the relevant piece of information.*

## 5.4.3 Extensions

In this section two extensions of the basic framework presented in the previous section will be briefly described.

**Extension 1: Range disclosures**

This version of the disclosure game can be seen as an extension of the previous model when the true worth of the company can take more than two values. Assume the true worth of the company can take three values: $G$, $S$, $B$ with $G > M > B > 0$. In Dye (1985), either the manager knows the true worth of the company or he/she does not know it at all. Consider now an intermediate situation where the manager can be *partially* informed. For example he/she knows that the true worth is either $M$ or $B$. In this case the manager can have up to six different information sets:

$$
\begin{aligned}
I &= \{k\}, \ k = G, M, B; \ \text{full information} \\
I &= \{B, M, G\}; \ \text{no information} \\
I &= \{B, M\} \ \text{or} \ \{M, G\}; \ \text{partial information}
\end{aligned}
\tag{5.33}
$$

It is obvious that now the statement *truthful disclosure* has a different meaning. When information is partial a truthful disclosure is necessarily a *range disclosure*: "the true worth of the firm is either $x$ or $y$". Hence, in this case we need to study the situation where range disclosure of this kind is allowed. Assume that disclosures can be range disclosures, but they cannot be completely false. Formally if $I$ is the range included in the information set of the manager and $D$ is the range disclosed, we assume that $I \subseteq D$. This means that, for example, if the manager knows that the true worth is $M$, he/she can disclose $\{M\}, \{M, G\}, \{B, M\}, \{B, G\}$, but he/she cannot disclose $\{B\}$ or $\{G\}$. A truthful disclosure is a disclosure such that $I \equiv D$.

Shin (1994) shows that an equilibrium disclosure strategy for this game is what he calls the *sanitization* strategy. That is, this strategy hides bad news and discloses good news. Consider again the case of $I = \{M\}$. In this case the fact that the true worth of the company is not $G$ is bad news, but the fact that the true worth of the company is not $B$ is good news. In this case the sanitization strategy implies the disclosure of the range $\{M, G\}$ so that good news is disclosed (i.e. the true worth is not $B$), but bad news is not disclosed (i.e. the true worth of the company is not $G$).

In equilibrium, buyers will anticipate this strategy and will respond by adopting a *sceptical* belief profile that takes as relatively more likely the lower values of the range disclosed. Hence, if $[M, G]$ is disclosed buyers will believe that $M$ is more likely than $G$. However, the manager could be simply partially informed, i.e., his/her information set could be $I = \{M, G\}$ and could be disclosing honestly everything he/she knows. This is the reason why buyers can never put zero probability on any of the values disclosed by the manager and the unravelling argument can never work completely in this model, no matter how *skeptical* buyers are.

**Extension 2: Different buyers**

In the basic disclosure game, the buyers are all equally capable of understanding the disclosure strategy adopted by the manager. A natural extension consists in assuming that different buyers differ in their ability to understand disclosures. This difference will give rise to different post-disclosure beliefs. Consequently different buyers will value the same company differently. For this reason, it is not obvious what price the market as a whole will quote for the company. Dye (1998) and Fishman and Hagerty (1997a) deal with this problem in a different way.

Dye (1998) extends the model with uncertainty about the flow of information and considers two different sets of buyers. Sophisticated buyers know whether the manager is informed or not. Unsophisticated buyers do not. If the manager is informed, he/she is fully informed. If disclosure takes place, it is truthful and both sets of buyers will quote the true worth of the company as the price. However the no disclosure event will be interpreted differently by the two sets of buyers. Sophisticated buyers will know for sure whether the manager is withholding some value relevant information or simply is not informed. Unsophisticated buyers will not be able to tell which of these two occurrences is true. The market price for the company is determined through a first price, sealed bid auction among the different buyers.

The optimal disclosure strategy in this model is defined by a cut-off point $x^c$. If the true worth of the company is strictly smaller than this cut-off point (i.e. $x < x^c$), then the manager, if informed, does not disclose. If $x \geq x^c$ an informed manager discloses.

Of course, the position of the cut-off point depends on the share of sophisticated buyers. The more sophisticated buyers there are the smaller is the cut-off point. In the two state model presented in the previous section the situation is similar to the case of uncertain flow of information and whether a manager with good news will disclose or not depends on whether the cut-off point is $B$, $G$ or above $G$.

Fishman and Hagerty (1997a) assume the manager is always fully informed. However, there is a group of buyers (uninformed customers) who are not able to interpret disclosures, even if disclosure takes place. For this reason these two groups of buyers will interpret differently the disclosure event and their valuation of the company will be different. In addition to that, Fishman and Hagerty (1997a) assume that the buyer not only decides whether to disclose or not (with disclosures being costless), but also quotes a price. In this particular respect, their model differs from the standard disclosure models where the price is determined after disclosure and comes from the market.

The presence of uninformed customers can break the unravelling argument. If the number of informed customers (those who understand disclosure) is sufficiently low, then there is a no disclosure equilibrium where the manager never discloses, no matter what the information is, and always quotes $P = E(x)$. Managers who know that the true worth of the company is above $E(x)$ have no incentive to disclose and charge a higher price, because most of the buyers will not understand the disclosure and simply won't buy.

## 5.4.4 Mandatory vs voluntary disclosure

The last question we have to deal with regards the regulation of disclosures. The comparison between Game 1 (adverse selection), Game 2 (free disclosures) and Game 3 (credible disclosures) tells us that disclosures of value relevant information can solve the adverse selection problem and they can do it only if they are credible. But we have also learnt that they should take place spontaneously, i.e., there is no need to make them compulsory. What is crucial is their credibility. If disclosures are credible, they should happen anyway. Hence, from this point of view, the aim of regulation should be to guarantee that disclosures are credible and not to impose them. Therefore, regulators should concentrate on the liability implications of disclosures and on their auditing. This is a quite general point.[9]

Notice the following.

**Remark 5** *If the market prices the company fairly, investors have no incentive to impose disclosure, because their expected payoff is zero. In fact, ex ante they always pay the fair expected price given the available information.*

**Remark 6** *If disclosures are credible anyway, disclosing companies have no interest in mandatory disclosure either. They can always disclose credibly if they want.*

**Remark 7** *In Game 5 the companies that suffer the adverse selection problem cannot do anything about it because they do not know they are good companies. Hence, they do not have the possibility to use disclosure strategies, no matter whether they are voluntary or mandatory.*

**Proposition 9** *In an efficient market, it seems relatively more important to guarantee the credibility of disclosures of value relevant information, than to actually impose those disclosures.*

Consider Game 4 (disclosure costs) and Game 5 (uncertain information flow). In this case some value relevant information is not disclosed because the benefits of disclosure are less than its costs or because the manager does not have the relevant information.

In these two cases, we have some scope for mandatory disclosure, because the withholding of information is a possibility. However it has to be proven that the benefit for society outweighs the costs for disclosing firms, because the private benefit is not enough to justify these disclosures. In Game 4 and 5 the effect of mandatory disclosure would be to bring the market price closer to the true worth of the company. But, in the simple model presented here, neither the selling manager nor the investors would gain *ex ante* from this. Hence there must be some social benefit in obtaining a price as close to the true worth of the company as possible other than the private benefit of the disclosing firm and/or the investors in order to justify a regime of mandatory disclosure.

**Proposition 10** *In an efficient market, mandatory disclosure requirements can play a role only if*

---

[9]It has been shown by Gigler (1994) that even completely free (cheap talk) disclosures can be informative when there are multiple users. This conclusion, however, does not change the fact that credible disclosures are more useful than completely free disclosures.

1. *the social benefits of disclosures are greater than their costs;*

2. *the case of absence of information is provided for and can be dealt with.*[10]

# 5.5 Conclusions

In the first part of this chapter it has been shown why financial reporting is far from being a mechanical activity, where the financial officer of a company simply applies some codified rules in order to produce the annual financial statements and the annual report. If we accept this point of view, then financial reporting becomes part of a company business strategy and in particular it plays a crucial role in the interaction between the company and the financial market. This is the reason why financial reporting problems can be studied with the lenses of economic theory.

Two approaches have been presented in the second part of the chapter: the signalling approach to accounting policy choice and the disclosure approach to the communication of value relevant information. The main results of these two approaches and their implication for financial reporting have also been presented.

We can conclude the chapter by considering what, if any, is the possible interaction between the two approaches presented. In the signalling approach a *costly* accounting policy is chosen in order to signal value relevant information. The disclosure approach tells us that value relevant information should be disclosed voluntarily if credible disclosures can be made. It is clear that in both approaches the object of communication is always some value relevant information. If a company decides that it wants to communicate some value relevant information to the market, it can choose between the two means: a costly accounting policy choice or a credible disclosure. How should this choice be made?

First of all, it has to be noticed that not all the value relevant information can be signalled through accounting policy choice. For example, it is difficult to use accounting policy choice to disclose range values. Hence, there are situations where direct disclosure is the only option.

However in many cases there is a choice between the two methods. If we assume that the costs and benefits of one method are not influenced by the simultaneous use of the other, then the most efficient method will be chosen. But it is possible that, for example, the cost of signalling is influenced by the level of simultaneous disclosures. Consider the case of debt

---

[10]For a more extensive discussion of this topic, see Fishman and Hagerty (1997b).

covenants analysed by Frantz (1997). An adequate level of disclosure can allow the breach of a particular debt covenant. When the costs and benefits of signalling and disclosing are linked, then it is very likely that the optimal financial reporting policy will be a mix of the two.

The issue of the simultaneous choice of an accounting policy and a disclosure strategy has not been fully addressed in the relevant literature. This appears to be an interesting route for future research.

# References

1] Akerlof, G.A. (1970), "The Market for 'Lemons'", *Quarterly Journal of Economics*, **89**, 488-500.

2] Beaver, W.H. (1998), *Financial Reporting: An Accounting Revolution*, 3rd edition, New Jersey, Prentice Hall.

3] Beaver, W.H. and J.S. Demski (1979), "The Nature of Income Measurement", *Accounting Review*, **54**, 38-46.

4] Crawford, V.P. and J. Sobel (1982), "Strategic Information Transmission", *Econometrica*, **50**, 1431-51

5] Cushing, B.E. and M.J. LeClere (1992), "Evidence on the Determinants of Inventory Accounting Policy Choice", *Accounting Review*, **67**, 355-66.

6] Dye, R.A. (1985), "Disclosure of Nonproprietary Information", *Journal of Accounting Research*, **23**, 123-45.

7] Dye, R.A. (1998), "Investor Sophistication and Voluntary Disclosures", *Review of Accounting Studies*, **3**, 261-87

8] Fishman, M.J. and K.M. Hagerty (1997a), "Mandatory vs Voluntary Disclosure in Markets with Informed and Uninformed Customers", mimeo, Northwestern University.

9] Fishman, M.J. and K.M. Hagerty (1997b), "Mandatory Disclosure", New Palgrave Dictionary.

10] Frantz, P. (1997), "Discretionary Accounting Choices: A Debt-Covenants Based Signalling Approach", *Accounting and Business Research*, **27**, 99-110.

11] Fudenberg, D. and J. Tirole (1991), *Game Theory*, Cambridge, MA, MIT Press.

12] Gigler, F. (1994), "Self-Enforcing Voluntary Disclosures", *Journal of Accounting Research*, **32**, 224-40.

13] Hughes, P. and E. Schwartz (1988), "The LIFO-FIFO Choice: An Asymmetric Information Approach", *Journal of Accounting Research*, **10**(S), 41-58.

14] Jung, W. and Y. Kwong (1988), "Disclosure When the Market Is Unsure of Information Endowment of Managers", *Journal of Accounting Research,* **26**, 146-53.

15] Milgrom, P. (1981), "Good News and Bad News: Representation Theorems and Applications", *Bell Journal of Economics,* **12**, 380-91.

16] Palepu, K.G., V.L. Bernard and P.M. Healy (1996), *Business Analysis & Valuation,* Cincinnati, Ohio, South-Western College Publishing.

17] Rankine, G. and E.K. Stice (1997), "Accounting Rules and the Signalling Properties of 20 Percent Stock Dividends", *Accounting Review,* **72**, 23-46.

18] Scott, W.R. (1997), *Financial Accounting Theory,* New Jersey, Prentice Hall.

19] Shin, H.S. (1994), "News Management and the Value of Firms", *RAND Journal of Economics,* **25**, 58-71.

20] Sunder, S. (1997), *Theory of Accounting and Control,* Cincinnati, Ohio, South-Western College Publishing.

21] Verrecchia, R. (1983), "Discretionary Disclosures", *Journal of Accounting and Economics,* **5**, 179-94.

22] Wagenhofer, A. (1990), "Voluntary Disclosure with a Strategic Opponent", *Journal of Accounting and Economics,* **12**, 341-62.

# Chapter 6

# R&D and information sharing

Dan Sasaki[1]

## 6.1  Introduction

This chapter is devoted to the strategic role of information in oligopoly, and more broadly, in monotone games in general.

From an informational point of view, **research** and **development** can both be interpreted as acquisition of information. The distinction, if any, is that the former is oriented more towards the revelation of **common states** (e.g., the state of demand in an industry, which affects *all firms* operating in the industry) whilst the latter is concerned more about **independent states** (e.g., a firm's idiosyncratic cost structure). An alternative way of interpreting research and development is to consider research as revelation of states, whether common or independent, as opposed to development referring to any form of activity which is meant to make a transition from one state to another, again whether common or independent, such as enhancing the

[1]The author is most indebted to Luca Lambertini, for his patient encouragement and suggestions. Parts of the research project overviewed in this chapter have been presented at: Princeton University, October 1995; Institute of Economics, University of Copenhagen, March 1996; University of Lund, November 1996; 11th Conference on Game Theory and Applications at Bocconi University, June 1997; Faculty of Economics, University of Tokyo, September 1997; Tokyo Metropolitan University, September 1997; and University of Melbourne, September 1999. Generous financial assistance from Faculty of Economics and Commerce, University of Melbourne, and from School of Business and Economics, University of Exeter, should also be acknowledged. Much of the material presented in this chapter is on the state-of-the-art frontier of research which is still actively developing. The author assumes the sole responsibility for any remaining shortcomings found in this chapter, and is open to further comments and discussions which may help enhance future research projects.

demand in a market by investing in advertisement or reducing production costs by "developing" a new set of manufacturing technology.

The central focus of this chapter is to analyse information acquisition as strategic investment, whether called research, development, or anything else, without restricting attention to any specific material form in which such investment is carried out or to any other institutional specificities including the definitions of "R&D" in corporate accounting or patenting regulations. The reason why the chapter title nevertheless includes "research" and "development" is because oligopoly provides one of the best economic examples for this theoretical subject. The essence of the analysis presented in this chapter is potentially applicable to various situations other than oligopoly.

As is trivially understood, research in its strictest sense, that is, acquisition of information about common states, is a *public good* if the acquired information always becomes observable to other players. It is noteworthy that what is known as **information sharing** is a subject *by no means* confined to this rather trivial public good problem. Namely, it is far less obvious whether information acquisition about independent states, and acquisition of information that does not become immediately observable to other players, can still have some aspects of public good. In particular, the latter category is the key essence of information sharing theory.

Some terms and concepts are to be clarified in the beginning, as they can be (and indeed have been) used with different meanings depending upon authors and upon contexts. In section 6.2, the basic concepts of *common states* and *independent states* are explained. Then follows an extensive discussion on the **value of information** in sections 6.3 through 6.7. Some strategic aspects of voluntary information transmission, or **communication**, are discussed in section 6.8. Then finally, section 6.9 embeds information acquisition in a broader context of strategic investment in general, and relates it to the existing game-theoretic analysis on strategic investment. Section 6.10 briefly concludes the chapter.

## 6.2   Information

*Information* is one of the most context-dependent terms in economics. In an informal context, it is often used synonymously with "knowledge". In a statistical context, it refers to a certain kind of statistic, that is, a function of observed data. In a game-theoretic context, it can refer to one of the following two contents. One is "information" *about other players' actions*. The informational configuration of the game in this sense is referred to as **informational (im)perfection**. The other is "information" *about the* *structure of the game.* The game's informational configuration in this sense is referred to as **informational (in)completion**. The latter is the notion of information discussed throughout this chapter.

Later in section 6.8, strategic incentives for (or against) **information transmission** between players are discussed. In general, transmission of information *about actions* is referred to as **coordination**, whereas transmission of information *about states* is referred to as **revelation**. As this chapter is exclusively devoted to *state contingency*, the kind of information transmission discussed later in this chapter is *revelation*, not coordination.

**Uncertainty** is an alternative term for informational incompletion (beware, however, that this term is occasionally misused referring to informational imperfection). In game theory and decision theory, the most common practice in handling informational incompletion, or uncertainty, is to parametrise the payoff function(s) in terms of stochastic **states**. This idea originates from Harsanyi (1967-68, 1973), hence this formulation of uncertainty is often referred to as Harsanyi uncertainty.

Conventionally, stochastic states are categorised into the following two classes, depending upon the form of state contingency of payoffs. One is **common states**, *directly* affecting *all* (or, at least, more than one) players' payoffs. Let $J$ denote the set of players, and $a = \{a_j\}_{j \in J}$ the players' actions. Then, in the presence of a common state $\omega$, player $i$'s payoff ($i \in J$) can be defined as a *stochastic variable* $\pi_i(a\,;\omega)$, which is a function of $a$ and the common state $\omega$.

The other is **independent states**. A player-specific independent state $\omega_i$ directly affects only player $i$'s payoffs. Other players' payoffs are not directly affected by $\omega_i$ *per se*, albeit possibly affected *indirectly through player i's action* $a_i$. Player $i$'s payoff is defined as a stochastic variable $\pi_i(a\,;\omega_i)$, a function of $a$ and the player's own state $\omega_i$ which is often referred to as the player's **type**. Note that the term "independent states" does not automatically imply that the *probability distributions* of types $\omega_i$ and $\omega_j$ ($i, j \in J$, $i \neq j$) are independent across players.

Independent states can be viewed as a special case of common states, where the common state $\omega$ is **separable** as $\omega = \{\omega_i\}_{i \in J}$ so that $\pi_i$ is constant in $\omega_j$ ($j \neq i$). Viewed differently, however, common states can in turn be reinterpreted as a special case of independent states, where all players' types are (commonly known to be) identically equal, i.e., $\omega_i = \omega$ for all $i \in J$. In either interpretation, for the game to be well-defined, the **prior** probability distributions of states must be *commonly known to all players at the beginning of the game* (also see section 6.8).

More formally, a **state space** is defined by a triple $\langle \Omega, \Sigma, \mu \rangle$ where $\Omega$ is the set of all feasible states ($\Omega = \underset{i \in J}{\times} \Omega_i$ in the case of independent states), $\Sigma$ is a $\sigma$-algebra defined over $\Omega$, and $\mu$ is a (prior) probability measure defined over $\Sigma$. This state space is common knowledge among all players.

Finally, **information** is conceptualised as the formation of any **posterior** $\mu_i$, which is another probability measure defined over $\Sigma$. When $\mu_i$ differs across players, the game is said to involve **asymmetric information**.

Obviously, in order to materialise the relevance of information, there must be some *contingent actions* that can be taken after the acquisition of information (or the abstinence therefrom).

## 6.3   Information sharing

Information sharing in its narrowest sense is for more than one player of a game sharing the same piece of information. It can occur either cooperatively or noncooperatively. In a broader, less restrictive sense, information sharing can refer to those situations where one player's information affects the **value of information** (see section 6.4) for other players. In the latter sense, one player's information need not be the same as other players' information.

Noncooperative information sharing can occur either when multiple players independently acquire information, or when information is **transmitted** (or more specifically, **revealed**) from one player to another. The former is discussed in sections 6.6, 6.7 and the latter in section 6.8 of this chapter.

Cooperative information sharing can occur either when there exist common benefits among players from precommitting to make certain pieces of information commonly known, or when players seek to *share costs* of information acquisition. The latter is important in many economic activities including **research joint ventures**,[2] but is outside the scope of this chapter which is devoted specifically to information in its standard game-theoretic sense.

---

[2] Even though investment decisions inside a joint venture are made cooperatively, participation in such a joint venture is still up to each individual firm's noncooperative decisions. Hence in general, an oligopoly game with the prospect of joint research can still involve an element of noncooperativeness. Thereby the *social* desirability of such cooperation hinges upon the delicate balance between the cost-saving benefit and the anticompetitiveness. See Katz (1986), d'Aspremont and Jacquemin (1988, 1990), Katz and Ordover (1990), Kamien *et al.* (1992), Suzumura (1992), Amir (2000) and Amir *et al.* (2000) for the cost issue (usually known as *effort duplication*), Grossman and Shapiro (1986), Brodley (1990), Jorde and Teece (1990), Shapiro and Willig (1990), Tao and Wu (1997) for theoretical policy recommendations, the National Cooperative Research Act (U.S.), EC Commission (1990), Goto and Wakasugi (1988) for antitrust issues. As for the interlink between joint R&D and tacit collusion in ensuing marketing stages, see Martin (1995), Lambertini *et al.* (1998, 2002) and Cabral (2000).

Game-theoretic literature on information sharing is extensive, covering both pure theory and economic applications including topics closely related to industrial organisation. Founding contributions include Novshek and Son- nenschein (1982), Clarke (1983a, 1983b), Singh and Vives (1984), Vives (1984), Gal-Or (1985, 1986), Sakai (1985, 1990, 1991), Okuno-Fujiwara *et al.* (1990), *inter alia*. Existing literature, however, offers relatively little cov- erage on the **hierarchy of information**. It turns out that theoretical tools available to this date are somewhat inadequate for this purpose altogether. This chapter provides only a minimal amount of theoretical discussion, with a minimal level of mathematical formality, in sections 6.4 through 6.8 in order to minimise the unnecessary distraction from economic interpretations. The potential theoretical complication is only briefly described in section 6.10, as it is beyond the immediate scope of industrial organization.

# 6.4   Value of information

The value of information is defined as the increment in a player's expected payoff when the player acquires information. More specifically, the value of that "information" which entails the transition from player $i$'s prior $\mu$ (which is in fact common across all players) to the player's posterior $\mu_i$ is defined as the difference between the player's expected payoff resulting from the posterior $\mu_i$ and that when the player does not acquire $\mu_i$ and remains with the un-updated prior $\mu$.

This definition is unambiguous when embedded in a single decision maker's problem. It may require, on the other hand, additional clarification when embedded in a multi-player game. This is because a player's information acquisition generally affects the value of information for other players, in the following two ways.

## 6.4.1   Superadditivity and subadditivity

Intuitively, super-/subadditivity of the value of information is about whether a player's information acquisition makes other players' information acquisi- tion more/less valuable. That is, information $\mu_i$ may have a higher/lower value for player $i$ when another player $j$ has information $\mu_j$ than when player $j$ has not updated the prior $\mu$. This *pairwise* notion of superadditivity and subadditivity of the value of information is used throughout this chapter.[3]

---

[3]This chapter follows the notions of super-/subadditivity, super-/submodularity, and strategic complementarity/substitutability as in Fudenberg and Tirole (1991).

Suppose, *ceteris paribus*, player $i$'s expected payoff is $\bar{\pi}_i[\rho_i, \rho_j]$ when these two players are informed with probabilities $\rho_i$, $\rho_j$ respectively, meaning that player $i$ has the posterior $\mu_i$ with probability $\rho_i$ and has not updated the prior $\mu$ with probability $1 - \rho_i$, and likewise that player $j$ has $\mu_j$ with probability $\rho_j$ and $\mu$ with probability $1 - \rho_j$. Then for player $i$, information $\mu_i$ has the value

$$\bar{v}_i[\rho_j] = \bar{\pi}_i[1, \rho_j] - \bar{\pi}_i[0, \rho_j]. \tag{6.1}$$

The value of information for player $i$ is said to be (strictly) **superadditive** to player $j$'s information if $\bar{v}_i'[\rho_j] > 0$, **subadditive** if $\bar{v}_i'[\rho_j] < 0$.

## 6.4.2   Hierarchy of information

In addition, in a multi-player game, the value of information can be affected by whether a player's information acquisition is observed by other players, and whether such observation is observed by others, and whether such observation of observation is observed by others, and so on.

Consider a two-player game for simplicity, where the two players simultaneously (in the sense of *mutually independently*) decide whether to acquire information or not. Let $\rho_i^0$ be the (true) probability that player $i$ is "informed" (has the posterior $\mu_i$), and $\rho_i^k$ denote player $i$'s belief about player $j$'s belief $\rho_j^{k-1}$, where $\{i, j\} = \{1, 2\}$, $k = 1, 2, 3, \ldots$. The expected equilibrium payoffs resulting from the **hierarchy of beliefs** $\rho = \{\rho_1^k, \rho_2^k\}_{k=0}^{\infty}$ are denoted by

$$\bar{\pi}_i[\rho] = \bar{\pi}_i \left[ \begin{array}{c} \rho_i^0, \rho_i^1, \rho_i^2, \ldots \\ \rho_j^0, \rho_j^1, \rho_j^2, \ldots \end{array} \right]. \tag{6.2}$$

When information acquisition is perfectly observable,

$$\rho_i^{2k} = \rho_j^{2k-1} = \begin{cases} 0 & \text{if player } i \text{ is uninformed,} \\ 1 & \text{if player } i \text{ is informed,} \end{cases} \quad \text{for all } k = 1, 2, 3, \ldots \tag{6.3}$$

hence the value of information is

$$\bar{v}_i[\rho_i^1, \rho_j^1] = \rho_j^0 \left( \bar{\pi}_i[1, 1] - \bar{\pi}_i[1, 0] \right) + (1 - \rho_j^0) \left( \bar{\pi}_i[0, 1] - \bar{\pi}_i[0, 0] \right). \tag{6.4}$$

On the other hand, when information acquisition is mutually unobservable, $\{\rho_1^k, \rho_2^k\}_{k=1}^{\infty}$ stay unaffected by players' information acquisition. Hence the value of information is simply

$$\bar{v}_i \left[ \{\rho_i^k\}_{k=1}^{\infty}, \{\rho_j^k\}_{k=0}^{\infty} \right] = \bar{\pi}_i \left[ \begin{array}{c} 1, \rho_i^1, \rho_i^2, \ldots \\ \rho_j^0, \rho_j^1, \rho_j^2, \ldots \end{array} \right] - \bar{\pi}_i \left[ \begin{array}{c} 0, \rho_i^1, \rho_i^2, \ldots \\ \rho_j^0, \rho_j^1, \rho_j^2, \ldots \end{array} \right]. \tag{6.5}$$

Note that, formally, $\rho_i^1$ is a subjective *probability distribution* of $\rho_j^0$. Likewise, $\rho_i^2$ is a probability distribution of $\rho_j^1$, i.e., a probability distribution over probability distributions of $\rho_i^0$, and so on. This formality, however, shall often be ignored in this chapter by treating $\rho_i^k$ ($k = 1, 2, 3, ...$) and its (subjective) mean interchangeably. This treatment, albeit mathematically informal, serves to facilitate analytical operations in section 6.6 (also see section 6.10).

# 6.5 Monotone games with incomplete information

For simplicity, assume $\Omega$ to be a subset of the real line. The belief held by player $i$ ($i \in J$), based upon which the player chooses an action $a_i$, is defined by a cumulative distribution function $y_i[\cdot]$ (which may or may not differ from the common prior $\mu$). Based upon this belief, the player's best reply function can be defined and denoted heretofore by $\alpha_i(a_{-i}; y_i)$, where $a_{-i} = \{a_j\}_{j \in (J \setminus \{i\})}$. A (strictly) **monotone game** is defined as a game satisfying the following.

- **Monotone Externality:** For any ordered pair of players $(i, j) \subseteq J$, either

$$\frac{\partial}{\partial a_j} \pi_i(a; \omega) > 0 \quad \text{for all} \quad a, \omega \tag{E+}$$

or

$$\frac{\partial}{\partial a_j} \pi_i(a; \omega) < 0 \quad \text{for all} \quad a, \omega \tag{E-}$$

This definition does not preclude the possibility that there can be a pair $i, j$ such that E+ holds for the order $(i, j)$ whilst E− holds for the order $(j, i)$. Likewise in the following *monotone modularity*.

- **Monotone Modularity:** For any ordered pair of players $(i, j) \subseteq J$, either

$$\frac{\partial}{\partial a_j} \alpha_i(a_{-i}; y_i[\cdot]) > 0 \quad \text{for all} \quad a_{-i}, y_i[\cdot] \tag{M+}$$

or

$$\frac{\partial}{\partial a_j} \alpha_i(a_{-i}; y_i[\cdot]) < 0 \quad \text{for all} \quad a_{-i}, y_i[\cdot] \tag{M-}$$

In particular, if M+ (resp., M−) holds for both $(i, j)$ and $(j, i)$, then the game is **supermodular** (resp., **submodular**) between players $i$ and $j$.

- **Monotone State:** For every player $i \in J$, whenever $y_i^1[\cdot]$ first-order stochastic dominates $y_i^2[\cdot]$, either

$$\alpha_i(a_{-i}\,;y_i^1[\cdot]) > \alpha_i(a_{-i}\,;y_i^2[\cdot]) \quad \text{for all} \ \ a_{-i} \qquad \text{(S+)}$$

or

$$\alpha_i(a_{-i}\,;y_i^1[\cdot]) < \alpha_i(a_{-i}\,;y_i^2[\cdot]) \quad \text{for all} \ \ a_{-i} \qquad \text{(S$-$)}$$

In addition, for analytical simplicity, we often confine our attention to those games which are **asymptotically stable**. A sufficient condition for asymptotic stability is for the reaction matrix

$$\left( \left( \frac{\partial}{\partial a_j}\, \alpha_i(a_{-i}\,;y_i[\cdot]) \right)_{i \in J} \right)_{j \in J} \qquad (6.6)$$

to be *positive definite*, where the main diagonal elements $\partial\left[\alpha_i(a_{-i}\,;y_i[\cdot])\right]/\partial a_i$ are reset to unity.

Monotone games can be found in many economic situations, especially in industrial organisation. Oligopoly games, when $\omega$ is a demand index, give typical examples of monotone games. Cournot oligopoly is a monotone game with E$-$, M$-$, S+ whilst Bertrand oligopoly is a monotone game with E+, M+, S+, insofar as firms supply *substitute products*. If firms are supplying *complement products*, a Cournot game has E+, M+, S+ whilst a Bertrand game has E$-$, M$-$, S+. If a duopolistic market is served by a quantity-setting firm and a price-setting firm supplying substitute products, then this duopoly game has E$-$, M$-$, S+ for the price setter (meaning $(i,j) =$ (price setter, quantity setter)) and E+, M+, S+ for the quantity setter.

Examples of monotone games are by no means confined to oligopoly games. *Oligopsony* is another class of monotone games in economics. Regarding $\omega$ as a *supply* index, "Cournot" (quantity bidding) oligopsony is a monotone game with E$-$, M$-$, S+, whereas "Bertrand" (price bidding) oligopsony has E$-$, M+, S$-$.

# 6.6 Information about common states

## 6.6.1 Preliminaries

Information sharing in its narrow sense refers to sharing information about common states. A typical economic example of such a situation is oligopoly with **demand uncertainty** (see, e.g., Sasaki, 2001). The state of demand is a common state, because it *directly affects all firms' profits*.

Acquisition of information about common states can be in one of the following two categories. One is to acquire it *overtly*, that is, the fact that a player has obtained information becomes commonly observable, even though the *content* of information may not be commonly shared. Namely, the state becomes **private information** in its strict sense (see Levin and Ponssard, 1979). In oligopoly with demand uncertainty, for example, this corresponds to the case where firms decide whether or not to set up pilot shops in order to assess the demand level in the market.

The other is to acquire information about the state *covertly*, i.e., the fact that a player has obtained information remains unobservable to other players. This is referred to as **secret information** (again see Levin and Ponssard, 1979). In the example of oligopoly with uncertain demand, this corresponds to the case where firms decide whether or not to conduct a consumer survey either by phone or by mail.

## 6.6.2 Simplified model

For analytical convenience, consider a two-player game where the payoffs are quadratic functions of actions and states. This can be viewed as a simple approximation of more general payoff structures, insofar as payoff functions are *smooth* (in the sense of twice continuous differentiability) in actions and states, and neither the stochastic fluctuations of states nor the contingent variations in optimal actions are too large to allow second-order Taylor approximation.

For extra simplicity, assume that the pure action space for each player is the real line (or a subset thereof), and that the state space is also unidimensional. The payoff for player $i$ can be expressed as

$$\pi_i(a_i, a_j; \omega) = [a_i \, a_j \, \omega \, 1] \begin{bmatrix} \pi_{i,i,i} & \pi_{i,i,j} & \pi_{i,i,s} & \pi_{i,i,k} \\ \pi_{i,j,i} & \pi_{i,j,j} & \pi_{i,j,s} & \pi_{i,j,k} \\ \pi_{i,s,i} & \pi_{i,s,j} & \pi_{i,s,s} & \pi_{i,s,k} \\ \pi_{i,k,i} & \pi_{i,k,j} & \pi_{i,k,s} & \pi_{i,k,k} \end{bmatrix} \begin{bmatrix} a_i \\ a_j \\ \omega \\ 1 \end{bmatrix} \tag{6.7}$$

where $\pi_{i,i,i} < 0$ in order to ensure an interior equilibrium, $\{i,j\} = \{1,2\}$. Also, without loss of generality we can assume that *the coefficient matrix is symmetric*.

The game consists of two stages. In the first stage, each player decides independently whether to observe the state. For further simplicity, each player can either observe the precise realisation of the state $\omega$, or not observe it at all and stay with the common prior. Costs associated with this information acquisition are disregarded for the time being for analytical simplicity,

yet can make the decision either for or against information acquisition more
realistic and less trivial (see subsection 6.6.5). The second stage is for the
players to choose, again simultaneously, their actions.

Due to the quadratic structure of the payoff function, the payoff maximising first-order condition becomes *linear*, thereby the expectation operator
becomes *separable*, i.e.

$$\frac{\partial}{\partial a_i} E\left[\pi_i(a_i, a_j; \omega)\right] = E\left[\frac{\partial}{\partial a_i}\pi_i(a_i, a_j; \omega)\right] = 0. \qquad (6.8)$$

It is for this analytical convenience that the quadratic form is chosen.

### 6.6.3   Private but not secret information acquisition

Assume that information acquisition is *mutually observable*. Let $a_i[1, \rho_i^1; \omega]$
denote player $i$'s equilibrium action when the player is informed of $\omega$, and
$a_i[0, \rho_i^1]$ when uninformed of $\omega$, given any belief $\rho_i^1$ about the other player
$j$'s information.

By the assumption that information acquisition is mutually observable,
$\rho_i^1 = 1$ if player $j$ is informed, $\rho_i^1 = 0$ if player $j$ is uninformed of $\omega$. On the
other hand, $\rho_i^0$ denotes the *ex ante* probability that player $i$ is informed of
the state $\omega$.

The first-order conditions are:

$$a_i[1, 1; \omega] = -\frac{\pi_{i,i,j}}{\pi_{i,i,i}} a_j[1, 1; \omega] - \frac{\pi_{i,i,s}}{\pi_{i,i,i}}\omega - \frac{\pi_{i,i,k}}{\pi_{i,i,i}};$$

$$a_i[1, 0; \omega] = -\frac{\pi_{i,i,j}}{\pi_{i,i,i}} a_j[0, 1] - \frac{\pi_{i,i,s}}{\pi_{i,i,i}}\omega - \frac{\pi_{i,i,k}}{\pi_{i,i,i}};$$

$$a_i[0, 1] = -\frac{\pi_{i,i,j}}{\pi_{i,i,i}} E\left[a_j[1, 0; \omega]\right] - \frac{\pi_{i,i,s}}{\pi_{i,i,i}}E[\omega] - \frac{\pi_{i,i,k}}{\pi_{i,i,i}}; \qquad (6.9)$$

$$a_i[0, 0] = -\frac{\pi_{i,i,j}}{\pi_{i,i,i}} E\left[a_j[0, 0]\right] - \frac{\pi_{i,i,s}}{\pi_{i,i,i}}E[\omega] - \frac{\pi_{i,i,k}}{\pi_{i,i,i}}.$$

Solving these four equations with four unknowns, the value of information
$v_i[\rho_j^0]$ is identified as

$$v_i[\rho_j^0] = \rho_j^0 E\left[\pi_i(a_i[1, 1; \omega], a_j[1, 1; \omega]; \omega) - \pi_i(a_i[0, 1], a_j[1, 0; \omega]; \omega)\right]$$

$$+ (1 - \rho_j^0)E\pi_i\left[(a_i[1, 0; \omega], a_j[0, 1]; \omega) - \pi_i(a_i[0, 0], a_j[0, 0]; \omega)\right]$$

$$= \left(\frac{(\pi_{i,j,j}\pi_{j,j,i}{}^2 - \pi_{i,i,i}\pi_{j,j,j}{}^2)(\pi_{i,i,s}\pi_{j,j,j} - \pi_{i,i,j}\pi_{j,j,s})}{\pi_{j,j,j}{}^2(\pi_{i,i,i}\pi_{j,j,j} - \pi_{i,i,j}\pi_{j,j,i})^2}\right)\rho_j^0$$

$$+\frac{2\pi_{j,j,i}(\pi_{i,i,s}\pi_{j,j,j} - \pi_{i,i,j}\pi_{j,j,s})(\pi_{i,j,s}\pi_{j,j,j} - \pi_{i,j,j}\pi_{j,j,s})}{\pi_{j,j,j}{}^2(\pi_{i,i,i}\pi_{j,j,j} - \pi_{i,i,j}\pi_{j,j,i})} \rho_j^0 \qquad (6.10)$$

$$\left. - \frac{\pi_{i,i,s}{}^2}{\pi_{i,i,i}}(1 - \rho_j^0)\right) \mathrm{Var}[\omega].$$

The determination of the sign of $v_i'[\rho_j^0]$ may seem slightly complicated, yet essentially hinges upon the signs of $\pi_{i,i,s}$ and $\pi_{i,i,j}$. In this regard, note first that each player's action can be "normalised" so as to make $\pi_{i,i,s} \geq 0$ for all players. Given this normalisation, in conjunction with the standard regularity assumption that $-\pi_{i,i,i} \gg |\pi_{i,i,j}|$ (which ensures asymptotic stability), the value of information for player $i$ tends to be:

- superadditive to player $j$'s information, i.e., $v_i'[\rho_j^0] > 0$, if $\pi_{i,i,j} > 0$;

- subadditive to player $j$'s information, i.e., $v_i'[\rho_j^0] < 0$, if $\pi_{i,i,j} < 0$.

In words, super-/subadditivity of the value of information is parallel to **super-/submodularity** of actions, respectively.

These properties can be given the following geometric intuition, which is illustrated in figure 6.1. In a **supermodular game**, where players' actions are mutually **strategic complements**, the state-dependent variation in player $i$'s actions is larger when the other player $j$ is also informed of the state (the thick horizontal arrow in the left diagram of figure 6.1) than when player $j$ is uninformed of the state and thus takes the same action irrespective of the state (the thin horizontal arrow in the left diagram of figure 6.1).

This intuitively indicates that player $i$'s utilisation of information about the state is heavier when the other player $j$ is also informed of the state, than when player $j$ is uninformed. Hence the *superadditivity* property characterising the value of information.[4]

In a **submodular game**, where players' actions are mutually **strategic substitutes**, the state-dependent variation in player $i$'s actions is smaller when the other player $j$ is also informed of the state (the thick horizontal arrow in the right diagram of figure 6.1) than when player $j$ is uninformed of the state and thus takes the same action irrespective of the state (the thin horizontal arrow in the right diagram of figure 6.1). The value of information hereby becomes *subadditive*.

---

[4]For more on strategic substitutability and complementarity, see Bulow *et al.* (1985).

**Figure 6.1:**   Super-/subadditive value of information

Supermodular (strategic complements)   Submodular (strategic substitutes)
Superadditive value of information        Subadditive value of information

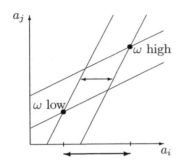
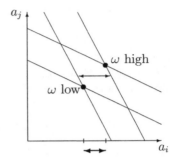

## 6.6.4   Secret information acquisition

Assume, alternatively, that information acquisition is mutually *unobservable*. Let $a_i[1, \rho_i^1, \rho_i^2, \dots ; \omega]$ denote player $i$'s second-stage equilibrium action when the player is informed of $\omega$, and $a_i[0, \rho_i^1, \rho_i^2, \dots]$ when uninformed of $\omega$, given any belief $\rho$. The first-order conditions for player $i$'s equilibrium action given $\rho = \widehat{\rho}$ is

$$a_i[1, \widehat{\rho}_i^1, \widehat{\rho}_i^2, \dots ; \omega] = -\frac{\pi_{i,i,j}}{\pi_{i,i,i}} \left( \widehat{\rho}_i^1 a_j[1, \widehat{\rho}_i^2, \widehat{\rho}_i^3, \dots ; \omega] \right.$$
$$\left. + (1 - \widehat{\rho}_i^1) a_j[0, \widehat{\rho}_i^2, \widehat{\rho}_i^3, \dots] \right) - \frac{\pi_{i,i,s}}{\pi_{i,i,i}} \omega - \frac{\pi_{i,i,k}}{\pi_{i,i,i}} ;$$

$$a_i[0, \widehat{\rho}_i^1, \widehat{\rho}_i^2, \dots] = -\frac{\pi_{i,i,j}}{\pi_{i,i,i}} \left( \widehat{\rho}_i^1 E\left[a_j[1, \widehat{\rho}_i^2, \widehat{\rho}_i^3, \dots ; \omega]\right] \right. \tag{6.11}$$
$$\left. + (1 - \widehat{\rho}_i^1) a_j[0, \widehat{\rho}_i^2, \widehat{\rho}_i^3, \dots] \right) - \frac{\pi_{i,i,s}}{\pi_{i,i,i}} E[\omega] - \frac{\pi_{i,i,k}}{\pi_{i,i,i}}$$

where $\{i, j\} = \{1, 2\}$. For a generic belief $\widehat{\rho}$ this system of four simultaneous equations is unidentifiable, as it involves as many as eight unknowns. However, for any system of beliefs which are internally and mutually consistent, in the sense of satisfying

$$\widehat{\rho}_i^{k+1} = \widehat{\rho}_j^k \qquad \text{for all } k = 1, 2, 3, \dots, \tag{6.12}$$

the foregoing simultaneous equations reduce to an identifiable system of four equations with four unknowns. The value of information is thereby identified as

$$v_i[\widehat{\rho}_i^1, \widehat{\rho}_j^1] = \widehat{\rho}_i^1 E\left[\pi_i(a_i[1, \widehat{\rho}_i^1; \omega], a_j[1, \widehat{\rho}_j^1; \omega]; \omega)\right.$$

$$-\pi_i(a_i[0, \widehat{\rho}_i^1], a_j[1, \widehat{\rho}_j^1; \omega]; \omega)] + (1 - \widehat{\rho}_i^1)\left[E\pi_i(a_i[1, \widehat{\rho}_i^1; \omega], a_j[0, \widehat{\rho}_j^1]; \omega)\right.$$

$$-\pi_i(a_i[0, \widehat{\rho}_i^1], a_j[0, \widehat{\rho}_j^1]; \omega)]$$

$$= \frac{-\pi_{i,i,i}(\pi_{i,i,s}\pi_{j,j,j} - \pi_{i,i,j}\pi_{j,j,s}\widehat{\rho}_i^1)^2}{(\pi_{i,i,i}\pi_{j,j,j} - \pi_{i,i,j}\pi_{j,j,i}\widehat{\rho}_i^1\widehat{\rho}_i^2)^2}\mathrm{Var}[\omega]. \tag{6.13}$$

If the monotone game is **asymptotically stable**, $\pi_{i,i,i}\pi_{j,j,j} > |\pi_{i,i,j}\pi_{j,j,i}|$, hence

$$\mathrm{sign}\left[\frac{\partial v_i[\widehat{\rho}_i^1, \widehat{\rho}_j^1]}{\partial \widehat{\rho}_i^2}\right] = \mathrm{sign}[\pi_{i,i,j}\pi_{j,j,i}] \tag{6.14}$$

insofar as $\widehat{\rho}_i^1 > 0$. This suggests that, as $\widehat{\rho}_j^2$ increases, i.e., when player $j$ believes that player $i$ is likely to be informed, the value of information for player $i$:

- increases if $\pi_{i,i,j}\pi_{j,j,i} > 0$, as in Cournot oligopoly (where $\pi_{i,i,j} < 0$, $\pi_{j,j,i} < 0$ if firms are substitute producers, or $\pi_{i,i,j} > 0$, $\pi_{j,j,i} > 0$ if they are complement producers) and Bertrand oligopoly (where $\pi_{i,i,j} > 0$, $\pi_{j,j,i} > 0$ if firms are substitute producers, or $\pi_{i,i,j} < 0$, $\pi_{j,j,i} < 0$ if they are complement producers);

- decreases if $\pi_{i,i,j}\pi_{j,j,i} < 0$, as in oligopoly where one firm sets a price and the other a quantity.

A geometric intuition of these results is provided in figure 6.2. If the second-stage actions are either mutually supermodular or mutually submodular, the variation in $a_i$ when player $i$ *unacquires* information given player $j$ believing that player $i$ is informed (thick arrows in the left two diagrams of figure 6.2) is larger than the variation in $a_i$ when player $i$ acquires information given player $j$ believing that player $i$ is uninformed (thin arrows in the left two diagrams of figure 6.2). If the second-stage actions are a strategic complement for one player and a strategic substitute for the other, then the value of information for player $i$ is lower when player $j$ believes player $i$ to be informed (thick arrows in the right diagram of figure 6.2) than when player $j$ believes player $i$ to be uninformed (thin arrows in the right diagram of figure 6.2).

**Figure 6.2:**   Value of information and hierarchy of beliefs

Mutually supermodular          Mutually submodular
$(\pi_{i,i,j}\pi_{j,j,i} > 0)$          $(\pi_{i,i,j}\pi_{j,j,i} > 0)$

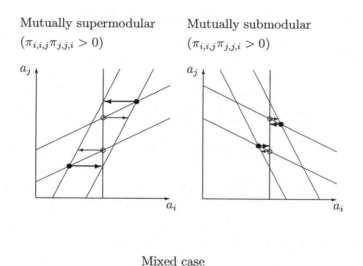

Mixed case
$(\pi_{i,i,j}\pi_{j,j,i} < 0)$

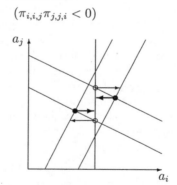

The effect of $\widehat{\rho}_j^2$, which determines superadditivity or subadditivity of the value of information, is slightly more complicated, although the essence is similar to the previous case of private (non secret) information acquisition. Assuming $\pi_{i,i,s}\pi_{j,j,j} < -|\pi_{i,i,j}\pi_{j,j,i}|$, superadditivity or subadditivity depends largely upon the sign of $\pi_{i,i,j}$. For instance, in symmetric Cournot oligopoly, if firms are substitute producers then $\pi_{i,i,j} < 0$, hence the value of information tends to be subadditive, otherwise if firms are complement producers then $\pi_{i,i,j} > 0$ and thus the value of information tends to be superadditive.

### 6.6.5 Discussion

The above analysis shows that the value of information is affected by the **monotone comparative statics** of the ensuing stage-game, in which actions are taken contingent upon the acquired information.

When information acquisition requires costs, each player's rational decision in the first stage is to acquire information if and only if its value exceeds the costs. This implies that, when information acquisition costs are relatively close to the value of information, there can be *multiple equilibria* as follows.

- When the value of information is *superadditive* between players, a player's information acquisition encourages another's information acquisition. Hence, there can be an *informed equilibrium* where both (all) players acquire information, and an *uninformed equilibrium* where neither player does (and also a stochastically mixed equilibrium).

- When the value of information is *subadditive*, a player's information acquisition discourages another's information acquisition. Hence, there can be multiple equilibria in each of which different players acquire information (aside from a mixed equilibrium).

This further suggests that, when there are many pieces of information available, superadditivity of the value of information tends to induce players to acquire the same set of information. This leads to *informational clustering*, or **ranked information** (the term frequently used in financial theory and general equilibrium theory). On the other hand, subadditivity of the value of information tends to induce different players to opt for disjoint sets of information, leading to **differential information**.

## 6.7 Information about independent states

Somewhat intriguingly, it is ambiguous whether common states are special cases of independent states, or *vice versa* (see section 6.2). Whichever interpretation is applied, it deserves heightened attention that "information" about independent states can refer to two distinct contents. One is for a player to uncover his or her *own* independent state. Development of a new product, or a new production technology, can be a prime example of this category, where the firm obtains information about its own cost structure. The other is for a player to obtain information about *other players'* types.

In industrial organisation, the acquisition of information about competing firms' cost structures can be done either by spying, by voluntary disclosure, or by forming multi-firm joint ventures.

Accordingly, information sharing can also refer to different contents. It can be for player $i$ to acquire player $j$'s idiosyncratic type $\omega_j$ and for player $j$ to uncover player $i$'s type $\omega_i$. It can also be for player $i$ to learn about her own type and for player $j$ to learn about his own type. Or alternatively, it can refer to players $i$ and $j$ sharing information about player $i$'s type, or about a third player's type.

Applying directly the analysis from the previous section, the following can be shown.

- Player $i$'s information acquisition about the player's own type $\omega_i$ and player $j$'s information acquisition about player $i$'s type $\omega_i$ always have mutually independent values, that is, their values are neither superadditive nor subadditive. This is because player $j$'s payoff function is not directly dependent upon $\omega_i$ so that, in the notation from the previous section, the coefficient $\pi_{j,j,s}$ is zero.

- For the same reason, player $i$'s information acquisition about player $j$'s type $\omega_j$ and player $j$'s information acquisition about player $i$'s type $\omega_i$ have mutually independent values.

- Player $i$'s information acquisition about her own type $\omega_i$ and player $j$'s information acquisition about $\omega_j$ have mutually independent values insofar as the *prior distributions of these types are uncorrelated*. If these types are positively correlated, the values of information are either superadditive or subadditive when the ensuing actions are supermodular or submodular, respectively. This is intuitively similar to the case of common states: in the limit, if types are *perfectly correlated*, then they reduce into common states. The opposite holds when types are negatively correlated.

## 6.8   Dual roles of communication

Sections 6.5 through 6.7 have been devoted to *independent information acquisition* by each player in isolation. A different angle in studying economics of information is to focus on *information transmission*, or **revelation** (see section 6.2), between players.

## 6.8.1 Preliminaries

Generally, the strategic effects of information transmission are twofold. Its obvious direct effect is to give the receiver that specific piece of information which the sender wants to convey, provided that the message be truthful and credible, if not *verifiable*. This in fact brings a side effect, which is to inform the receiver of the fact that the sender has the information.

These two sides of a coin act differently depending upon the situation *prior* to the cheap talk. The former, the direct effect, emerges when the receiver has been uninformed prior to the message. Otherwise, if the receiver happens to have the same information independently, this transmitted information becomes redundant and thus has no direct effect. The latter, the side effect, is present whether the receiver is informed or uninformed beforehand. Furthermore, the former is always unverifiable, whereas the latter *is* effectively verifiable when the receiver is previously informed, even though the message is unverifiable *per se*.

Hence the main question here is: does cheap talk occur more easily when the receiver is relatively poorly informed so that he is in need of informational help, or when he is relatively well informed? A typical and simple analytical example of a situation where players have conflicting interests in information acquisition is the following.

## 6.8.2 The sender-receiver model

The state $\omega$ is a real number, of which the unconditional c.d.f. is $F(\omega)$ and is commonly known. There is an event V, conditional upon which the c.d.f. of $\omega$ becomes $V(\omega)$. The prior probability that this event occurs is $v$. Assume that $V(\cdot)$ first-order stochastic dominates $F(\cdot)$.

The game involves two players, referred to as the sender and the receiver hereinafter, and consists of two stages. At the very beginning of the game, event V randomly may or may not take place. Conditional upon the event V, at the beginning of the first stage, the sender and the receiver are exogenously and independently informed of the event with probabilities $s$ and $r$, respectively. In the first stage of the game, the sender can send either a message "V" or no message to the receiver. The message itself is unverifiable in either case. The information structure can be summarised by the tree in figure 6.3. Thick arrows indicate truthful information transmission.

The second stage is a simultaneous-move *monotone game* as defined in section 6.5, where each player's pure action space is the real line, or a subset thereof.

It can be shown that if there is a triple $(s, r, v)$ for which a truth-telling equilibrium exists, then there is an $r^* \in (0,1)$ such that

- there is an $s^* \in (0,1)$ such that there exists a truth-telling equilibrium for any $s \in [s^*, 1)$, $r \in [r^*, 1)$ and $v \in (0,1)$;

- there is a $v^* \in (0,1)$ such that there exists a truth-telling equilibrium for any $s \in (0,1)$, $r \in [r^*, 1)$ and $v \in (0, v^*]$.

**Figure 6.3:** The first stage of the sender-receiver game

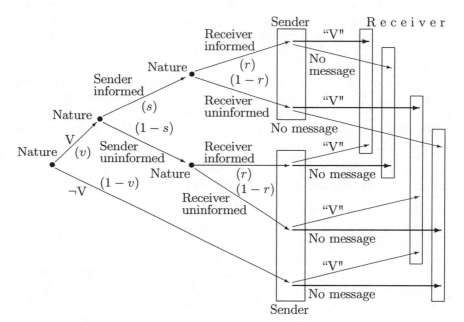

### 6.8.3 Discussion

By construction, a monotone game provides systematic incentives for the sender either always to overstate or always to understate the state (no pun intended). This is why truthful revelation is strategically unsustainable in the sheer absence of verifiability.

When information is shared, i.e., when the receiver already has the same piece of information as the sender does, it serves to restore verifiability. Hence it can, under some conditions, restore incentive compatibility of voluntary communication.

Also, given that information is already shared, the main informative content of inter-player communication is no longer the revelation of state information *per se*, but the transmission of higher-order hierarchical information. Viewed in this way, information sharing not only affects the value of information but also the content of informational revelation.

# 6.9 Information acquisition as strategic investment

The existing literature on strategic investment relies mostly upon the framework of *monotone comparative statics*. The seminal paper by Fudenberg and Tirole (1984) shows the relation between investment incentives and strategic characteristics of the contemplated investment, i.e., whether investment leads to more aggressive actions or less aggressive actions later on.

Undoubtedly, information acquisition can be viewed as a kind of investment. Also, as has been shown throughout this chapter, it certainly brings strategic effects when embedded in games. Hence, information acquisition in games can qualify as strategic investment. However, there is a certain degree of difficulty in applying the traditional monotone comparative statics to strategic information acquisition. This is due to the fact that, even in monotone games, information acquisition does not make the player's later actions uniformly more aggressive or uniformly less aggressive.

This is precisely the essence of information acquisition: it is for the player to determine whether to play aggressively or not. This prevents the traditional analytical framework of monotone comparative statics from being applied directly to strategic information acquisition in general.

In other words, information acquisition (whether strategic or not) is a device which enables the decision maker to choose the state-dependent optimal level of "aggression". If, on the other hand, the decision maker decides not to invest in information acquisition, then by rational expectation, he/she should choose an "unbiased" level of action. This is why, *on average*, information acquisition entails neither overaction nor underaction.

Viewed differently, the investment in information acquisition requires *second-order* monotone comparative statics, as opposed to most of the other kinds of strategic investment being analysed by means of *first-order* monotone comparative statics.

## 6.10   Conclusion

This chapter has taken a brief game-theoretic (albeit mathematically informal) overview on information acquisition in a specific but fairly broad class of state-contingent games. The qualitative relation between the value of information and the monotone comparative statics of those actions which are to depend upon the acquired information about the state(s) can be applied in many economic games including some of the most typical industrial organisation models.

In addition to familiar industrial economics applications, state-contingent games leave immense room for further theoretical research. From the standpoint of decision theory, state contingency has a potential to create logical inconsistency, especially when modelled with an infinite hierarchy of beliefs. In standard decision theory and game theory, *all players must share a common prior* about the state distribution; otherwise the initial node of the decision tree cannot be well-defined. More structurally, in terms of the state generating process, the true distribution of states can be drawn randomly from a distribution of distributions. Then, all players must share a common prior about the distribution of distributions. Likewise, they must share a common prior about the distribution of distributions of distributions, and so on. Namely, the common prior must encompass the whole of the infinite hierarchy of beliefs. However, from the point of view of the state generating process, every extra order added to this hierarchy of distributions adds a chance node which *precedes* the existing (sub)tree in which all the lower-order beliefs and distributions are embedded. Hence, an infinite hierarchy of distributions means that the tree extends *infinitely backwards*, preponing the initial node into the "infinite past". This, too, precludes a well-defined initial node. Hence an initial node can *never* be well-defined!

This potential complication has been conveniently avoided in this chapter, by keeping the hierarchical structure deliberately vague. This is because the main focus of the chapter (and of the book) should be on industrial organisation rather than more general game theory and decision theory.

## References

1] Amir, R. (2000), "Modelling Imperfectly Appropriable R&D Via Spillovers", *International Journal of Industrial Organization*, **18**, 1013-32.
2] Amir, M., R. Amir and J. Jin (2000), "Sequencing R&D Decisions in a Two-Period Duopoly with Spillovers", *Economic Theory*, **15**, 297-317.

3] Brodley, J.F. (1990), "Antitrust Law and Innovation Cooperation", *Journal of Economic Perspectives*, **4**, 97-112.

4] Bulow J.I., J.D. Geanakoplos and P.D. Klemperer (1985), "Multimarket Oligopoly: Strategic Substitutes and Complements", *Journal of Political Economy*, **93**, 488-511.

5] Cabral, L.M.B. (2000), "R&D Cooperation and Product Market Competition", *International Journal of Industrial Organization*, **18**, 1033-47.

6] Clarke, R.N. (1983a), "Oligopolists Don't Want to Share Information", *Economics Letters*, **11**, 33-6.

7] Clarke, R.N. (1983b), "Collusion and the Incentives for Information Sharing", *Bell Journal of Economics*, **14**, 383-94.

8] d'Aspremont, C. and A. Jacquemin (1988), "Cooperative and Noncooperative R&D in Duopoly with Spillovers", *American Economic Review*, **78**, 1133-7.

9] d'Aspremont, C. and A. Jacquemin (1990), "Cooperative and Noncooperative R&D in Duopoly with Spillovers: Erratum", *American Economic Review*, **80**, 641-2.

10] EC Commission (1990), *Competition Law in the European Communities*, Volume I, *Rules Applicable to Undertakings*, Brussels-Luxembourg.

11] Fudenberg, D. and J. Tirole (1984), "The Fat Cat Effect, the Puppy Dog Ploy, and the Lean and Hungry Look", *American Economic Review, Papers and Proceedings*, **74**, 361-68.

12] Fudenberg, D. and J. Tirole (1991), *Game Theory*, Cambridge, MA, MIT Press.

13] Gal-Or, E. (1985), "Information Sharing and Oligopoly", *Econometrica*, **53**, 329-43.

14] Gal-Or, E. (1986), "Information Transmission - Cournot and Bertrand Equilibria", *Review of Economic Studies*, **53**, 85-92.

15] Goto, A. and R. Wakasugi (1988), "Technology Policy", in R. Komiya, M. Okuno and K. Suzumura (eds), *Industrial Policy of Japan*, New York, Academic Press.

16] Grossman, G. and C. Shapiro (1986), "Research Joint Ventures: An Antitrust Analysis", *Journal of Law, Economics and Organization*, **2**, 315-37.

17] Harsanyi, J. (1967-68), "Games with Incomplete Information Played by Bayesian Players", *Management Science*, **14**, 159-82, 320-34, 486-502.

18] Harsanyi, J. (1973), "Games with Randomly Disturbed Payoffs: A New Rationale for Mixed-Strategy Equilibrium Points", *International Journal of Game Theory*, **2**, 1-23.

19] Jorde, T.M. and D.J. Teece (1990), "Innovation and Cooperation: Implications for Competition and Antitrust", *Journal of Economic Perspectives*,

4, 75-96.

20] Kamien, M., E. Muller and I. Zang (1992), "Cooperative Joint Ventures and R&D Cartels", *American Economic Review*, **82**, 1293-1306.

21] Katz, M.L. (1986), "An Analysis of Cooperative Research and Development", *RAND Journal of Economics*, **17**, 527-43.

22] Katz M.L. and J.A. Ordover (1990), "R&D Cooperation and Competition", *Brookings Papers on Economic Activity*, Special issue, 137-91.

23] Lambertini, L., S. Poddar and D. Sasaki (1998), "Standardization and the Stability of Collusion", *Economics Letters*, **58**, 303-10.

24] Lambertini, L., S. Poddar and D. Sasaki (2002), "Research Joint Ventures, Product Differentiation and Price Collusion", *International Journal of Industrial Organization*, **20**, 829-54.

25] Levin, P. and J.P. Ponssard (1979), "The Value of Information in Some Nonzero Sum Game", *International Journal of Game Theory*, **6**, 221-29.

26] Martin, S. (1995), "R&D Joint Ventures and Tacit Product Market Collusion", *European Journal of Political Economy*, **11**, 733-41.

27] Novshek, W. and H. Sonnenschein (1982), "Fulfilled Expectations Cournot Oligopoly with Information Acquisition and Release", *Bell Journal of Economics*, **13**, 214-18.

28] Okuno-Fujiwara, M., A. Postlewaite and K. Suzumura (1990), "Strategic Information Revelation", *Review of Economic Studies*, **57**, 25-47.

29] Sakai, Y. (1985), "The Value of Information in a Simple Duopoly Model", *Journal of Economic Theory*, **36**, 36-54.

30] Sakai, Y. (1990), "Information Sharing and Oligopoly: Overview and Evaluation - Part I. Alternative Models with a Common Risk", *Keio Economic Studies*, **27**, 17-41.

31] Sakai, Y. (1991), "Information Sharing and Oligopoly: Overview and Evaluation - Part II. Private Risks and Oligopoly Models", *Keio Economic Studies*, **28**, 51-71.

32] Sasaki, D. (2001), "The Value of Information in Oligopoly with Demand Uncertainty", *Journal of Economics*, **73**, 1-13.

33] Shapiro, C. (1986), "Exchange of Cost Information in Oligopoly", *Review of Economic Studies*, **53**, 433-46.

34] Shapiro, C. and R. Willig (1990), "On the Antitrust Treatment of Production Joint Ventures", *Journal of Economic Perspectives*, 4, 113-30.

35] Singh, N. and X. Vives (1984), "Price and Quantity Competition in a Differentiated Duopoly", *RAND Journal of Economics*, **15**, 546-54.

36] Suzumura, K. (1992), "Cooperative and Noncooperative R&D in an Oligopoly with Spillovers", *American Economic Review*, **82**, 1307-20.

37] Tao, Z. and C. Wu (1997), "On the Organization of Cooperative Research and Development", *International Journal of Industrial Organization*, **15**, 573-96.

38] Vives, X. (1984), "Duopoly Information Equilibrium: Cournot and Bertrand", *Journal of Economic Theory*, **34**, 71-94.

# Chapter 7

# Differential oligopoly games

Roberto Cellini and Luca Lambertini[1]

## 7.1  Introduction

The aim of this chapter consists in introducing the reader to the dynamic models of oligopoly. In particular, we want to outline the basics of the theory of differential games and provide the reader with a brief survey of the literature concerning its applications to industrial organisation. It is surprising that the most part of standard microeconomic analysis - and specifically the theory of industrial organisation - has been developed in static contexts, although this is clearly at odds with reality. Even the issue of strategic interaction among firms over time has been modelled mostly through the tools of repeated games, which are inherently static in that the constituent game repeats unchanged over time.

The theory of differential games originated from the work of Isaacs (1954), in the form of unpublished reports of the RAND Corporation, accounting for his research activity in the previous five years, at least. The reason why differential game theory remained for a long time at the margin of research in economics is certainly to be found in the fact that Isaacs, as well as many of his colleagues working in the same field or in related fields, was in fact appointed by the US Government to deal with military problems related to the Cold War.[2] Much the same can be told about their Russian counterparts.

---

[1] We thank Dan Sasaki for very helpful comments and suggestions. The usual disclaimer applies.

[2] This is the case for Arrow, Bellman, Nash, von Neumann, Tucker and many others. A very enjoyable account of the activity at RAND Corporation in the early fifties can be found in Nasar (1998). Relevant applications of differential game theory to military issues

In both cases, the products of research started being published in the mid-sixties (Isaacs, 1965; Pontryagin, 1966), and, as a result of this delay, their applications to economics are extremely recent and relatively few.

Most of the applications of differential game theory are to be found in the field of industrial organisation,[3] and, more precisely, they can be partitioned into four groups:

**I.** Oligopoly games with dynamic prices

**II.** Oligopoly games with capital accumulation for production

**III.** R&D games

**IV.** Advertising games

In this survey, we give an account of I-III.[4] The chapter is organised as follows. First, the foundations of differential games are laid out, together with the Hamiltonian solution method (section 7.2). Then, we introduce the simplest way to treat dynamics in a market game, reviewing games with dynamic prices where firms bear solely variable costs, i.e., there is no capital accumulation of any kind (section 7.3). The subsequent step consists in describing both Cournot and Bertrand competition with capital accumulation for production (section 7.4). Finally, we survey games of innovation, where investment is aimed at achieving either process or product innovation (section 7.5). Concluding comments are in section 7.6.

## 7.2   Technical features

Here, we briefly illustrate the cornerstones of the theory of differential games, namely, the notions of

---

include Brito (1972), Taylor (1978), Intriligator and Brito (1984, 1989).

[3] Several applications can also be found in macroeconomics. See Pau (1975), Pindyick (1977), Başar *et al.* (1986), Pohjola (1986), Başar and Salmon (1988), van der Ploeg and de Zeeuw (1989), de Zeeuw and van der Ploeg (1991). Moreover, another important field of application is environmental economics, where the main issue in this respect is the exploitation of exhaustible resources (see Levhari and Mirman, 1980; Clemhout and Wan, 1986; Kaitala, 1986, *inter alia*).

[4] Jørgensen (1982) and Feichtinger *et al.* (1994) provide exhaustive surveys of differential games with advertising. See also Leitmann and Schmitendorf (1978); Feichtinger (1983); Dockner and Feichtinger (1986). Another topic tackled in the differential game literature is the exploitation of exhaustible resources. In this regard, see Reinganum and Stokey (1985), *inter alia*; for a survey, see Clemhout and Wan (1994). All these topics are exhaustively treated in Dockner *et al.* (2000).

- state variable and control variable

- objective functions of players

- information and related solution concepts

## 7.2.1 The state variable and the control variable

In any dynamic setting, at least one variable changes over time, depending on its past values as well as the players' choices. We define this variable as the *state variable*. An example pertaining to industrial organisation may be a firm's productive capacity or installed capital, which depends upon both the capacity held by the firm in past periods and its current investment decisions. Insofar as there exists strategic interaction among firms, both the optimal investment at any point in time, and the resulting evolution of capacity over time, depend upon the investment undertaken by all other firms. The actions of players at any time $t$ consist in setting the so-called *control variables*. In the jargon of the aforementioned example, current investment is the control variable of the generic firm $i$, that must set it optimally over time.

Let the game unravel over $t \in [0, T]$.[5] Define the set of players as $\mathbb{P} \equiv \{1, 2, 3, ..., N\}$. Moreover, let $x_i(t)$ define the state variable for player $i$.[6] Formally, its dynamics can be described by the following:

$$\frac{dx_i(t)}{dt} \equiv \dot{x}_i(t) = f\left(x_i(t), \{u_i(t)\}_{i=1}^N\right) \qquad (7.1)$$

where $\{u_i(t)\}_{i=1}^N$ is the vector of players' actions at time $t$, i.e., it is the vector of the values of control variables at time $t$.

The value of the state variables at the beginning of time $(t = 0)$ is assumed to be known: $\{x_i(0)\}_{i=1}^N = \{x_{0,i}\}_{i=1}^N$. The behaviour of the state variable over time represents a dynamic constraint for each player. As long as the state variable affects each player's optimal decisions, and there exists a feedback from the players' actions to the value of each state variable, strategic interdependence among players emerges.

---

[5] The time horizon of the game may well be infinitely long. See sections 7.4 and 7.5 for models where $t \in [0, \infty)$.

[6] The state variable might be unique for all players, but it is not necessarily so. In the above example, it is certainly not, because the accumulation of capacity or capital characterises every individual firm in the market, possibly in different ways. See section 7.5 for cases where $x(t)$ is indeed common to all players.

## 7.2.2 The objective function

Each player has an objective function, to be either maximised or minimised, depending upon the way we define payoff functions (i.e., whether payoffs denote gains or losses). The function is defined as the discounted value of the flow of payoffs over time. Define the instantaneous payoff accruing to player $i$ at time $t$ as $\pi_i(t)$, and, for the sake of simplicity, suppose $\pi_i(t)$ is a gain (or profit). Of course, the instantaneous payoff must depend upon the choices made by player $i$ as well as his rivals, that is, $\pi_i(t) = \pi_i\left(x_i(t), x_{-i}(t), u_i(t), u_{-i}(t)\right)$, where $u_{-i}(t)$ summarises the actions of all other players at time $t$. Player $i$'s objective is then

$$\max_{u_i(t)} J_i \equiv \int_0^T \pi_i(t)e^{-\rho t}dt \qquad (7.2)$$

where the factor $e^{-\rho t}$ discounts future gains. Observe that the discount rate $\rho$ has no index, due to the simplifying assumption that all players discount future payoffs at the same constant rate. In order to solve his optimisation problem, each player sets the value of his control variable $u_i(t)$ in each period, so that he actually chooses a time path for his control, under the dynamic constraint represented by the behaviour of the state variable (7.1).

## 7.2.3 Information

What is the relevant information set available to each player at any date $t \in [0, T]$? Dynamic game theory distinguishes three cases:

**Open-Loop Information (OLI)** Common knowledge consists only in the state of the world, i.e., the vector of values of the state variables, at initial time $t = 0$. At this date, each player sets the path of his control variable (taking into account the expected behaviour of all other players). All decisions are taken at $t = 0$, and applied accordingly by players during the whole relevant time span.

**Feedback Information (FI)** Players are assumed to know, at any $t$, the state of the world at $t - 1$, so that the information set at time $t$ can be summarised by the vector of values of the state variables of all players at $t - 1$, defined as $X(t - 1) \equiv \{x_1(t - 1), x_2(t - 1), ..., x_N(t - 1)\}$ (or $X(t - \varepsilon)$, where $\varepsilon$ is positive and arbitrarily small, if the game is specified in continuous time).

**Closed-Loop Information (CLI)** Under closed-loop (history-dependent) information, players are assumed to know at date $t$ the whole previous history of the game over $[0, t)$.

The above information sets give rise to (i) different behaviour on the part of agents, and consequently (ii) different equilibria, according to which type of information is assumed.[7] In general, a Nash equilibrium under OLI is not subgame perfect (or, strongly time consistent). Nevertheless, in the remainder, we will illustrate industrial organisation models under OLI. This solution is weakly time consistent, in the sense that, if one considers the game over the truncated interval $[\sigma, T]$, where $\sigma \in (0, T)$, its solution coincides with the solution to the original game over the same interval, provided that agents have played optimally over $[0, \sigma)$.[8] In line of principle, the CLI solution is preferable in that it is subgame perfect. However, it should be noted that the choice may depend upon the context. Indeed, the main difference between OLI and CLI is that in the former, players decide by looking at the clock (i.e., calendar time), while in the latter, they decide by looking at the stock (i.e., the past history of the game). Whether the second picture is more realistic than the first has to be evaluated within the specific environment of the model being used, in relation with the kind of story the model itself tries to account for (Clemhout and Wan, 1994, p. 812).

## 7.2.4 Equilibrium concepts

Exactly like in static games, we may describe strategic interaction between players in different ways. First of all, we may suppose that each player takes all his opponents' choices as give, in which case the relevant equilibrium concept, i.e., the Nash equilibrium, can be defined as usual: a set of strategy paths is a Nash equilibrium if each player consider his own action as optimal given the other players' behaviour, and even after having observed such behaviour.

Second, we may consider the Stackelberg equilibrium, where the leader takes into account the follower's best reply, so that the reaction function

---

[7]It is worth mentioning that the same labels also apply to strategies, so that a player is said to adopt a closed- or open-loop or feedback strategy. Moreover, if the game is defined in such a way that strategies depend upon the *state* but not upon *time*, they are often referred to as Markovian (see Reinganum and Stokey, 1985; Fudenberg and Levine, 1988; Başar and Olsder, 1995; Clemhout and Wan, 1994; Dockner *et al.*, 2000).

[8]The limitations affecting open-loop solutions are well known (Kydland, 1977; Spence, 1979; see also Fudenberg and Tirole, 1991, pp. 520-36). In line of principle, it would be preferable to solve a differential game under either CLI or, even better, FI, rather than under OLI. It can be shown that there are classes of games for which the open-loop and the closed-loop solutions coincide (see Reinganum, 1982b; Mehlmann and Willing, 1983; Fershtman, 1987). For a survey of these classes of games, see Dockner *et al.* (2000). For an exhaustive discussion of time consistency and subgame perfection in differential game theory, see Mehlmann (1988, ch. 4) and Başar and Olsder (1995, chs. 5 and 6).

of the follower must be inserted into the leader's problem as an additional constraint.

Third, players can cooperate, i.e., they can adopt a common objective function defined, for instance, by the sum of individual discounted flows of payoffs. In the field of industrial organisation, this is the case when, e.g., firms build up a cartel in order to maximise joint profits w.r.t. their investment in R&D to reduce marginal production costs or to introduce new products.

## 7.2.5   Optimisation over time

Solving a differential game amounts to solving a problem of dynamic optimisation with several agents interacting strategically with each other. We are not going into the formal details of dynamic optimisation;[9] rather, we confine to reporting some operative rules to solve a differential game. Namely, we present the Hamilton technique.

Consider the following problem for player $i$ :[10]

$$\max_{u_i(t)} J_i \equiv \int_0^T \pi_i\left(x_i(t), x_{-i}(t), u_i(t), u_{-i}(t)\right) e^{-\rho t} dt \tag{7.3}$$

$$s.t. \frac{dx_i(t)}{dt} \equiv \dot{x}_i(t) = f\left(x_i(t), \{u_i(t)\}_{i=1}^N\right) \tag{7.4}$$

where $x_i(t)$ and $u_i(t)$ denote player $i$'s state variable and control variable, respectively. We introduce now the Hamiltonian function, defined as follows:

$$\mathcal{H}_i\left(x_i(t), u_i(t)\right) \equiv \left[\pi_i\left(x_i(t), x_{-i}(t), u_i(t), u_{-i}(t)\right) \right. \tag{7.5}$$
$$\left. + \lambda_i(t) \cdot f\left(x_i(t), \{u_i(t)\}_{i=1}^N\right)\right] \cdot e^{-\rho t}$$

where $\lambda_i(t) = \mu_i(t)e^{\rho t}$ is an auxiliary variable, called the *co-state variable*, its interpretation being much the same as that attached to Lagrange multipliers in static constrained optimisation problems. That is, the co-state variable can be seen as the shadow price of a variation of the state variable.

The first order conditions (FOCs) for the solution of the dynamic problem are:

$$\frac{\partial \mathcal{H}_i\left(x_i(t), u_i(t)\right)}{\partial u_i(t)} = 0 \tag{7.6}$$

---

[9]We refer the reader interested in a thorough exposition of methods for dynamic optimisation and differential games to Chiang (1992) and Mehlmann (1988) or Başar and Olsder (1995), respectively. Both theories are thouroughly treated in Kamien and Schwartz (1981) and Dockner *et al.* (2000). A brief technical exposition is in Friedman (1994).

[10]Note that player $i$ may face either a maximisation or a minimisation problem. In the remainder, we will focus on the former case.

and

$$-\frac{\partial \mathcal{H}_i\left(x_i(t), u_i(t)\right)}{\partial x_i(t)} = \frac{\partial \lambda_i(t)}{\partial t} \tag{7.7}$$

along with the initial condition $x_i(0) = x_0$ and a transversality condition, which sets the final value (at time $T$) of the state and/or co-state variables. In problems defined over an infinite time horizon, it is very common to set

$$\lim_{t \to \infty} \lambda_i(t) \cdot x_i(t) = 0 \tag{7.8}$$

as the transversality condition. It amounts to saying that the "monetary" value of the state variable at infinity is nil.

In analysing dynamic settings, we are also generally interested in evaluating whether a *steady state* exists, i.e., a vector of variables which possesses the desirable property that, whenever players reached the steady state, then all the relevant variables would remain unchanged thereafter.

A steady state equilibrium may not exist, or, if it does, it may not be unique.[11] Last but not least, a steady state equilibrium may exhibit different features as far as its stability is concerned. More precisely, the steady state equilibrium can be:

**A.** a *stable (unstable) node*, when the system non-cyclically converges to (diverges from) that steady state, regardless of where it starts from;

**B.** *stable along a saddle path*, when there exists one and only one time path leading to the steady state;

**C.** a *stable (unstable) focus*, when the system cyclically converges to (diverges from) the steady state;

**D.** a *vortex*, when the system orbits around the steady state in a perpetual motion.

Define the steady state as the vector $\{x^*, u^*\}$. This vector is the outcome of the dynamic system:

$$\begin{cases} \dfrac{dx(t)}{dt} \equiv \dot{x}(t) = f(x, u) = 0, \\[2mm] \dfrac{du(t)}{dt} \equiv \dot{u}(t) = g(x, u) = 0. \end{cases} \tag{7.9}$$

---

[11] There exists also the possibility that a steady state be meaningless from an economic standpoint. See below, sections 7.4 and 7.5.

The dynamic equations in (7.9) can be linearised around the steady state point through a first order Taylor expansion, so that the system (7.9) can be written in matrix notation as follows:

$$
\begin{bmatrix} \dot{x} \\ \dot{u} \end{bmatrix} = \Xi \begin{bmatrix} (x - x^*) \\ (u - u^*) \end{bmatrix} + \Psi \qquad (7.10)
$$

where $\Xi$ is the Jacobian matrix of partial derivatives evaluated at $\{x^*, u^*\}$:

$$
\Xi \equiv \begin{bmatrix} f_x & f_u \\ g_x & g_u \end{bmatrix} \Bigg|_{x^*, u^*}
$$

and $\Psi = \{f(x^*, u^*), g(x^*, u^*)\}$ is a column vector whose components are zero, since $f(\cdot, \cdot)$ and $g(\cdot, \cdot)$ are nil when evaluated at $\{x^*, u^*\}$.[12] The stability properties of the system in the neighbourhood of the steady state depend upon the trace and determinant of matrix $\Xi$. In particular, the system produces a saddle when the determinant is negative. Of course, in looking for steady states, we have to ascertain whether optimality conditions (7.6-7.7) are indeed compatible with $dx(t)/dt = 0$ and $du(t)/dt = 0$.

As a last remark on steady state Nash equilibria, observe that the analysis of the properties of a dynamic system is conceptually distinct from and independent of the issue of the equilibrium of a differential game. We have a Nash equilibrium when each agent plays the best response to all his opponents' actions. From the standpoint of the analysis of a dynamic system, "equilibrium" means that variables are stationary over time. Both issues are relevant when we focus upon a steady state Nash equilibrium, i.e., a state where the system (the market, if we refer to industrial organisation examples) stays, provided each agent plays his optimal strategy.

We are now in a position to proceed to a selected overview of the existing literature on dynamic oligopoly games. In the next section, we expose a model where firms produce without capital, with variable costs only, and dynamics enters the picture through the evolution of market price over time. Then, in the following sections, we focus upon the dynamics of capital accumulation over time, aimed either at producing final consumption goods, or at achieving process or product innovations through R&D activities.

---

[12]Notice that we have dropped index $i$. This is admissible if players are symmetric, so that the state and control variables are symmetric in equilibrium.

## 7.3 Dynamic prices

Probably the simplest way to think about the dynamics of market interaction consists in assuming that prices evolve over time according to some acceptable rules. That is, it consists in taking price as the state variable. This is the problem analysed in Simaan and Takayama (1978) and Fershtman and Kamien (1987).[13] In this section, we present a simplified version of the model.

Consider an oligopoly where, at any $t \in [0, \infty)$, $N$ firms produce quantities $q_i(t)$, $i \in \{1, 2, ..., N\}$, of the same homogeneous good at a total cost $C_i(t) = cq_i(t) - [q_i(t)]^2/2$. In each period, market demand is $\widehat{p}(t) = A - B \sum_{i=1}^{N} q_i(t)$. Hence, the problem of firm $i$ is:

$$\max_{q_i(t)} J_i = \int_0^\infty e^{-\rho t} \, q_i(t) \cdot \left[ p(t) - c - \frac{1}{2} q_i(t) \right] \, dt \qquad (7.11)$$

subject to:

$$\frac{dp(t)}{dt} \equiv \dot{p}(t) = w \left\{ \widehat{p}(t) - p(t) \right\} \qquad (7.12)$$

$$p(0) = 0; \text{ and } p(t) \geq 0 \text{ for all } t \in [0, \infty] . \qquad (7.13)$$

Notice that the dynamics described by (7.12) establishes that price adjusts proportionately to the difference between the price level given by the inverse demand function and the current price level, the speed of adjustment being determined by the constant $w$. This amounts to saying that the price mechanism is sticky, that is, firms face menu costs in adjusting their price to the demand conditions deriving from consumers' preferences: they may not (and, in general, they will not) choose outputs so that the price reaches immediately the "correct" market clearing level, given by $\widehat{p}(t)$. The Hamiltonian function is:

$$\mathcal{H}_i(t) = e^{-\rho t} \left\{ \pi_i(t) + \lambda_i(t) w \left[ A - B \sum_{i=1}^{N} q_i(t) - p(t) \right] \right\} \qquad (7.14)$$

where $\pi_i(t) = q_i(t) [p(t) - c - q_i(t)/2]$; $\lambda_i(t) = \mu_i(t) e^{\rho t}$, and $\mu_i(t)$ is the costate variable associated with $p(t)$. The supplementary variable $\lambda_i(t)$ is introduced to ease calculations as well as the remainder of the exposition. Consider the FOC w.r.t. $q_i(t)$, calculated using (7.14):

$$\frac{\partial \mathcal{H}_i(t)}{\partial q_i(t)} = p(t) - c - q_i(t) - \lambda_i(t) B w = 0 . \qquad (7.15)$$

---

[13]See also Mehlmann (1988, ch. 5) for an exhaustive exposition of both contributions. An interesting application of this setup can be found in Dockner and Haug (1990), who study optimal trade policies in an international duopoly. On this issue, see also Cheng (1987) and Driskill and McCafferty (1996).

This yields the optimal open-loop output for firm $i$, as follows:[14]

$$q_i(t) = \begin{cases} p(t) - c - \lambda_i(t)Bw & \text{if } p(t) > c + \lambda_i(t)Bw \\ 0 & \text{otherwise.} \end{cases} \qquad (7.16)$$

The remaining conditions for optimum are:

$$-\frac{\partial \mathcal{H}_i(t)}{\partial p(t)} = -q_i(t) + \lambda_i(t)w = \frac{\partial \mu_i(t)}{\partial t} \Rightarrow \qquad (7.17)$$

$$\frac{\partial \lambda_i(t)}{\partial t} = \lambda_i(t)(w + \rho) - q_i(t) \, ;$$

$$\lim_{t \to \infty} \mu_i(t) \cdot p(t) = 0 \, . \qquad (7.18)$$

Differentiating (7.16) and using (7.17), we obtain:

$$\frac{dq_i(t)}{dt} = \frac{dp}{dt} - Bw\left[(\rho + w)\lambda_i(t) - q_i(t)\right] . \qquad (7.19)$$

Now, substitute into (7.19) (i) $dp/dt = w\{\widehat{p}(t) - p(t)\}$, with $\widehat{p}(t) = A - NBq(t)$, where a symmetry assumption is introduced for an individual firm's output; and (ii) $w\lambda_i(t) = [p(t) - c - q(t)]/B$ from (7.16). This yields:

$$\frac{dq(t)}{dt} = wA + (w + \rho)c - (2w + \rho)p(t) + [wB(1 - N) + w + \rho]q(t). \qquad (7.20)$$

Note that $dq(t)/dt = 0$ is a linear relationship between $p(t)$ and $q(t)$. This, together with $dp(t)/dt = 0$, also a linear function, fully characterises the steady state of the system. The dynamic system can be immediately rewritten in matrix form as follows:

$$\begin{bmatrix} \dot{p} \\ \dot{q} \end{bmatrix} = \Xi \begin{bmatrix} p \\ q \end{bmatrix} + \begin{bmatrix} wA \\ wA + (w + \rho)c \end{bmatrix}, \qquad (7.21)$$

$$\Xi \equiv \begin{bmatrix} -w & -wBN \\ -(2w + \rho) & w + \rho - wB(N - 1) \end{bmatrix}.$$

As the determinant of the above $2 \times 2$ Jacobian matrix $\Xi$ is negative, the equilibrium point is a saddle, with

$$q^* = \frac{(A - c)(w + \rho)}{(w + \rho)(1 + BN) + wB} \, ; \, p^* = A - BNq^* \, . \qquad (7.22)$$

---

[14]In the remainder, we consider the positive solution. Obviously, the derivation of the steady state entails non-negativity constraints on price and quantity, that we assume to be satisfied.

# 7.4 Capital accumulation for production

Here, we present a model encompassing several contributions concerning the need for firms to invest in capital over time in order to produce the final goods to be supplied to consumers (Kamien and Schwartz, 1979; Fershtman and Muller, 1984; Cellini and Lambertini, 1998; see also Spence, 1979). The following exposition follows Cellini and Lambertini (1998).

Consider a market where $N$ single-product firms offer differentiated products over $t \in [0, \infty)$. At any time $t$, the inverse demand function for variety $i$ is (see Spence, 1976):

$$p_i(t) = A - Bq_i(t) - D \sum_{j \neq i} q_j(t) \qquad (7.23)$$

where $D \in [0, B]$ is the symmetric degree of substitutability between any pair of varieties. If $D = B$, products are completely homogeneous; if $D = 0$, strategic interaction disappears and firms are independent monopolists. The direct demand function obtains by inverting (7.23):

$$q_i(t) = \frac{A}{B + D(N - 1)} - \frac{[B + D(N - 2)]p_i(t) + D \sum_{j \neq i} p_j(t)}{[B + D(N - 1)](B - D)}. \qquad (7.24)$$

Producing any variety $i$ requires physical capital $k$, accumulating over time to create capacity. At any $t$, the output level is $y_i(t) = f(k_i(t))$, with $f' \equiv \partial f(k_i(t))/\partial k_i(t) > 0$ and $f'' \equiv \partial^2 f(k_i(t))/\partial k_i(t)^2 < 0$.

A reasonable assumption is that $q_i(t) \leq y_i(t)$, that is, the level of sales is at most equal to the quantity produced. Excess output is reintroduced into the production process yielding accumulation of capacity according to the following process à la Ramsey (1928):

$$\frac{\partial k_i(t)}{\partial t} = f(k_i(t)) - q_i(t) - \delta k_i(t) \qquad (7.25)$$

where $\delta$ denotes the rate of depreciation of capital. In order to simplify further the analysis, suppose that unit variable cost is constant and equal to zero. The cost of capital is represented by the opportunity cost of intertemporal relocation of unsold output. Firm $i$'s instantaneous profits $i$ are

$$\pi_i(t) = p_i(t)q_i(t). \qquad (7.26)$$

Firm $i$ maximises the discounted flow of its profits:

$$J_i = \int_0^\infty e^{-\rho t} \pi_i(t) \, dt \qquad (7.27)$$

under the constraint (7.25) imposed by the dynamics of the state variable $k_i(t)$. Notice that the state variable does not enter directly the objective function. It can be assumed, alternatively, that all firms behave as either quantity setters or price setters. Hence, the control variable is either $q_i(t)$ when all firms are Cournot agents, or $p_i(t)$ in the case where firms adopt a Bertrand behaviour.

### 7.4.1 Cournot competition

When firms compete in quantities, substitute (7.23) in (7.27) to get the relevant objective function of firm $i$:

$$J_i = \int_0^\infty e^{-\rho t} \, q_i(t) \cdot \left[ A - Bq_i(t) - D \sum_{j \neq i} q_j(t) \right] \, dt \qquad (7.28)$$

which must be maximised w.r.t. $q_i(t)$, under (7.25). The corresponding Hamiltonian function is:

$$\mathcal{H}_i(t) = e^{-\rho t} \cdot \left\{ q_i(t) \left[ A - Bq_i(t) - D \sum_{j \neq i} q_j(t) \right] \right. \qquad (7.29)$$
$$\left. + \lambda_i(t) \left[ f(k_i(t)) - q_i(t) - \delta k_i(t) \right] \right\}$$

where $\lambda_i(t) = \mu_i(t) e^{\rho t}$, and $\mu_i(t)$ is the co-state variable associated with $k_i(t)$.

The solution of firm $i$'s problem follows from conditions (7.6), (7.7) and (7.8), appropriately written for the present model. Specifically, the necessary and sufficient conditions for a path to be optimal are:

$$\frac{\partial \mathcal{H}_i(t)}{\partial q_i(t)} = A - 2Bq_i(t) - D \sum_{j \neq i} q_j(t) - \lambda_i(t) = 0; \qquad (7.30)$$

$$-\frac{\partial \mathcal{H}_i(t)}{\partial k_i(t)} = \frac{\partial \mu_i(t)}{\partial t} \Rightarrow \frac{\partial \lambda_i(t)}{\partial t} = [\rho + \delta - f'(k_i(t))] \, \lambda_i(t); \qquad (7.31)$$

$$\lim_{t \to \infty} \mu_i(t) \cdot k_i(t) = 0. \qquad (7.32)$$

From (7.30) we obtain

$$q_i(t) = \frac{A - D \sum_{j \neq i} q_j(t) - \lambda(t)}{2B} \qquad (7.33)$$

which can be differentiated w.r.t. time to get

$$\frac{dq_i(t)}{dt} = \frac{-D \sum_{j \neq i} (dq_j(t)/dt) - d\lambda_i(t)/dt}{2B}. \qquad (7.34)$$

Thanks to (7.31), the expression in (7.34) simplifies as follows:

$$\frac{dq_i(t)}{dt} = \frac{1}{2B}\left[\left(f'(k_i(t)) - \rho - \delta\right)\lambda_i(t) - D\sum_{j\neq i}\frac{dq_j(t)}{dt}\right]. \tag{7.35}$$

In order to simplify calculations and to obtain an analytical solution, we adopt the following assumption, based on firms' *ex ante* symmetry:

$$\sum_{j\neq i} q_j(t) = (N-1)q_i(t) \tag{7.36}$$

so that

$$\sum_{j\neq i}\frac{dq_j(t)}{dt} = \frac{(N-1)dq_i(t)}{dt}.$$

Thanks to symmetry, in the remainder of this section we may drop the index of the firm. As a further simplification, we also drop the indication of time. Using (7.36), together with (7.33) and (7.31), we rewrite (7.35) as follows:

$$\frac{dq}{dt} = (f'(k) - \rho - \delta) \cdot \frac{A - (2B + D(N-1))q}{2B + D(N-1)}. \tag{7.37}$$

We are now able to draw a phase diagram in the space $\{k, q\}$, in order to characterise the steady state equilibrium. The locus $\dot{q} \equiv dq/dt = 0$ is given by $q = A/(2B + D(N-1))$ and $f'(k) = \rho + \delta$ in figure 7.1.

Notice that the horizontal locus $q = A/(2B+D(N-1))$ denotes the usual equilibrium solution we are well accustomed to from the existing literature dealing with static market games (see, e.g., Singh and Vives, 1984; Majerus, 1988).

The two loci partition the space $\{k, q\}$ into four regions, where the dynamics of $q$ is determined by (7.37), as summarised by the vertical arrows.

The locus $\dot{k} \equiv dk/dt = 0$ as well as the dynamics of $k$, depicted by horizontal arrows, derive from (7.25). Steady states, denoted by $M, L$ along the horizontal arm, and $P$ along the vertical one, are identified by intersections between loci.

**Figure 7.1:**   Cournot competition

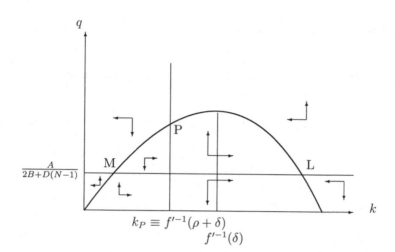

$$k_P \equiv f'^{-1}(\rho + \delta)$$
$$f'^{-1}(\delta)$$

It is worth noting that the situation illustrated in figure 7.1 is only one out of five possible configurations, due to the fact that the position of the vertical line $f'(k) = \rho + \delta$ is independent of demand parameters, while the horizontal locus $q = A/(2B+D(N-1))$ shifts upwards (downwards) as $A$ ($B$, $D$ and $N$) increases. Therefore, we obtain one out of five possible regimes:

[1] There exist three steady state points, with $k_M < k_P < k_L$ (this is the situation depicted in figure 7.1).

[2] There exist two steady state points, with $k_M = k_P < k_L$.

[3] There exist three steady state points, with $k_P < k_M < k_L$.

[4] There exist two steady state points, with $k_P < k_M = k_L$.

[5] There exists a unique steady state point, corresponding to $P$.

An intuitive explanation for the above taxonomy can be provided, in the following terms. The vertical locus $f'(k) = \rho + \delta$ identifies a constraint on optimal capital embodying firms' intertemporal preferences, i.e., their common discount rate. Accordingly, maximum output level in steady state would be that corresponding to (i) $\rho = 0$, and (ii) a capacity such that $f'(k) = \delta$. Yet, a positive discounting (that is, impatience) induces producers to install a smaller steady state capacity, much the same as happens in the well known Ramsey model (Ramsey, 1928).[15] On these grounds, define this level of $k$ as the *optimal capital constraint*, and label it as $\widehat{k}$. When the reservation price $A$ is very large (or $B$, $D$, $N$ are low), points $M$ and $L$ either do not exist (regime [5]) or fall to the right of $P$ (regimes [2], [3] and [4]). Under these circumstances, the capital constraint is operative and firms choose the capital accumulation corresponding to $P$. As we will see below, this is fully consistent with the dynamic properties of the steady state points.

Notice that both steady state points located along the horizontal locus entail the same levels of sales. As a consequence, point $L$ is surely inefficient in that it requires a higher amount of capital. Point $M$, as already mentioned above, corresponds to the optimal quantity emerging from the static version of the game. It is hardly necessary to emphasise that this solution encompasses both monopoly (either when $N = 1$ or when $D = 0$) and perfect competition (as, in the limit, $N \to \infty$).[16] In point $M$, $d\pi_i(t)/dq_i(t) = 0$, that is, the marginal instantaneous profit is nil.

Now we come to the stability analysis of the above system. The joint dynamics of $q$ and $k$ can be described by linearising (7.37) and (7.25) around $(k^*, q^*)$, to get what follows:

$$
\begin{bmatrix} \dot{k} \\ \dot{q} \end{bmatrix} = \Xi \begin{bmatrix} (k - k^*) \\ (q - q^*) \end{bmatrix}
\tag{7.38}
$$

where

$$
\Xi \equiv \begin{bmatrix} f'(k) - \delta & -1 \\ \dfrac{A - (2B + D(n-1))q}{2B + D(n-1)} f''(k) & -(f'(k) - \rho - \delta) \end{bmatrix}.
$$

The stability properties of the system in the neighbourhood of the steady state depend upon the trace and determinant of the $2 \times 2$ Jacobian matrix $\Xi$. In studying the system, we confine to steady state points. The trace of $\Xi$ is $tr(\Xi) = \rho > 0$, whereas the determinant $\Delta(\Xi)$ varies according to the point where it is evaluated. Consider the above taxonomy.

---

[15] For a detailed exposition of the Ramsey model, we refer the reader to Blanchard and Fischer (1989, ch. 2).

[16] The analysis of dynamic monopoly with capital accumulation dates back to Evans (1924). See Chiang (1992) for a recent exposition of the original model by Evans, as well as later developments.

**Regime [1].** In $M$, $\Delta(\Xi) < 0$, hence this is a saddle point. In $P$, $\Delta(\Xi) > 0$, so that $P$ is an unstable focus. In $L$, $\Delta(\Xi) < 0$, and this is again a saddle point, with the horizontal line as the stable arm.

**Regime [2].** In this regime, $M$ coincides with $P$, so that we have only two steady states which are both saddle points. In $M = P$, the saddle path approaches the saddle point from the left only, while in $L$ the stable arm is again the horizontal line.

**Regime [3].** Here, $P$ is a saddle; $M$ is an unstable focus; $L$ is a saddle point, as in regimes [1] and [2].

**Regime [4].** Here, points $M$ and $L$ coincide. $P$ remains a saddle, while $M = L$ is a saddle whose converging arm proceeds from the right along the horizontal line.

**Regime [5].** Here, there exists a unique steady state point, $P$, which is also a saddle point.

We can sum up the above discussion as follows. The unique efficient and non-unstable steady state point is $P$ if $k_P < k_M$, while it is $M$ if the opposite inequality holds. Such a point is always a saddle. Individual equilibrium output is $q_M^C = A/(2B + D(N-1))$ if the equilibrium is identified by point $M$, or the level corresponding to the optimal capital constraint $\widehat{k}$ if the equilibrium is identified by point $P$. The reason is that, if the capacity at which marginal instantaneous profit is nil is larger than the optimal capital constraint, the latter becomes binding. Otherwise, the capital constraint is irrelevant, and firms' decisions in each period are solely driven by the unconstrained maximisation of single-period profits. It is apparent that, in the present setting, firms always operate at full capacity.[17] When optimal output is $q_M^C$, per firm instantaneous profits in steady state are

$$\pi_M^C = \frac{A^2 B}{[2B + D(N-1)]^2} \tag{7.39}$$

while they are $\pi_P^C = f\left(\widehat{k}\right)\left\{A - [B + D(N-1)]f\left(\widehat{k}\right)\right\}$ if optimal output is $f\left(\widehat{k}\right)$.[18]

---

[17]The possibility for firms to choose capacity strategically has been extensively debated in static models (Levitan and Shubik, 1972; Kreps and Scheinkman, 1983; Davidson and Deneckere, 1986; Osborne and Pitchik, 1986).

[18]Our approach generalises the analysis in Fershtman and Muller (1984). They do

## 7.4.2 Bertrand competition

Consider now the alternative setting where firms compete in prices. In this case, the demand function is (7.24), and firm $i$'s dynamic problem is:

$$\max_{p_i(t)} J_i = \int_0^\infty \frac{e^{-\rho t} \, p_i(t)}{B + D(N-1)} \cdot \left\{ A - \frac{[B + D(N-2)]p_i(t)}{B - D} \right. \tag{7.40}$$
$$\left. + \frac{D}{B - D} \sum_{j \neq i} p_j(t) \right\} \, dt$$

$$s.t. \quad \dot{k}_i(t) = f(k_i(t)) - \delta k_i(t) - \left\{ \frac{A}{B + D(N-1)} \right.$$

$$- \frac{[B + D(N-2)]p_i(t)}{[B + D(N-1)](B - D)} + \frac{D}{[B + D(N-1)](B - D)} \sum_{j \neq i} p_j(t) \right\}. \tag{7.41}$$

The corresponding Hamiltonian function is now relatively straightforward. On the basis of FOCs, and using the symmetry assumption $\sum_{j \neq i} p_j = (N-1)p_i$, the necessary and sufficient conditions for the optimal path obtain:

$$\dot{p} \equiv \frac{dp}{dt} = 0; \; \dot{k} \equiv \frac{dk}{dt} = 0, \tag{7.42}$$

along with the standard transversality condition

$$\lim_{t \to \infty} \vartheta(t) \cdot k(t) = 0, \tag{7.43}$$

where $\vartheta(t)$ is the co-state variable associated with $k(t)$. The explicit derivation of expressions (7.42) is left to the reader, as well as the pertaining phase diagram in the space $\{k, p\}$. The locus $\dot{k} = 0$ is a convex curve, while the locus $\dot{p} = 0$ consists of the two orthogonal lines along which $f'(k) = \rho + \delta$ (as in the Cournot case) and

$$p^* = \frac{A(B - D)}{2(B - D) + D(N - 1)}, \tag{7.44}$$

respectively. The analysis of the price-setting case is qualitatively analogous to the case of quantity-setting behaviour. There exist one, two or three

---

not consider demand conditions, and suppose that instantaneous individual profits are everywhere increasing in each firm's own capital (see their assumption 2, p. 325). In our terminology, they only identify the equilibrium in $P$ along the vertical locus $f'(k) = \rho + \delta$. They are prevented from reaching an equilibrium like point $M$, in that the horizontal locus $q = A/(2B + D(N-1))$ does not appear in their model.

steady state points, according to the relative position of the two loci. From the analysis of the dynamic properties of the system, we draw the following conclusions. The unique efficient and non-unstable steady state point is $P$ if $k_P < k_M$, while it is $M$ if the opposite holds. This is always a saddle point. Individual equilibrium output is

$$q_M^B = \frac{A\left[B + D(N-2)\right]}{(2(B-D) + D(N-1))\left(B + D(N-1)\right)} \tag{7.45}$$

in $M$, or the level corresponding to the optimal capacity constraint $\widehat{k}$ in $P$. In the former case, instantaneous steady state profits per firm are

$$\pi_M^B = \frac{A^2(B-D)\left[B + D(N-2)\right]}{\left[2(B-D) + D(N-1)\right]^2\left[B + D(N-1)\right]} \tag{7.46}$$

while $\pi_P^B = \pi_P^C = \widehat{k}\left\{A - \left[B + D(N-1)\right]\widehat{k}\right\}$ if optimal output is $\widehat{k}$.

### 7.4.3  The social optimum

From a social planner's viewpoint, the choice between prices and quantities is completely immaterial. Moreover, in this case the symmetry assumption can be adopted from the outset, so that market demand for each product writes as $p = A - (B + D(N-1))q$, where $q$ is the individual firm's level of sales. Instantaneous social welfare, defined as the sum of consumer surplus and firms' profits, is

$$sw(t) = \frac{Nq(t)}{2}\left[2A - (B + D(N-1))q(t)\right]. \tag{7.47}$$

The resulting optimum problem for the social planner can be written as follows:

$$\max_q \quad SW = \int_0^\infty e^{-\rho t} sw(t)\, dt \tag{7.48}$$

$$s.t. \quad \frac{\partial k(t)}{\partial t} = f(k(t)) - q(t) - \delta k(t). \tag{7.49}$$

The solution of the social optimum problem is formally equivalent to what we carried out in the section dealing with Cournot behaviour under all respects, with the exception of the unconstrained optimal sales level, which here is

$$q_M^S = \frac{A}{B + D(N-1)}\,. \tag{7.50}$$

This output level is obviously larger than both the Cournot and the Bertrand levels, if the capital constraint is not binding, while the three regimes are indistinguishable from one another when the capital constraint becomes operative in the Cournot setting. Intuitively, there can be cases where the constraint binds under social planning and/or Bertrand behaviour but not under Cournot competition. Hence, if $k_P > k_M$ in all regimes, then $q_M^S > q_M^B > q_M^C$. Iff $k_P \leq k_M$ in the Cournot setting, then the optimal efficient point corresponds to $k_P = f'^{-1}(\rho + \delta)$ in all regimes, with $q_P^S = q_P^B = q_P^C$.

A straightforward implication of the above proposition is that, when the capital accumulation constraint comes into operation in all settings, the three regimes are observationally equivalent. In particular, the following relevant conclusion can be drawn. If $k_P > k_M$ in all regimes, then $SW^S \geq SW^B \geq SW^C$; otherwise, $SW^S = SW^B = SW^C$.[19] The first chain of inequalities on the ranking of social welfare levels across regimes replicates the established wisdom according to which social planning is more efficient than Bertrand competition, and both are more efficient than Cournot competition, as long as products are differentiated and the number of firms is finite. In this case, social welfare is the same irrespective of the market regime only when the number of firms becomes infinitely large. Social planning and Bertrand competition coincide also when products are perfect substitutes. The second result in the above corollary indicates that the type of market competition is irrelevant if the allocation of resources is driven only by the dynamic accumulation constraint.

# 7.5    Product and process innovation

Research in the economics of innovation has focused upon two different issues, process and product innovation, the first having received more attention than the second. However, the differential game approach to both problems has produced relatively few contributions. In this section, we present two models, dealing, respectively, with (i) product innovation in a framework of perfect certainty and (ii) a stochastic race for a generic technological breakthrough, that might turn into either a new product or a new (and cheaper) production process for existing products.

---

[19] As is usually done in the existing literature on static oligopoly competition, these inequalities are calculated *for a given number of firms* (see Vives, 1985; Okuguchi, 1987). It can be shown that the incentive to enter vanishes faster under price than under quantity competition, so that we might expect the number of firms to be larger in the Cournot steady state. This may reverse the above inequalities on output and social welfare levels, and make Cournot socially more desirable than Bertrand (see Cellini *et al.*, 1999).

### 7.5.1   R&D activity for product innovation

Here, we use the same demand structure as in section 7.4, except that we assume that the degree of substitutability, $D$, is the result of R&D activity. Thus, $D$ is the steady state variable common to all firms, and we suppose that there is no capacity constraint on firms' output. Notice that investing to reduce $D$ amounts to investing in product differentiation. We investigate two alternative situations. In the first, firms make their decisions non-cooperatively, with respect to both the R&D investment and the market behaviour. Here, we reach an Arrowian conclusion according to which the amount of resources invested by the industry in product differentiation is increasing in the number of firms, i.e., one of the determinants of the intensity of market competition. In the second setting, we model the behaviour of an R&D cartel made up by all firms, which continue to behave non-cooperatively in setting their respective output levels. In this case, the main result is that the R&D cartel invests more than the sum of their expenditures when they pursue independent product innovation, and therefore obtains a higher degree of product differentiation.

**The setup**

We use the same setup as in the previous section. Consider a market where $N$ single-product firms sell differentiated products over $t \in [0, \infty)$. Market competition takes place à la Cournot. The demand structure is (7.23). At any time $t$, the output level $q_i(t)$ is produced at constant returns to scale, for a given $D$, and we normalise marginal (and average) costs to zero.

We assume that, at the initial instant $t = 0$, $D = B$, so that firms may produce the same homogeneous good through a technology which is public domain.[20] Product differentiation may increase (that is, $D$ may decrease) through firms' R&D investment according to:

$$\frac{\partial D(t)}{\partial t} = -\frac{K(t)}{1 + K(t)} \cdot D(t) \equiv -\frac{k_i(t) + \sum_{j \neq i} k_j(t)}{1 + \left[k_i(t) + \sum_{j \neq i} k_j(t)\right]} \cdot D(t) \qquad (7.51)$$

with $k_i(t) \geq 0 \ \forall \ i$. The above dynamics of product differentiation can be interpreted as follows. The industry overall R&D expenditure is $K(t)$, while $k_i(t)$ is individual investment. Given the symmetric nature of product differentiation in this model, there exists a complete spillover effect in the R&D process. Notice that the externality effect we consider here entails that the

---

[20] The idea that $D$ depends upon the behaviour of firms has been investigated in static models by Harrington (1995); Lambertini and Rossini (1998); Lambertini et al. (1998).

outcome of R&D activity is public domain via the demand function. On the contrary, the externality effects usually considered in the literature are associated with information leakage or transmission (see, *inter alia*, d'Aspremont and Jacquemin, 1988). The R&D technology defined by (7.51) exhibits decreasing returns to scale. As a result, $D(t)$ is non-increasing over time, and would approach zero if $K(t)$ tended to infinity.

The instantaneous profit is $\pi_i(t) = p_i(t)q_i(t) - k_i(t)$. Each firm aims at maximising the discounted value of its flow of profits $J_i = \int_0^\infty e^{-\rho t}\pi_i(t) \, dt$ under the dynamic constraint (7.51) concerning the state variable $D(t)$. The control variables are $q_i(t)$ and $k_i(t)$.

## Non-cooperative R&D

Suppose firms choose non-cooperatively both R&D efforts and output levels. The solution concept we adopt is the open-loop Nash equilibrium. The objective function of firm $i$ is:

$$J_i = \int_0^\infty e^{-\rho t} \left\{ q_i(t) \cdot \left[ A - Bq_i(t) - D(t) \sum_{j \neq i} q_j(t) \right] - k_i(t) \right\} \, dt \quad (7.52)$$

to be maximised w.r.t. $q_i(t)$ and $k_i(t)$, under (7.51). The corresponding Hamiltonian function is:

$$\mathcal{H}_i(t) = e^{-\rho t} \cdot \left\{ Aq_i(t) - B(q_i(t))^2 - D(t)q_i(t) \sum_{j \neq i} q_j(t) - k_i(t) \right. \quad (7.53)$$

$$\left. + \lambda_i(t)[-\frac{k_i(t) + \sum_{j \neq i} k_j(t)}{1 + \left[ k_i(t) + \sum_{j \neq i} k_j(t) \right]} \cdot D(t)] \right\}$$

where $\lambda_i(t) = \mu_i(t)e^{\rho t}$, $\mu_i(t)$ being the co-state variable associated to $D(t)$. Necessary and sufficient conditions for a path to be optimal are:

$$\frac{\partial \mathcal{H}_i(t)}{\partial q_i(t)} = A - 2Bq_i(t) - D(t) \sum_{j \neq i} q_j(t) = 0; \quad (7.54)$$

$$\frac{\partial \mathcal{H}_i(t)}{\partial k_i(t)} = -1 - D(t)\lambda_i(t) \frac{1}{\left( 1 + k_i(t) + \sum_{j \neq i} k_j(t) \right)^2} = 0; \quad (7.55)$$

$$-\frac{\partial \mathcal{H}_i(t)}{\partial D(t)} = \frac{\partial \mu_i(t)}{\partial t} \Rightarrow \quad (7.56)$$

$$\frac{\partial \lambda_i(t)}{\partial t} = q_i(t) \sum_{j \neq i} q_j(t) + \lambda_i(t) \left( \frac{k_i(t) + \sum_{j \neq i} k_j(t)}{1 + \left[ k_i(t) + \sum_{j \neq i} k_j(t) \right]} + \rho \right);$$

$$\lim_{t \to \infty} \mu_i(t) \cdot D(t) = 0. \tag{7.57}$$

We introduce the usual symmetry assumption involving no loss of generality: $q_i(t) = q_j(t) = q(t)$, and $k_i(t) = k_j(t) = k(t)$. This implies $\sum_{j \neq i} q_j(t) = (N-1)q(t)$ and $\sum_{j \neq i} k_j(t) = (N-1)k(t)$.

From (7.54) we get the individual equilibrium output:[21]

$$q(t) = \frac{A}{2B + (N-1)D(t)}. \tag{7.58}$$

Hence, the first order condition (7.55) rewrites as

$$-\lambda(t) = \frac{[1 + Nk(t)]^2}{D(t)}. \tag{7.59}$$

Moreover, (7.56) simplifies as follows:

$$\frac{\partial \lambda(t)}{\partial t} = (N-1)[q(t)]^2 + \frac{N\lambda(t)k(t)}{1 + Nk(t)} + \lambda(t)\rho. \tag{7.60}$$

From (7.59) we obtain $k(t)$, which can be differentiated w.r.t. $t$ to characterise the dynamics of investment. With this aim, first observe that

$$\begin{aligned} [1 + Nk(t)]^2 &= -\lambda(t)D(t) \Rightarrow \\ Nk(t) &= -1 + \sqrt{-\lambda(t)D(t)} \end{aligned} \tag{7.61}$$

which allows one to write

$$N\frac{\partial k(t)}{\partial t} = \frac{1}{2\sqrt{-\lambda(t)D(t)}} \cdot \left\{ -D(t)\frac{\partial \lambda(t)}{\partial t} - \lambda(t)\frac{\partial D(t)}{\partial t} \right\}. \tag{7.62}$$

Then, plugging (7.60) into $\partial k(t)/\partial t$ and rearranging, one obtains:

$$\frac{\partial k(t)}{\partial t} = \frac{1}{2N}\sqrt{\frac{D(t)}{-\lambda(t)}} \cdot \left\{ -\lambda(t)\rho - (N-1)[q(t)]^2 \right\}. \tag{7.63}$$

This can be further simplified by substituting the co-state variable with (7.59), to get:

$$\frac{\partial k(t)}{\partial t} = \frac{1}{2N(1 + Nk(t))} \cdot \left\{ \frac{\rho}{D(t)}[1 + Nk(t)]^2 - (N-1)[q(t)]^2 \right\} \tag{7.64}$$

---

[21]Which, again, coincides with the standard outcome of Cournot models with product differentiation (Singh and Vives, 1984; Majerus, 1988).

which obviously holds for all $D(t) \in (0, B]$. If $D(t) = 0$, optimal per period investment is $k(t) = 0$.

We are now able to assess the overall dynamic properties of the model, which is fully characterised by (7.64) and $\partial D(t)/\partial t = -Nk(t)D(t)/(1 + Nk(t))$. The latter equation establishes that $\partial D(t)/\partial t < 0$ for all $k(t) \in (0, \infty)$ and for all $D(t) \in (0, B]$; while $\partial D(t)/\partial t = 0$ if $k(t) = 0$ or $D(t) = 0$. In the latter case, it is immediate to verify that $\partial q(t)/\partial t$ is also nil. Moreover, observe that

$$\frac{\partial k(t)}{\partial t} \propto \frac{\rho}{D(t)} \left[1 + Nk(t)\right]^2 - (N - 1)[q(t)]^2. \tag{7.65}$$

Thus, using equilibrium output (7.58), we have:

$$\frac{\partial k(t)}{\partial t} > 0 \text{ iff } k(t) > \frac{1}{N} \left[ \frac{A\sqrt{(N - 1)D(t)}}{[2B + (N - 1)D(t)]\sqrt{\rho}} - 1 \right]. \tag{7.66}$$

Of course, we want to investigate the dynamics of the system in the positive quadrant of the space $\{D, k\}$, which is described in figure 7.2. The locus $\partial D(t)/\partial t = 0$ corresponds to the axes. The locus $\partial k(t)/\partial t = 0$ draws a curve over the admissible range of parameter $D$, which, depending upon parameter values, may or may not cross the horizontal axis within the same range, i.e., $D \in (0, B]$. If it does, the associated degree of substitutability in steady state is

$$D^* = \frac{A^2 - 4B\rho - A\sqrt{A^2 - 8B\rho}}{2(N - 1)\rho}. \tag{7.67}$$

See Cellini and Lambertini (2002) for details concerning the conditions ensuring that $D^* \in (0, B]$. When no steady state exists, the model becomes trivial, in that the only admissible strategy is $k(t) = 0$ at every $t$, implying that firms are stuck with homogeneous products forever.

**Figure 7.2:** Dynamics in the space $(D, k)$

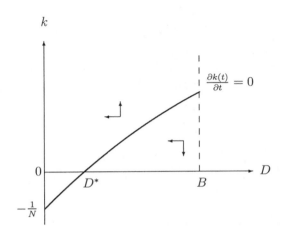

As to the stability of the system, it remains to be stressed that, whenever $D^* \in (0, B]$, it is a saddle, and it can obviously be approached only along the north-east arm of the saddle path.

We now proceed to the comparative statics on $D^*$ w.r.t. all the relevant parameters. From (7.67), it immediately appears that, *ceteris paribus*, $D^*$ is decreasing in the number of firms. That is, the steady state degree of product differentiation is increasing in the intensity of market competition. This result can be interpreted in the light of the debate between the polar positions of Schumpeter (1942) and Arrow (1962), concerning the relationship between the intensity of market competition and the incentives to invest in R&D (for a survey, see Reinganum, 1989). Here, R&D efforts are aimed at increasing product differentiation. Overall, any increase in the number of firms reduces equilibrium profits, and this effect can be offset by investing a larger amount of resources in order to decrease the degree of substitutability among products. When $N = 1$, the anti-Schumpeterian flavour of these considerations is evident, since the monopolist has no incentive at all to invest.

Unsurprisingly, one finds that $\partial D^*/\partial A > 0$ and $\partial D^*/\partial B < 0$. Given that $A/B$ yields a measure of market size and profitability, any increase in this ratio induces firms to invest less in product differentiation.

As a final remark, $\partial D^*/\partial \rho < 0$ can be given the following interpretation. As the discount rate $\rho$ increases, the present value of future profits shrinks. This can be balanced by a higher investment in product differentiation. Bluntly speaking, an increase in $\rho$ reduces, *ceteris paribus*, firms' capability to spend as measured by the incoming profit flows. Yet, a reduction in $D^*$ does indeed restore endogenously firms' profitability and, consequently, their incentive to invest so as to offset the negative effects produced by higher discounting. This amounts to saying that, in this model, the income effect outweighs the intertemporal substitution effect.

## Cooperative R&D

We consider the situation where firms behave non-cooperatively in the market phase, while they activate an R&D cartel wherein they choose investments in product differentiation so as to maximise joint profits, as is commonly assumed in the existing (static) literature on this topic (d'Aspremont and Jacquemin, 1988; Kamien *et al.*, 1992). This entails maximising

$$J_i = \int_0^\infty e^{-\rho t} \left\{ q_i(t) \cdot \left[ A - Bq_i(t) - D(t) \sum_{j \neq i} q_j(t) \right] - k(t) \right\} dt \quad (7.68)$$

subject to the dynamic constraint:

$$\frac{\partial D(t)}{\partial t} = -\frac{K(t)}{1 + K(t)} \cdot D(t) \equiv -\frac{Nk(t)}{1 + Nk(t)} \cdot D(t); \quad k(t) \geq 0 . \quad (7.69)$$

It is worth noting that here $k(t)$ has no subscript, since we impose symmetry across firms in the R&D phase from the outset. This is meant to grasp the idea that the R&D cartel optimises w.r.t. $K(t)$ and then symmetrically charges each firm of its own share $k(t) = K(t)/N$ of the investment carried out by the whole cartel. Notice also that this procedure is equivalent to what we usually observe in static R&D models (Katz, 1986; d'Aspremont and Jacquemin, 1988; Kamien *et al.*, 1992; Suzumura, 1992, *inter alia*), where firms' behaviour is described by a two-stage game. In the first, a single agent (the cartel) chooses the symmetric investment level maximising cartel profits; in the second, firms compete in the relevant market variable.

Adopting the usual procedure, we find that the candidate steady state level of $D$ is

$$\widehat{D} = \frac{NA^2 - 4B\rho - A\sqrt{N^2A^2 - 8B\rho N}}{2(N - 1)\rho} . \quad (7.70)$$

Then, $\widehat{D} \in [0, B]$ iff $A^2 \geq (N + 1)^2 B\rho/[N(N - 1)]$. Again, see Cellini and Lambertini (2002) for further details.

We are now able to characterise the main result, namely, that $\widehat{D} < D^*$ when both exist. This amounts to saying that product substitutability in steady state is lower under R&D cooperation than under non-cooperative behaviour. Accordingly, both the per firm and the aggregate steady state output levels are larger when an R&D cartel operates.

This has some relevant implications as to the established wisdom on the investment behaviour of R&D cartels, according to which an R&D cartel invests less than a decentralised industry, if technological spillovers are low enough, and conversely.[22] Hence, with low spillovers, an R&D cartel can be successful in mitigating the well known wasteful duplication of efforts affecting competitive industries. However, this literature deals with process rather than product innovations. Consequently, spillover effects operate within the R&D activity. In our setting, there exists a full spillover effect from each firm's investment to its competitors through consumer preferences, i.e., there is no wasteful duplication of efforts.[23] Therefore, the ultimate implication of the externality is to drive the R&D cartel's investment well beyond that resulting from independent ventures. An alternative viewpoint to interpret the above results is that, given the non-cooperative behaviour of firms in setting the output levels, cartelisation in the development phase can produce higher profits for its members only by increasing differentiation. Observe that firms could invest less in product differentiation, while raising collusive profits in the marketing phase. However, the current legislation stimulates cost saving in R&D, while prohibiting collusion in prices or quantities (on this point, see Lambertini et al., 1998, 2002).

This discussion ultimately leads to the comparative appraisal of social welfare levels in the two settings. The utility function of the representative consumer is:

$$U(t) = A \sum_i q_i(t) - \frac{1}{2} \left[ B \sum_{i=1}^{N} (q_i(t))^2 + D(t) \sum_i \sum_{j \neq i} q_i(t) q_j(t) \right] \quad (7.71)$$

whose maximisation under the usual budget constraint $Y(t) \geq \sum_i p_i(t) q_i(t)$ yields the demand functions (7.23). Accordingly, consumer surplus is $CS(t) \equiv U(t) - \sum_i p_i(t) q_i(t)$ and social welfare is $SW(t) \equiv \sum_i \pi_i(t) + CS(t)$. Under the symmetry assumption, and given that $k = 0$ in steady state, welfare simplifies as follows:

$$SW = NAq - \frac{Nq^2}{2} [B + D(N-1)]. \quad (7.72)$$

---

[22] Cf. d'Aspremont and Jacquemin (1988, p. 1135); Kamien et al. (1992, proposition 1, p. 1301). See also Katz and Ordover (1990), for an exhaustive survey.

[23] Setting up a research joint venture would indeed eliminate duplication completely, in that firms would jointly proceed to the development of a single good. In the present model this would trivially imply that they should not invest at all and market the undifferentiated good available at $t = 0$.

Now it suffices to plug the equilibrium output (7.58) (which, for any given value of $D$, is the same irrespective of the behaviour of firms in the R&D phase) into (7.72) and differentiate w.r.t. $D$ to verify that $\partial SW/\partial D < 0$ everywhere, which implies that the R&D cartel produces a higher welfare than independent ventures do. This is due to the fact that firms exploit product differentiation, and consequently consumers purchase larger quantities at the cartel equilibrium as compared to the case of fully non-cooperative behaviour.[24]

## 7.5.2   R&D races under uncertainty

So far, we have treated innovation as an enterprise whose outcome is perfectly known from the outset. However, one could stress that innovation is an uncertain adventure. Firms are subject to technological uncertainty, in that they are unable to foresee with certainty the R&D investment globally required for any of them to achieve an innovation. In addition to this, each firm is subject to the uncertainty associated with the possibility of a rival's pre-emptive breakthrough. Accordingly, R&D activity has been modelled in stochastic environments in the differential game approach. Kamien and Schwartz (1972, 1976) and Reinganum (1981, 1982a) are the most relevant contributions in the field of stochastic differential games of innovation. Here, we broadly follow Reinganum (1981, 1982a). Suppose $N$ firms compete over $t \in [0, T]$ for a technological innovation, that might lead either to a new and cheaper production process for an existing commodity, or to a new good. Suppose the innovation date for firm $i$ is a random variable $\tau_i$ distributed according to $F_i(t) = \Pr\{\tau_i \leq t\}$, with dates $\tau_i$ being i.i.d.. The model is worked out under the assumption that the *innovator* gets a patent of infinite duration over the innovation, but there exists the possibility of imitation due to imperfect patent protection, so that all other firms may continue to operate with the technology already available before the innovation, or imitate the innovator.[25] If the innovation occurs at $\tau = \min_i \tau_i$, the innovator is firm $j$ with $\tau_j = \tau$. Independency implies:

$$F(t) = \Pr\{\tau \leq t\} = 1 - \prod_{i=1}^{N} [1 - F_i(t)] . \qquad (7.73)$$

---

[24] The possibility that, in dynamic models, cartels generate welfare advantages as compared to non-cooperative equilibria is discussed in Fershtman and Pakes (2000) and Pakes (2001).

[25] This amounts to saying that the profits from the innovation accrue solely to the winner, but the innovation is *non-drastic*, i.e., it does not create a monopoly for the innovator. In this respect, we follow Reinganum (1982a). For the consequences of the alternative assumption that *the winner takes all*, see Reinganum (1981). For further discussion on these issues, see Tirole (1988, ch. 10) and Reinganum (1989), *inter alia*.

We define as $k_i(t)$ the intensity of the research effort of firm $i$ at time $t$, with the R&D cost being $C_i(t) = [k_i(t)]^2 / 2$, and introduce the assumption that firm $i$'s conditional probability of innovation at date $t$ (the *hazard rate*) is

$$\frac{dF_i(t)}{dt} \equiv \dot{F}_i(t) = \beta k_i(t) [1 - F_i(t)] \; ; \; \beta > 0; \; F_i(0) = 0. \qquad (7.74)$$

In contrast with the models reviewed so far, here the market interaction and the resulting per period profits are blackboxed. Define the present value of the innovation to the winner as $V_W$, and the present value to the loser(s) of an alternative technology as $V_L$.[26] The expected profit flow of firm $i$ is then:

$$J_i^e = \int_0^T \left\{ V_W \dot{F}_i(t) \prod_{j \neq i} [1 - F_j(t)] + V_L \sum_{j \neq i} \dot{F}_j(t) \prod_{m \neq j} [1 - F_j(t)] \right.$$
$$\left. - \frac{[k_i(t)]^2}{2e^{\rho t}} \prod_{j=1}^N [1 - F_j(t)] \right\} dt. \qquad (7.75)$$

In order to simplify the exposition, define $\ln[1 - F_i(t)] = -\beta x_i(t)$, so that it is possible to write firm $i$'s problem as:[27]

$$J_i^e = \int_0^T e^{-\beta \sum_{j=1}^N x_j(t)} \left[ \beta V_W k_i(t) + \beta V_L \sum_{j \neq i} k_j(t) - \frac{[k_i(t)]^2}{2e^{\rho t}} \right] dt \qquad (7.76)$$

$$s.t. \; \dot{x} \equiv \frac{dx_i(t)}{dt} = k_i(t) \, , \; x_i(0) = 0. \qquad (7.77)$$

The game characterised as in (7.76-7.77) has a unique open-loop Nash equilibrium. Using the following transformation:

$$\eta = \exp \left\{ -\alpha \beta \sum_{j=1}^N x_j(t) \right\} \qquad (7.78)$$

and provided $\alpha \neq 0$, we may write the Hamiltonian function:

$$\mathcal{H}_i(t) = \eta^{\frac{1}{\alpha}} \left[ \beta V_W k_i(t) + \beta V_L \sum_{j \neq i} k_j(t) - \frac{[k_i(t)]^2}{2e^{\rho t}} \right] - \mu_i \alpha \beta \eta - \sum_{j=1}^N k_j(j) \quad (7.79)$$

---

[26]The payoff $V_L$ could be the profit resulting from the use of an inferior technology available after the innovator's breakthrough. Obviously, $V_L < V_W$.

[27]Reinganum (1981, 1982a) assumes that, for any firm $i$, the probability of being the innovator at any date $t$ is positively related to the amount of knowledge $\kappa_i(t)$ accumulated by the same date:

$$\Phi_i [\kappa_i(t)] = 1 - \exp \{-\beta \kappa_i(t)\}$$

with $\dot{\kappa} \equiv d\kappa_i(t)/dt = \nu_i(t)$ being the rate at which knowledge accumulates over time.

from which we obtain:

$$k_i^*(t, \alpha, \eta) = \left[ V_W - \alpha \lambda_i(t) \eta^{(\alpha-1)/\alpha} \right] \beta e^{\rho t} \tag{7.80}$$

where $\lambda_i(t)$ must satisfy:

$$\dot{\lambda}_i \equiv \frac{d\lambda_i(t)}{dt} = -\frac{\partial \mathcal{H}_i}{\partial \eta} - \sum_{j \neq i} \frac{\partial \mathcal{H}_i}{\partial k_i} \cdot \frac{\partial k_i^*}{\partial \eta} \; ; \; \lambda_i(T) = 0. \tag{7.81}$$

From (7.80) it can be ascertained that increasing the prize ($V_W$) for the innovation induces firm $i$ to increase the (optimal) R&D effort. The opposite obviously holds for an increase in $\alpha$ and/or $\eta$.

A cooperative solution can also be adopted (see Reinganum, 1981, pp. 31-3). In such a case, firms would maximise joint profits w.r.t. the collective R&D effort. Reinganum (1981, pp. 34-6) shows that R&D cooperation allows firms to reduce wasteful effort duplication. Put the other way around, rivalry induces players to invest in R&D at a uniformly higher rate than cooperation does. The other side of the coin is that non-cooperative behaviour allows firms to innovate earlier than they would under cooperative behaviour.[28] Hence, the question whether cooperation is better than rivalry is elusive, and so are the implications for antitrust policy and R&D subsidisation as well.

# 7.6  Concluding remarks

In this chapter, we have provided the reader with a summary of the toolbox of differential game theory, with a brief collection of examples of its applications to oligopoly settings. Although exhaustiveness is far beyond the scope of our exposition, we believe that the foregoing overview suffices to grasp the investigative power of differential game theory with respect to the research currently undertaken in the field of industrial organisation. In particular, differential games properly highlight the role of time in strategic interactions where some form of capital accumulates over time. This feature remains often out of reach in static multi-stage models, where, by definition, no costly dynamic accumulation exists.

Several fruitful applications of the above theoretical settings can be envisaged. A few obvious examples immediately spring to mind: models of

---

[28]This holds when the outcomes of innovative activity can be privately retained. The conclusion is completely reversed if the results obtained by R&D activity are public domain, i.e., if they fully leak out to rivals.

intertemporal capital accumulation can be used to study the dynamic implications (and therefore the optimal design) of taxation (see Baldini and Lambertini, 2002) or, in trade models, tariffs and other policy measures on the steady state levels of production and capacity (see Dockner and Haug, 1990, 1991; Calzolari and Lambertini, 2002). Differential games of R&D can be extended to investigate, e.g., the effectiveness of subsidies in accelerating technical progress. Hopefully, future research will produce a stream of contributions in this direction, which could reshape our understanding of industry dynamics in more realistic terms.

# References

1] Arrow, K.J. (1962), "Economic Welfare and the Allocation of Resources for Invention", in R. Nelson (ed.), *The Rate and Direction of Industrial Activity*, Princeton, NJ, Princeton University Press.

2] Baldini, M. and L. Lambertini (2002), "Profit Taxation and Capital Accumulation in Dynamic Oligopoly Models", working paper no. 431, Dipartimento di Scienze Economiche, Università degli Studi di Bologna.

3] Başar, T. and G.J. Olsder (1982, 1995, 2nd edition), *Dynamic Noncooperative Game Theory*, San Diego, Academic Press.

4] Başar, T. and M. Salmon (1988), "On the Convergence of Beliefs and Policy to a Rational Expectations Equilibrium in a Dual Policy Problem", in D. Laussel, W. Marois and A. Soubeyran (eds), *Monetary Theory and Policy*, Berlin, Springer-Verlag, pp. 207-23.

5] Başar, T., S.J. Turnovsky and V. d'Orey (1986), "Optimal Strategic Monetary Policies in Dynamic Interdependent Economies", in T. Başar (ed.), *Dynamic Games and Applications in Economics*, Lecture Notes in Economics and Mathematical Systems, vol. 265, Berlin, Springer-Verlag, pp. 134-78.

6] Blanchard, O. and S. Fischer (1989), *Lectures on Macroeconomics*, Cambridge, MA, MIT Press.

7] Brito, D.L. (1972), "A Dynamic Model of an Armaments Race", *International Economic Review*, **13**, 359-75.

8] Calzolari, G. and L. Lambertini (2002), "Tariffs vs Quotas in a Model of Trade with Capital Accumulation", in R. Neck (ed.), *Proceedings of the IFAC Symposium on Modelling and Control of Economic Systems (SME 2001)*, Oxford, Pergamon Press.

9] Cellini, R. and L. Lambertini (1998), "A Dynamic Model of Differentiated Oligopoly with Capital Accumulation", *Journal of Economic Theory*, **83**, 145-55.

10] Cellini, R. and L. Lambertini (2002), "A Differential Game Approach to Investment in Product Differentiation", *Journal of Economic Dynamics and Control*, **27**, 51-62.

11] Cellini, R., L. Lambertini and G.I.P. Ottaviano (1999), "Welfare in a Differentiated Oligopoly with Free Entry: A Cautionary Note", Discussion paper 99/9, Department of Economics, University of Bologna (Rimini Centre).

12] Cheng, L. (1987), "Optimal Trade and Technology Policy: Dynamic Linkages", *International Economic Review*, **28**, 757-76.

13] Chiang, A.C. (1992), *Elements of Dynamic Optimization*, New York, McGraw-Hill.

14] Clemhout, S. and H.Y. Wan, Jr. (1986), "Common Property Exploitations under Risks of Resource Extintions", in T. Başar (ed.), *Dynamic Games and Applications in Economics*, Lecture Notes on Economics and Mathematical Systems, vol. 265, Berlin, Springer-Verlag, pp. 267-88.

15] Clemhout, S. and H.Y. Wan, Jr. (1994), "Differential Games. Economic Applications", in R.J. Aumann and S. Hart (eds), *Handbook of Game Theory*, Amsterdam, North-Holland, vol. 2, ch. 23, pp. 801-25.

16] d'Aspremont, C. and A. Jacquemin (1988), "Cooperative and Noncooperative R&D in Duopoly with Spillovers", *American Economic Review*, **78**, 1133-7.

17] Davidson, C. and R. Deneckere (1986), "Long-Run Competition Capacity, Short-Run Competition in Price, and the Cournot Model", *RAND Journal of Economics*, **17**, 404-15.

18] de Zeeuw, A. and F. van der Ploeg (1991), "Difference Games and Policy Evaluation: A Conceptual Framework", *Oxford Economic Papers*, **43**, 612-36.

19] Dockner, E. and G. Feichtinger (1986), "Dynamic Advertising and Pricing in an Oligopoly: A Nash Equilibrium Approach", in T. Başar (ed.), *Dynamic Games and Applications in Economics*, Lecture Notes on Economics and Mathematical Systems, vol. 265, Berlin, Springer-Verlag, pp. 238-51.

20] Dockner, E. and A. Haug (1990), "Tariffs and Quotas under Dynamic Duopolistic Competition", *Journal of International Economics*, **29**, 147-59.

21] Dockner, E.J. and A.A. Haug (1991), "The Closed Loop Motive for Voluntary Export Restraints", *Canadian Journal of Economics*, **3**, 679-85.

22] Dockner, E.J., S. Jørgensen, N. Van Long and G. Sorger (2000), *Differential Games in Economics and Management Science*, Cambridge, Cambridge University Press.

23] Driskill, R. and S. McCafferty (1996), "Industrial Policy and Duopolistic Trade with Dynamic Demand", *Review of Industrial Organization*, **11**, 355-73.

24] Evans, G.C. (1924), "The Dynamics of Monopoly", *American Mathematical Monthly*, **31**, 75-83.

25] Feichtinger, G. (1983), "The Nash Solution of an Advertising Differential Game: Generalization of a Model by Leitmann and Schmitendorf", *IEEE Transactions on Automatic Control*, **28**, 1044-8.

26] Feichtinger, G., R.F. Hartl and P.S. Sethi (1994), "Dynamic Optimal Control Models in Advertising: Recent Developments", *Management Science*, **40**, 195-226.

27] Fershtman, C. (1987), "Identification of Classes of Differential Games for Which the Open-Loop is a Degenerated Feedback Nash Equilibrium", *Journal of Optimization Theory and Applications*, **55**, 217-31.

28] Fershtman, C. and M.I. Kamien (1987), "Dynamic Duopolistic Competition with Sticky Prices", *Econometrica*, **55**, 1151-64.

29] Fershtman, C. and E. Muller (1984), "Capital Accumulation Games of Infinite Duration", *Journal of Economic Theory*, **33**, 322-39.

30] Fershtman, C. and A. Pakes (2000), "A Dynamic Oligopoly with Collusion and Price Wars", *RAND Journal of Economics*, **31**, 207-36.

31] Friedman, A. (1994), "Differential Games", in R.J. Aumann and S. Hart (eds), *Handbook of Game Theory*, Amsterdam, North-Holland, vol. 2, ch. 22, pp. 781-99.

32] Fudenberg, D. and D.K. Levine (1988), "Open-Loop and Closed-Loop Equilibria in Dynamic Games with Many Players", *Journal of Economic Theory*, **44**, 1-18.

33] Fudenberg, D. and J. Tirole (1991), *Game Theory*, Cambridge, MA, MIT Press.

34] Intriligator, M.D. and D.L. Brito (1984), "Can Arms Races Lead to the Outbreak of War?", *Journal of Conflict Resolution*, **28**, 63-84.

35] Intriligator, M.D. and D.L. Brito (1989), "A Dynamic Heuristic Game Theory Model of an Arms Race", in F. van der Ploeg and A. de Zeeuw (eds), *Dynamic Policy Games in Economics*, Amsterdam, North-Holland, pp. 73-90.

36] Isaacs, R. (1954), "Differential Games, I, II, III, IV", Reports RM-1391, 1399, 1411, 1486, RAND Corporation.

37] Isaacs, R. (1965), *Differential Games*, New York, Wiley.

38] Jørgensen, S. (1982), "A Survey of Some Differential Games in Advertising", *Journal of Economic Dynamics and Control*, **4**, 341-69.

39] Kaitala, V. (1986), "Game Theory Models of Fisheries Management: A Survey", in T. Başar (ed.), *Dynamic Games and Applications in Economics*, Lecture Notes on Economics and Mathematical Systems, vol. 265, Berlin, Springer-Verlag, pp. 252-66.

40] Kamien, M.I. and N. Schwartz (1972), "Timing of Innovations under Rivalry", *Econometrica*, **40**, 43-60.

41] Kamien, M.I. and N. Schwartz (1976), "On the Degree of Rivalry for Maximum Innovation Activity", *Quarterly Journal of Economics*, **90**, 245-60.

42] Kamien, M.I. and N. Schwartz (1979), "Optimal Capital Accumulation and Durable Good Production", *Zeitschrift für National Ökonomie*, **37**, 25-43.

43] Kamien, M.I. and N. Schwartz (1981), *Dynamic Optimization*, Amsterdam, North-Holland.

44] Kamien, M.I., E. Muller and I. Zang (1992), "Cooperative Joint Ventures and R&D Cartels", *American Economic Review*, **82**, 1293-1306.

45] Katz, M.L. (1986), "An Analysis of Cooperative Research and Development", *RAND Journal of Economics*, **17**, 527-43.

46] Katz, M.L. and J.A. Ordover (1990), "R&D Cooperation and Competition", *Brookings Papers on Economic Activity*, Special issue, 137-91.

47] Kreps, D. and J. Scheinkman (1983), "Quantity Precommitment and Bertrand Competition Yield Cournot Outcomes", *Bell Journal of Economics*, **14**, 326-37.

48] Kydland, F.E. (1977), "Equilibrium Solutions in Dynamic Dominant Player Models", *Journal of Economic Theory*, **15**, 307-24.

49] Lambertini, L., S. Poddar and D. Sasaki (1998), "Standardization and the Stability of Collusion", *Economics Letters*, **58**, 303-10.

50] Lambertini, L., S. Poddar and D. Sasaki (2002), "Research Joint Ventures, Product Differentiation and Price Collusion", *International Journal of Industrial Organization*, **20**, 829-54.

51] Lambertini, L. and G. Rossini (1998), "Product Homogeneity as a Prisoner's Dilemma in a Duopoly with R&D", *Economics Letters*, **58**, 297-301.

52] Leitmann, G. and W. Schmitendorf (1978), "Profit Maximization through Advertising: A Nonzero Sum Differential Game Approach", *IEEE Transactions on Automatic Control*, **23**, 646-50.

53] Levhari, D. and L.J. Mirman (1980), "The Great Fish War: An Example Using A Dynamic Cournot-Nash Solution", *Bell Journal of Economics*, **11**, 322-34.

54] Levitan, R. and M. Shubik (1972), "Price Duopoly and Capacity Constraints", *International Economic Review*, **13**, 111-23.

55] Majerus, D. (1988), "Price vs Quantity Competition in Oligopoly Supergames", *Economics Letters*, **27**, 293-7.

56] Mehlmann, A. (1988), *Applied Differential Games*, New York, Plenum Press.

57] Mehlmann, A. and R. Willing (1983), "On Nonunique Closed-Loop Nash Equilibria for a Class of Differential Games with a Unique and Degenerate Feedback Solution", *Journal of Optimization Theory and Applications*, **41**, 463-72.

58] Nasar, S. (1998), *A Beautiful Mind: A Biography of John Forbes Nash, Jr.*, New York, Simon & Schuster.

59] Okuguchi, K. (1987), "Equilibrium Prices in the Bertrand and Cournot Oligopolies", *Journal of Economic Theory*, **42**, 128-39.

60] Osborne, M. and C. Pitchik (1986), "Price Competition in a Capacity-Constrained Duopoly", *Journal of Economic Theory*, **38**, 238-60.

61] Pakes, A. (2001), "A Framework for Applied Analysis in Dynamic I.O.", Plenary Lecture, 28th Annual Conference of the European Association for Research in Industrial Economics, Dublin, August 30-September 2, 2001.

62] Pau, L.F. (1975), "A Differential Game among Sectors in a Macroeconomy", *Automatica*, **11**, 473-85.

63] Pindyick, R.S. (1977), "Optimal Economic Stabilization Policies under Decentralized Control and Conflicting Objectives", *IEEE Transactions on Automatic Control*, **22**, 517-30.

64] Pohjola, M. (1986), "Applications of Dynamic Game Theory to Macroeconomics", in T. Başar (ed.), *Dynamic Games and Applications in Economics*, Lecture Notes on Economics and Mathematical Systems, vol. 265, Berlin, Springer-Verlag, pp. 103-33.

65] Pontryagin, L.S. (1966), "On the Theory of Differential Games", *Uspekhi Mat. Nauk*, **21**, 219-74.

66] Ramsey, F.P. (1928), "A Mathematical Theory of Saving", *Economic Journal*, **38**, 543-59. Reprinted in J.E. Stiglitz and H. Uzawa (1969, eds), *Readings in the Modern Theory of Economic Growth*, Cambridge, MA, MIT Press.

67] Reinganum, J. (1981), "Dynamic Games of Innovation", *Journal of Economic Theory*, **25**, 21-41.

68] Reinganum, J. (1982a), "A Dynamic Game of R&D: Patent Protection and Competitive Behavior", *Econometrica*, **50**, 671-88.

69] Reinganum, J. (1982b), "A Class of Differential Games for Which the Closed Loop and Open Loop Nash Equilibria Coincide", *Journal of Optimization Theory and Applications*, **36**, 253-62.

70] Reinganum, J. (1989), "The Timing of Innovation: Research, Development and Diffusion", in R. Schmalensee and R. Willig (eds), *Handbook of Industrial Organization*, vol. 1, Amsterdam, North-Holland.

71] Reinganum, J. and N. Stokey (1985), "Oligopoly Extraction of a Common Property Natural Resource: The Importance of the Period of Commitment in Dynamic Games", *International Economic Review*, **26**, 161-73.

72] Schumpeter, J.A. (1942, 2nd edition), *Capitalism, Socialism and Democracy*, New York, Harper.

73] Simaan, M. and T. Takayama (1978), "Game Theory Applied to Dynamic Duopoly Problems with Production Constraints", *Automatica*, **14**, 161-6.

74] Singh, N. and X. Vives (1984), "Price and Quantity Competition in a Differentiated Duopoly", *RAND Journal of Economics*, **15**, 546-54.

75] Spence, M. (1976), "Product Differentiation and Welfare", *American Economic Review*, **66**, 407-14.

76] Spence, M. (1979), "Investment Strategy and Growth in a New Market", *Bell Journal of Economics*, **10**, 1-19.

77] Suzumura, K. (1992), "Cooperative and Noncooperative R&D in an Oligopoly with Spillovers", *American Economic Review*, **82**, 1307-20.

78] Taylor, J.G. (1978), "Differential-Game Examinations of Optimal Time-Sequential Fire-Support Strategies", *Naval Research Logistics Quarterly*, **25**, 323-56.

79] Tirole, J. (1988), *The Theory of Industrial Organization*, Cambridge, MA, MIT Press.

80] van der Ploeg, F. and A. de Zeeuw (1989, eds), *Dynamic Policy Games in Economics*, North-Holland, Amsterdam.

81] Vives, X. (1985), "Efficiency of Bertrand and Cournot Equilibria with Product Differentiation", *Journal of Economic Theory*, **36**, 166-75.

# Index